STUDIES
IN
MODERN
PHILOLOGY
16

STUDIES IN MODERN PHILOLOGY

Series Editors
Károly Manherz
János Szávai

AKADÉMIAI KIADÓ, BUDAPEST

MIHÁLY SZEGEDY-MASZÁK

LITERARY CANONS:
NATIONAL AND INTERNATIONAL

AKADÉMIAI KIADÓ, BUDAPEST

This book has been sponsored by the
Office of Higher Education Programmes (FPI)

ISBN 963 05 7785 2

HU ISSN 0236-9591

Published by Akadémiai Kiadó H-1117 Budapest, Prielle Kornélia u. 4.

Printed in Hungary
by PXP Ltd., Budapest

Contents

On the Uses and Limits
of Multiculturalism

One of the ambiguities of the eighteenth century is that it was the period in which Europe reached maturity in historical understanding and turned to mononationalism in culture. The complex relations between these two facts proved to have far-reaching consequences for later developments. Jean-Jacques Rousseau and others insisted that the role to be played by cultural products was "de renforcer le caractère national,"[1] and Herder gave special emphasis to the binary opposition between organic and imitative culture. Historians, philosophers, and writers inspired by their ideas compared the fate of a nation to a teleological process. Having the confidence that a certain pattern could be discerned in the development of a nation, they told a highly constructed story in the form of an edifying tale, explaining the essence of a national literature by a hypostatized national psychology.

As I have argued elsewhere, in the present age the Romantic concept of national character can no longer be regarded as a narrative paradigm in what is loosely called the Western world.[2] It has become customary to speak of multiculturalism and global citizenship. In 1967 Heidegger characterized modern art in the following way: "Ihre Werke entspringen nicht mehr den prägenden Grenzen einer Welt des Volkhaften und Nationalen. Sie gehören in die Universalität der Weltzivilisation."[3] Yet the emergence of new cultures in Africa, Asia, or Canada, as well as the cult of a search for roots and the rise of ethnic history in the United States suggest that it may be too early to speak of globalization. Furthermore, as a result of the collapse of the Warsaw Pact and the decline of the international Communist movement, more national cultures seem to be active in Europe today than ever before. In view of this, it seems preferable to accept a third op-tion, different from both a nostalgic return to a Humboldtian view of culture as expression of national identity and a utopistic form of universalism. Such an intermediate and rather self-contradictory position was taken by Jacques Derrida when he gave the following definition at a conference on European identity: "l'histoire d'une culture suppose sans doute un cap identifiable, un *telos* vers lequel le mouvement, la mémoire et la promesse, l'identité, fut-ce comme différence à soi, rêve de se rassembler."[4]

How can we arrive at a legitimate evaluation of different cultures? In a postcolonial age this seems to be a very difficult question. On the one hand, the strict hierarchy inherited from a Eurocentric past has to be avoided; on the other hand, it is hardly deniable that cultural movements tend to establish centres of their own. It would be futile to deny that most of the initiatives associated with the Enlightenment originated in Britain, France, and Germany, just as most people would admit that between the middle of the eighteenth century and the 1820s the best music was composed by Gluck, Joseph Haydn, Wolfgang Amadeus Mozart, Beethoven, and Franz Schubert. Yet the opposition between centre and periphery may imply a strictly linear view of history and even a kind of cultural imperialism. The importance of a nineteenth- or twentieth-century painting is often judged in terms of a teleological process leading from Classicism to Romanticism, Impressionism, Postimpressionism, avant-garde, and Postmodernism. Multiculturalism may offer an alternative that would make it possible to see different traditions. From such a perspective doubts could be raised about the legitimacy of the overwhelming consensus that between 1870 and 1940 Paris was the centre in the visual arts, whereas after 1940 this centre shifted to New York.

In any case, it is difficult to speak from a centre about peripheral cultures. To what extent can it be taken for granted that the substance of generic or historical concepts is the same when applied to cultures other than those in which their definition had been originally developed? Is it justifiable, for instance, to speak about elegies in old Chinese literature?[5] Does it help any reader understand the works of Endre Ady, Hungarian poet and publicist, if he is called a Symbolist, and is it possible to speak of Postmodernism in countries that have not experienced the advantages and disadvantages of a consumer society? The danger is that the hermeneutic process is stopped too early and too easily when the unfamiliar is quickly reduced to the familiar. The so-called minor cultures are often treated as imperfect replicas, their history is viewed in terms of derivativeness and *décalage*, displacement in time and space.

8

It seems somewhat problematic to conceptually deduce progress or delay or to define the contemporaneity of the noncontemporaneous unless you can locate a centre with absolute certainty. The assumption that a culture is either central or marginal is closely related to the Classicist legacy – the manners of the court are opposed to those of the provinces –, and it is by no means obvious that this ideal can be used in the interpretation of the cultures of the last two centuries. If the impersonal and agnostic Mallarmé is considered to be the crucial figure of Symbolism, it may seem doubtful whether a writer who used not only discursive prose but also verse as an instrument of political message can be associated with this movement. When a Hungarian is asked about Symbolism in his literature, he may try to "sell" Ady as a representative of that movement and thereby avoid the nominalist-realist debate, but the question remains unanswered whether the concept of Symbolism, closely tied to a rejection of both self-expression and didacticism, is helpful for the understanding of Ady's egotistical sublime, political Messianism, or Calvinism. The interpretation may be so reductive that it can hardly be called a form of historical understanding. In a similar way, it is possible to have reservations about the legitimacy of characterizing as Postmodern writing that affirms Christian values.

The dilemma of cosmopolitanism vs. provincialism, the tension between the legacies of universalism and relativism cannot be regarded as outmoded. Colonialism has taught us that if the distance between two cultures is too great, no merging of horizons seems possible. As Goethe wrote to Herder in 1796: "Die Fremde hat ein fremdes Leben und wir können es uns nicht zu eigen machen, wenn es uns gleich als Gästen gefällt."[6]

The historical nature of understanding is closely related to the intertextual nature of meaning and may be the reason why the dialogue of cultures is not a matter of good intentions. You cannot enter a tradition, you have to stand in it. "Traditions ist nichts, was Einer lernen kann, ist nicht ein Faden, den Einer aufnehmen kann, wenn es ihm gefällt; so wenig, wie es möglich ist, sich die eigenen Ahnen auszusuchen."[7] There are limits to multicultural understanding ("Rezepzionsschwelle"), just as there are different degrees of translatability, depending on the distance between the source and the target language.

Displaced natives and refugees are always exposed to multicultural influence. A special category is represented by expatriates who decide to leave a homeland which they regard as provincial. In the late nineteenth and early twentieth centuries Americans from Henry James and Edith

Wharton to Gertrude Stein, Ezra Pound, and T. S. Eliot settled in Europe, because they missed high culture in the New World. Painters and sculptors moved to Paris because they viewed it as the place where visual artists were validated, certified, accredited. In many of these cases the interaction of different cultures led to greater complexity of meaning. Yet it would be a mistake to ignore the risks of *dépaysement*. The French poems of T. S. Eliot are generally considered to be mediocre, the films Fritz Lang made in America are inferior to those he directed in Germany, the later works of Stravinsky are less innovative than the three ballets of his early "Russian" period, and a decline of integrity has been ascribed to the last compositions of Bartók. When Pierre Boulez detected "un piétinement" and "trop de clichés dans l'écriture et la construction" in such a work as the *Concerto for Orchestra* (first performed in Boston in December 1944), he suggested that the composer's attempt to meet the demands of the American public proved to be self-destructive.[8]

It is easier to condemn ethnocentrism and cultural imperialism than to have anything more than a superficial knowledge of other cultures. While no legitimate interpretation of literature can be given by scholars whose reading is limited to texts in one language, some works of verbal art – especially those in which ambiguity and polyvalence can be traced back to the signifier, or in which connotations are based on etymology – can be understood only in the original by those who have a full command of the language in a very broad sense, including the history of the language. Interpretive communities and practices cannot exist without an intimate knowledge of certain conventions. The relative absence of great orchestral conductors in the late twentieth century, for example, may suggest that interpretive traditions built up gradually by several generations may die out if radical changes occur in the cultural climate.

A scholar's awareness of the limitations of his/her knowledge of other cultures may lead him/her to the belief that he/she can only develop historically relevant interpretations of the literature written in his/her mother tongue. It is only in such cases that a true reading occurs or takes place – in the sense the words "Es ereignet sich aber das Wahre," taken from Hölderlin's late hymn *Mnemosyne*, have been applied to interpretation.[9]

One of the advantages of multiculturalism is that it points to the provincial nature of monolithic concepts of *Weltgeschichte*. The works György Lukács wrote in his middle period, between the two world wars, his frequent use of the labels progressive and reactionary, might serve as a warning that *Weltgeschichte* may involve a uniform idea of teleology that makes cultural dialogue impossible and may give rise to totalitarian consequences. The interpretation of *Epochenschwelle* as developed by Hans Blumenberg, Reinhart Koselleck, and Hans Robert Jauß is incomparably more sophisticated, but even this concept implies a universalism that may relegate some cultures to the periphery. Nor can I accept the argument made by some of the critics of these universalist ideas. I would say tentatively and with great respect for those who use the term that it is somewhat misleading to speak of Eurocentrism. While it is important to remember that European imperialism has certainly distorted the understanding of the legacy of mankind, it is a dangerous temptation to ignore the cultural diversity of Europe.

In the first half of the twentieth century there were two types of intellectuals who introduced the concept of multiculturalism. Some ventured into this field out of intellectual curiosity – Western specialists of Oriental languages are obvious examples –, others were forced to insist on the dialogue between different cultures by the vagaries of fate or the tragedies of history. Paul Celan, a Jewish poet born in Bukovina, decided to write in the language of the people whose politicians had sent him to a death camp, yet he combined the language of Hölderlin, Nietzsche, and Heidegger with Hebrew and Yiddish. A similar dialogism is exemplified by the activity of Vladimir Nabokov. In the 1920s he started his career as an avant-garde novelist and poet in exile. Because of the limited chances of a writer with a small public consisting of Russian émigrés, he had to switch to the English language in middle age, during World War II. The next decade brought him international success, and by the 1960s his works became regarded as an epitome of multiculturalism. *Speak, Memory* (1966) and *Ada* (1969) were written about pre-revolutionary Russia in English by a writer living in Switzerland. In 1967 he gave the following answer to the question as to whether he had any conspicuous flaw as a writer:

"The absence of a natural vocabulary. [...] Of the two instruments in my possession, one – my native tongue – I can no longer use, and this is not only because I lack a Russian audience, but also because the excitement of verbal adventure in the Russian medium had faded away gradually after I turned to English in 1940. My English, this second instrument I have always had, is however a stiffish, artificial thing, which may be all right for describing a sunset or an insect, but which cannot conceal poverty of syntax and paucity of domestic diction when I need the shortest road

11

between warehouse and shop. An old Rolls Royce is not always preferable to a plain jeep."[10]

Of course, I would accept the view that comparative literature has legitimacy only if there are degrees of translatability. It is more possible to read *Bleak House* in translation than *Atemkristall*, a sequence of short and cryptic lyrics by Celan. However tempting the universalism of some Enlightenment thinkers, the Romantics may remind us that literary works are language-dependent. In the early twentieth century there were avant-garde journals in most parts of Europe and in America which aimed at the creation of an international literary climate. My guess is that the illusion of Valéry Larbaud, Ivan Goll, and Lajos Kassák has been lost by now. While in music and possibly even in the visual arts it is easier to speak of an international canon, in literature there are no institutions that are comparable to concert halls or museums. There exists a public which can equally appreciate the works of Hokusai and Giovanni di Paolo or Lassus and Cage, but it would be difficult to find many readers with a historical understanding of the poetry of both Tu Fu and Shakespeare. I admire and enjoy *The Dream of the Red Chamber* more than many European or American novels, but I cannot claim to be able to develop a historical interpretation of this work.

The self-contradiction in Derrida's definition – culture as identity and *différance* – suggests that history is knowledge of alien experience, yet it is also constituted by memory. "Zuletzt kann niemand aus den Dingen, die Bücher eingerechnet, mehr heraushören, als er bereits weiss," wrote Nietzsche,[11] and one of the possible implications of his remark is that if the distance between the text and the reader is too great, no continuity, ellipsis, or disruption of tradition can be felt and no historical understanding seems possible. It may be easier to learn about the place of a text in history than to acquire a sense of history in that text. "Durch sein Gedicht stiftet der Dichter Gedächtnis," says Gadamer.[12] The historical nature of understanding is closely related to the intertextual character of meaning and may be the main reason why there are limits to the fruitfulness of creative misinterpretation. When reading in Hungarian, I can have an awareness of intertextuality that is natural, almost instinctive, whereas if I read Celan, my memories of Hölderlin and Rilke will depend on my studies which relate to ideas about the text rather than to the text itself. While perusing Keats or Ashbery, Milton and Stevens are not in my ear, so I am at a disadvantage in comparison with a native speaker, who has a kind of organic contact with texts in that language and therefore is better able to sense the contest that takes place between those texts. If you know more, you can afford to be more flexible, relaxed, and spontaneous in your reading, whereas if you know less, your response might be somewhat stiff and unoriginal. It is not difficult to see a failure of historical understanding in the way the verse of Poe was read by Baudelaire, Mallarmé, and Valéry. Historically relevant interpretations have to be based on a sense of continuity and discontinuity in the history of a semiotic system, some assessment of the relation between precursor and ephebe.

It is one thing to assert that "il n'y a pas de hors texte,"[13] because the inner/outer dichotomy has to be deconstructed, and quite a different one to question the existence of traditions of interpretation. The third *Brandenburg Concerto* as conducted by Furtwängler is interesting yet somewhat misleading, because Furtwängler ignored the basic rules of Baroque music making. His excuse was that the institutions of music making had changed so radically in the nineteenth century that it seemed impossible to recreate eighteenth-century conditions in the twentieth. While the Romantic interpretive tradition made his reading of Bach at least partly justifiable, it would be difficult to make such historical claim for Glenn Gould's recording of Beethoven's opus 57, which may shed more light on the Canadian pianist's idiosyncratic ideas on artistic flaws in the works composed by Beethoven in his middle period than on the "Appassionata" sonata. In his interpretation preserved in a 1967 CBS recording, the first ("Allegro assai") movement lasts 14 minutes and 57 seconds, in sharp contrast to the versions by Arthur Schnabel and Edwin Fischer, recorded for His Master's Voice in 1933 and 1935, in which the same movement lasts 8 minutes and 56 seconds and 8 minutes and 35 seconds, respectively. An excessively slow performance of an "Allegro" movement composed in the Classical sonata form may be compared to a "Nachdichtung" that is too free to be accepted as a translation. No hermeneutic dialogue is developed, no "Horizontverschmelzung"[14] occurs, and the primacy of self-understanding leads to arbitrary interpretation. Such cases may remind us that it is easier to insist on multiculturalism than to do justice to its requirements, since understanding is mediation rather than self-expression or contemplation.

If cultural relativism has some legitimacy in music, it plays an even more crucial role in the historical understanding of literature. Reading in one's mother tongue necessitates interpretive stategies different from those followed when reading in a foreign language or in translation. The international status and accessibility of a language undoubtedly affects the reception of literary works. English, French, German, Russian, Chinese, and Spanish are taught as second or "foreign" languages. This makes it easier to view the literature in these languages from the outside. In the case of Albanian, Estonian, or Mongolian it would be difficult to speak of the perspective of the outsider, since the community of readers with Albanian, Estonian, or Mongolian as a second language must be rather small. Intercultural hermeneutics is a fascinating field, but in some cases it seems more possible than in others. The range of reading positions in the case of an Estonian poem is so narrow in comparison with a novel originally written in English that the interpretive strategies might be radically different in the two cases and it is virtually impossible to use the methods of *Wirkungsgeschichte* or *Rezeptionsästhetik* in the first case.

The world is extremely fragmented and yet the canons, highly institutionalized and based on accessibility, are very rigid. In view of the increasing globalization and standardization – what some call Americanization – all countries have to address two issues. Since the humanities will no longer be centred in the study of national cultures, all the institutions of secondary and higher education need to be restructured. The rise of comparative studies will ask not only for a rearrangement of departments but also for publications which can meet the new demands. To make some progress, it would be advisable to deconstruct the opposition between Western and non-Western cultures and examine the distinction between "great" and "small" literatures. If it is true that Western poetics is mimetic, whereas the conception of literature characteristic of east Asia is "affective-expressive,"[15] the task of comparative scholars is to attempt reinterpretations of both cultures from a double perspective. The evaluation of individual literatures involves even more difficult problems, including the relations between aesthetic value and accessibility, so-called high and popular culture. In any case, without a radical opening up of the international canon comparative literature research cannot justify its legitimacy in the future. Multiculturalism will change both research and teaching in ways that are hardly predictable at the present moment. One of the far-reaching consequences will be a rethinking of history, together with an undermining and possible restructuring of the cultural legacy of mankind.

Notes

1 Jean-Jacques Rousseau, *Lettre à M. D'Alembert.* Paris: Garnier, 1960, 137.

2 "The Idea of National Character: A Romantic Heritage," in Peter Borner ed., *Concepts of National Identity: An Interdisciplinary Dialogue.* Baden-Baden: Nomos, 1986, 45–61.

3 Martin Heidegger, "Die Herkunft der Kunst und die Bestimmung des Denkens," in *Denkerfahrungen 1910–1976.* Frankfurt am Main: Vittorio Klostermann, 1983, 140.

4 Jacques Derrida, *L'autre cap, suivi de La démocratie ajournée.* Paris: Les Éditions de Minuit, 1991, 22–23.

5 Ferenc Tőkei, *A kínai elégia születése: K'ü Jüan és kora.* Budapest: Akadémiai Kiadó, 1959. In French translation: *Naissance de l'élégie chinoise.* Paris: Gallimard, 1968.

6 Cited by Alois Wierlacher, "Mit fremden Augen oder: Fremdheit als Ferment: Überlegungen zur Begründung einer interkulturellen Hermeneutik deutscher Literatur," in Dietrich Krusche/Alois Wierlacher (Hrsg.), *Hermeneutik der Fremde.* München: Iudicium, 1990, 59.

7 Ludwig Wittgenstein, *Culture and Value* (*Vermischte Bemerkungen*). Chicago: The University of Chicago Press, 1984, 76.

8 Pierre Boulez, "Béla Bartok," in *Relevés d'apprenti.* Paris: Seuil, 1966, 304.

9 Paul de Man, "Foreword to Carol Jacobs, *The Dissimulating Harmony*" (1978), in *Critical Writings, 1953–1978.* Minneapolis: University of Minnesota Press, 1989, 221.

10 "Vladimir Nabokov: An Interview," *The Paris Review,* no. 41, Summer-Fall 1967, 110.

11 Friedrich Nietzsche, *Ecce homo.* Berlin: Walter de Gruyter and Co., 1969, 297–298.

12 Hans-Georg Gadamer, *Wer bin Ich and wer bist Du? Ein Kommentar zu Paul Celans Gedichtfolge "Atemkristall."* Frankfurt am Main: Suhrkamp, 1986, 131.

13 Jacques Derrida, *De la grammatologie.* Paris: Minuit, 1967, 227.

14 Hans-Georg Gadamer, *Wahrheit und Methode: Grundzüge einer philosophischen Hermeneutik.* Tübingen: C. C. Mohr (Paul Siebeck), 1986, 347, 401.

15 Earl Miner, *Comparative Poetics: An Intercultural Essay on Theories of Literature.* Princeton, NJ: Princeton University Press, 1990, 19.

The Illusion of (Un)certainty: Canon Formation in a Postmodern Age

"Stets Gewohntes
nur magst du verstehn:
doch was noch nie sich traf,
danach trachtet mein Sinn."

"Wanted things
Thou alone canst conceive,
Whereas my spirit broods
On things not yet brought forth."
(English translation by Margaret Armour.)

1. The Concept

Wotan's reproach to Fricka, in the first scene of Act II of *Die Walküre,* is a characteristic example of the continuous debate between the upholders and the critics of what Nietzsche called the "canon of certainty."[1] Although at the end of the twentieth century there may be a stronger sympathy for the anarchism haunting Wagner's God than for the conservatism of his wife, it cannot be denied that both positions prove to be illusory in the tetralogy.

Attempts made to freeze taste seem to be an indispensable element of history. There are no naive or innocent readers. A truly original interpretation of a work of art is almost impossible to develop since we are always under the influence of judgements made by others prior to our actual experience. These preconceptions are related to what may be referred to as canons.

The literal meaning of the word is "rod," but it is used as a metaphor for "measure," in opposition to "Apocrypha," which originally denotes "hidden ones," but also refers to "spurious texts."[2] The metaphoric nature of these two terms suggests not only that the distinction between authentic and inauthentic is variable but also that canons are fictional contructs and their destruction can be no more decisive than their creation.

One may be tempted to believe that canon formation in the West is a concept borrowed from Biblical scholarship. This is not so. Scholars who study the development of the Biblical canon admit that the model for the canonization of Christian writings was "the Alexandrian custom of drawing up lists of authors whose writings in a given literary genre were widely regarded as standard works. These exemplars were called 'canons'."[3] The grammarians of Alexandria gave the name "canon" to a collection of Greek texts "worthy of being followed as models because of the purity of their language."[4] Having reached a fossilized form, the prestige of this standard collection was unquestionable; it provided people with a referential criterion or standard by which the rectitude of opinions, value-judgements, and even actions was determined.

Although the making of canons may have started before Christianity, there is no doubt about the great influence exerted by Western theology on the process of canon formation. The Council of Trent, in 1546, played an important role by closing the Biblical canon, just as in the last two centuries the decline of the influence of the Church has contributed to the rise of cultural relativism.

A canon decides what products of culture are significant for us. Based on a sense of tradition, it is a body of knowledge, an incarnation of history. The stabilization of tradition into a canon means that a set of texts gains a reputation for serving as a "measuring rod." A catalogue or list is compiled and a fixed collection of texts makes its authority felt. A line of succession is established which assumes that the earlier works are major facts in the background of their successors, although "what one great original artist learns from another is the hardest kind of 'influence' to define, even when we see it to have been of the profoundest importance."[5]

A canon is a concept used in cultural history. The term stands for a standardized corpus which represents an organic whole with rules of its own. There are two pitfalls to be avoided when defining canon formation. A canon is neither a mere flourish of popularity nor an isolated body of great works devoid of any contextual character. Ezra Pound seems to have been aware of both dangers when he defined the concept in such terms: "Certain books form a treasure, a basis, once read they will serve you for the rest of yr. lives." The dynamic aspect is certainly not absent from his statement that those works can be considered canonical which "grow ever more luminous as one's experience increases."[6] More static and normative is T. S. Eliot's approach. For him the concept represents a "permanent standard, by which we can compare one civilization with another, and by which we can make some guess at the improvement or decline of our own."[7]

As to the criteria for determining the canonicity of a work, the first thing to be remembered is that every canon is based on value-judgements which constitute a hierarchy. All confirmations and disconfirmations of a value-judgement take place within this system. For those who share a canon, the values underlying it must appear as self-evident. Supported by unreasoned habits, canonicity is always settled by convention, it is "a necessity that is not chosen, but chooses, a necessary paramount to deliberation that admits no discussion, and demands no evidence."[8] In other words, canonicity has a certain resemblance to the status of proper nouns. You are not supposed to try to prove the greatness of a work you regard as canonical, you simply name it. The value of Homer's *Iliad*, Dante's *Commedia*, or Goethe's *Faust* is often taken for granted. So much so that their textual character is concealed and it may seem almost impossible to read them.

Still, canons can be viewed also from another perspective. Once you look upon a canon from the outside, it appears not as a given but as a created, artificial system. Wotan, as a nonbeliever, questions the value system which is taken as self-evident by Fricka.

Canons survive, but they can also be revived, rediscovered, and restored. The conscious effort to shape or to destroy canons proves that what we have here is a Janus-faced concept "which can refer either to the legacy of the past that has survived unquestioned into the present or to a conscious assimilation of this legacy."[9]

Just as the Bible is more than the sum of its parts, so a canon as a whole may be more than the sum of the entities it includes. Believers in such a significant unity are convinced that they can understand and enjoy one part of it better for having read another. Since all canons depend on established values, they cannot be created by mere individual effort. No individual can compensate for "what his ancestry and his country for some generations have failed to do."[10] The certainty involved is often bound up with the idea of hereditary succession. In so far as it is the outcome of tradition, it cannot be willed but must happen.

There is no denying that canon formation is related to temporality. In literature, the ideal of the canon fell into disrepute when Latin ceased to be the *lingua franca* of learning. In music, canon formation became possible only at a somewhat late stage. As a musicologist argues: "In the previous centuries the repertory consisted of music of the present generation and the one or two preceding generations [...]. Under such conditions of evanescence the idea of a canon is scarcely thinkable. After around 1800 or

1820, however, when new music entered the repertory, old music did not always drop out. [...] Increasingly the repertory assumed a historical dimension."[11]

Canons may have been more static in non-Western cultures because in the Western world artistic developments were often a history of changing generations – at least since the Renaissance – whereas the Asiatic developments, for instance, extended over greater stretches of time. A much more rigid patriarchal and/or despotic socio-political system may – at least partly – explain why canonicity played a more important role in Asian than in Western culture. The *Shih Ching* (sometimes called *The Classic Anthology Defined by Confucius*), a collection of 305 poems which existed more or less in the present form even before Confucius, has been a canonized anthology for the past twenty centuries. With the possible exception of the Bible, there was no book in the Western world that could exert such a profound influence on cultural products.

Taking the temporal aspect into consideration, it is possible to view a canon as a grammar of institutionalized expectations. Since there are "social roles canons can play as selective memories of traditions or ideals,"[12] they can also be defined as strategic constructs by which communities maintain their own interests.

The debate between Wotan and Fricka suggests that for the nonbeliever or "outsider" authority and legitimacy are not given. The recognition of the canonical status of certain works is almost always the result of a long and gradual process in the course of which some works, regarded as authoritative from some perspective, are separated from a much larger body of literature. A text can start its journey toward traditionhood only if it represents certain communal values. Canon formation consists of taking apart and putting together. It is a constant process of revaluation which proceeds by way of selection, moving from many to fewer items. There may be fluctuations during the growth and gradual recognition of a canon. During some periods it can be narrowed; in others broadened. What is called Augustan may be viewed as the result of a freezing of taste, whereas our own age may prove to be one of the fairly eclectic stages in history. The complex interrelations between conservation and correction reflect a wide range of different degrees of canonical authority, rather than a mere dichotomy of canonical and noncanonical literature. It is at least partly because of the rise and fall of canonical works that cultural history must be rewritten at regular intervals.

There are, to be sure, competing works that possess temporary and local canonicity, and some texts may even be withdrawn from canon usage before the limits of the canon become progressively clarified. Some critics aim at closing, others at opening the canon. For György Lukács, F. R. Leavis, or Yvor Winters the temptation to make a sharp delineation with regard to the canon was stronger than for their contemporaries, Dezső Kosztolányi, Virginia Woolf, and Ezra Pound. In their search for the highest authority, the former showed a far more lively feeling for an uncompromising Yea or Nay; they were more often disposed to assert that the books which they rejected had no authenticity.

Canon formation and the rise and fall of artistic and ideological trends are interrelated. At the peak of a literary movement, the previously unsettled elements of a canon become crystallized and fixed so that the distinction between recognized and disputed works becomes clear-cut and the canon ceases to be open-ended. In contrast to such periods of consolidation, transitions from the dominance of one movement to that of another may be characterized by elasticity in the boundaries of the literature revered and used by a given interpretive community. In the last decades of the 18th century the rise of Romanticism in Britain awakened doubts concerning the relevance of the Neoclassical canon. Burke gave the following characterization of this period: "Duration is no object to those who think little or nothing has been done before their time, and who place all their hopes in discovery."[13]

Accurate as this description may be of the age of Cowper and Wordsworth, it cannot apply to all ages of unsettled beliefs. The eclecticism of the late twentieth century, the distrust of all canons – what some call the Postmodern condition – may be the result of having too much historical awareness or at least of having access to too many objects inherited from the past.

In any case, canons cannot exist without creative forgetfulness and constant restructuring. Literature or art is not an immanent essence but a pragmatic concept. What is memorable for one community will not necessarily reflect artistic or even historical value for another. All movements decanonize texts; in their early stages the fringes of the emerging canon may even remain unsettled for generations. There may be a wide range between updating and the complete destruction of a previous canon. At the end of the twentieth century, after the virtual disappearance of some creative and interpretive traditions in narrative, music, or painting, with the emergence of new types of cultural activity, we may take Foucault's idea of epistemological ruptures seriously and ascribe no more than a limited relevance to T. S. Eliot's conservative and rather abstract definition of canonic changes: "What happens when a new work of art is created is something that happens simultaneously to all the works of art which preceded it. The existing monuments form an ideal order among themselves, which is modified by the introduction of the new (the really new) work of art among them. The existing order is complete before the new work arrives; for order to persist after the supervention of novelty, the whole existing order must be, if ever slightly, altered."[14]

Along with composition, canonicity also involves another activity, which I would call transmission. The question as to how a canon can be tested is quite difficult to answer. When I call *The Ambassadors* a great novel, what gives me this certainty? What kind of grounds can I have for trusting a canon? I can give reasons or refer to value-judgements made by others. Ideally these two forms of legitimacy are complementary to one another. As verbal processes, they reflect the interrelations between commentaries and metacommentaries. Whenever it is asserted that a certain work is canonical, the formulation goes together with its application. The constative and performative aspect of the speech act cannot be separated. Carl Dahlhaus is one of the most lucid analysts of canonicity, but he might be wrong in maintaining the distinction between "aesthetic" and "factual judgement" ("Sachurteil"),[15] because the constative and performative aspects of canon formation are inseparable.

A canon is alive only if it is based on a historical sense which is a heritage that is to be taken for granted yet is not directly accessible, but must be obtained. To clarify this ambiguity, one could rely upon psychological, sociological, and historical considerations. In other words, canonicity can be defined only with the help of the concepts of value, community, institution, and history.

2. Canons and Values

Canons create a hierarchy rather than a chronological sequence. Aesthetic judgements are never merely subjective; all evaluation is bound up with the idea of the canon. Taste implies discrimination, and a value judgement is justifiable only if the one who makes it has certain criteria. With the help of these he draws a line between masterpieces and works which are well outside what he considers the mainstream. Thus, canonicity is based on a distinction between the essential and the accidental. Pound, for instance, in his *Guide to Kulchur,* tried to teach his reader to discriminate between the man of genius and second-rate or "suburban" minds who are the recorders of an age.

Ideally, there is a correspondence between real value and conventional respectability, but no historian of culture can ignore the drastic revaluations which have been made in the past. In fact, it is almost true to say that it is possible to speak about history only because of the constant devaluation of the past. Cultural conservatism may involve a concern for a preexistent canon, but it often finds itself in opposition to currents which propagate some kind of counterculture. Protestantism certainly undermined earlier canons, and later on Liberalism played a similar role. The struggle for democracy was a struggle for self-government; it had to reject the idea of canonicity, which is always based on authority. The political implications of this opposition are obvious.

In our age it is sometimes suggested that even the greatest masterpieces are dated because there are no transhistorical values. The idea of a postcanonical form of culture may have been anticipated by Nietzsche and Heidegger. Following Heidegger's lead, some Deconstructionists are wont to observe that Postmodernism means "taking for granted that there was nothing essentially human which had gradually been realized, gradually emerged from heteronomous rule, in the course of history."[16]

The eclecticism of the Postmodern age may indicate that the distinction between the essential and the accidental, the central and the peripheral, is a vestige of the metaphysical tradition. The old and the new, the canonical and the noncanonical coexist in unpredictable ways, and the juxtaposition of varied cultural forms tends to collapse their historical specificity. As a result, the idea of the canon may be replaced by the cult of *bricolage.*

There is a poem by John Ashbery which first appeared in his volume *Self-portrait in a Convex Mirror* (1975). Its title – *The Tomb of Stuart Merrill* – is symptomatic of Postmodern eclecticism. What Ashbery insists on is his admiration for the poetry of a noncanonical Symbolist. "The canons are falling / One by one," as the poem says. The idea of an ordered tradition is discarded as irrelevant. The past "only builds up out of fragments." While earlier iconoclasts aspired to undermine the existing canon with the (conscious or unconscious) intention of establishing a counter-canon, the Postmodern artist does not believe in the permanence of values. The close of Ashbery's poem reads as follows:

> "Father!" "Son!" "Father I thought we'd lost you
> In the blue and bluff places of the Aegean:
> Now it seems you're really back."
> "Only for a while, son, only for a while."
> We can go inside now.

The Postmodern condition has undermined the very basis of evaluation. The new conditions are the results of a decline of historical consciousness, a loss of belief in the end of history. "Still, it remains to be seen how far man can do without teleology,"[17] whether the Postmodern condition represents a new era marked by the relativity of all values, or a transition similar to earlier crises which led to a restructuring of cultural heritage. Romanticism, for instance, also seemed to have invalidated earlier canons and placed great emphasis on individual experience, *Erlebnis;* yet in the long run the change proved to be far from decisive: canonicity had not lost its relevance.

It is characteristic that one of the most influential representatives of Deconstruction criticism, Paul de Man, hardly ever tried to analyze the culture of the later twentieth century. No less telling is the following admission at the close of his critical remarks on the canonic implications in the works of one of his European contemporaries: "try as I may, when I seem to be reproaching Jauss for not freeing himself from classical constraints, I am not more liberated from them than he is."[18] Although it is possible to argue that the holocaust represents a fundamental rupture in Western civilization,[19] it is hardly accidental that most of the statements about the death of cultural canons and of "high art" and of "the sense of connecting the present with the past"[20] are being made not in Europe but in the U.S.A. The range is very wide between the sweeping generalizations of publicists and the sophisticated forms of a disbelief in canons. Central Europeans may be reminded of a rather vulgar or at least canonical type of Marxism when reading that "the hierarchal view of literature at its heart is a vestige of a defunct, class-structured society, no longer viable in the world of mass communications and advanced technology."[21] By contrast, serious consideration can be given to the pragmatic thinker's idea that "there is no correct way of describing or picturing or perceiving *'the world',* but rather that there are many equally right but conflicting ways – and thus, in effect, many actual worlds."[22] Despite the considerable difference between these two attitudes to canonicity, a European may feel that both represent the same American sense of the past which can be symbolized also by those collections of art objects which are not arranged by chronology. Needless to say, a non-chronological perspective may be extremely refreshing. London, Paris, Munich, or Vienna cannot offer anything comparable to the West Gallery of the Frick Collection, with paintings by Gerard David, Turner, Rembrandt, Velázquez, El Greco, Goya, Jacob van Ruysdael, Hobbema, and Corot in one and the same room.

Art is not only a thing of the past but also a forgetting or suppression of history. The disintegration of canons may lead to a broader taste which is not based on a policy of systematic exclusion. Still, the freedom ahead may be more limited than expected. The loss of faith in the Western cultural heritage may provoke a search for alternatives which are more strictly canonical. The great Chinese painters, for example, were far more faithful followers of their predecessors than their European counterparts. The stylistic subtleties within their tradition may be less recognizable for outsiders than for those brought up on that culture. A more eclectic approach to culture may lead to greater superficiality, as a great American writer argued when comparing the culture of his own age with that of vanished societies, in a book published in 1903: "We have more things than they, but we have less and less room for them, either in our lives or in our minds; so that even if our taste is superior we have less the use of it, and thereby, to our loss, less enjoyment of our relations. The quality of these suffers more and more from the quantity, and it is in the quantity alone that we today make anything of a show."[23]

It seems probable that a statement like "*The Ambassadors* is a great novel" can be relevant only if certain preconceptions are shared by the speaker and the listener. Most people would argue that it has more credibility if the speaker can recall the pleasure he felt when reading the book than if he is induced to believe in the greatness of that work merely on the basis of what someone else has told him. Yet it would be misleading to forget that every individual value-judgement presupposes a canon. "The game of doubting itself presupposes certainty"[24] so that even when I deny greatness to a certain work of art, I have a canon in my mind. As readers we learn to judge, and experience teaches us to discriminate; but our activity is always a hermeneutic process through which we adapt some canon to reflect these activities and experiences. Because of this, it is more appropriate to say "I believe *The Ambassadors* is a great novel," than to assert that "I know *The Ambassadors* is a great novel."

3. Canon and Community

One of the proofs of the dependence of culture upon canons is that in most communities there are standard texts which people must have read, or rather lived with, to be considered educated. Frames of mind characteristic of certain periods can be described with the help of those monuments of other times and places which the representatives of the periods in question tried to assimilate. The type of secondary school called the "gymnasium" played a decisive role in Central Europe, in the second half of the nineteenth and early decades of the twentieth century, partly because it expected students to read the same books. Thus the gymnasium represented a social contract, a consensus of informed opinion. The study of certain monuments of the past was a means for students to become acculturated into the middle class. Although the social bias underlying the selection of cultural products taught was just as undeniable as in the English-speaking countries, where "working class people were trained in literature courses to see themselves through literature created mainly by another class" and "women were trained to see themselves through literature created by the opposite sex,"[25] the disappearance of these schools led to a decline in the prestige of general culture. Arguing that taste should not be a social privilege, the Communists disqualified it. Once sharp discontinuities prevailed in the cultural heritage, the very expression "well-educated" ceased to have a meaning.

If it is true that certain periods and regions are dominated by a *koiné,* a unified poetic, pictorial, or musical sign system, then style can be viewed as an aspect of the sharing of canons by a community. In this sense one may speak about a classical style in the music of Central Europe in the years 1780–1810. This example suggests that canon formation may lead to the consolidation of style not only in creation but also in interpretation. To put it another way, canonicity is related to conventions of reading, viewing, or listening. Those forms of art which are heavily dependent upon technology and the market – ceramics or novelwriting are obvious examples – may be more canonical than others, which give more room for individual achievements, but the difference is only one of degree. The idea of the canon is inseparable from the mode of existence of the work of art.

A canon always asks for a traditional code of behaviour. Since canon formation is affected by the size of the community, this can serve as a basis for making distinctions between different types of canons. Ethnomusicologists speak of *small-group canons* which may "emerge as a response to modernization and a means of emphasizing more intimate cultural expressions against a backdrop perceived as homogeneous." A second type has been called *mediated canon*. In this case the coherence of the style "inevitably benefits from channels of communication and the distribution of mass-produced" literature or music.[26] A third type I would call *imagined canon,* since it relies on a virtual community. Imagined canons represent attempts at centralizing a repertory with the aim of giving a conscious response to the need of cultural identification. Therefore, imagined canons are often transformed into actual canons, for example in the processes of nation-building. Nationalism is certainly related to canon formation. While *Weltliteratur* is still an imagined canon, some national canons have become highly conventionalized.

Canons play a major role in creating the identity, legitimacy, and self-image of communities. A national canon is closely tied to the way of life of a community whose members speak the same language. Thanks to this canon, "the artist, the poet, the philosopher, the politician and the laborer will have a culture in common, which they do not share with other people of the same occupations."[27]

In the Western world most national canons were established in the nineteenth century. In the later twentieth century environmental change tends to undermine the criteria of not only national but also other canons inherited from the past. Urbanization has not merely diminished the significance of ethnic and linguistic barriers; it has also blurred the edges between the articulate and the inarticulate, art and non-art, music and noise, cultural training and natural laws; and the new landscape has altered the concept of the poetic.

Change in the canon means that some works move from the core to the boundary, whereas others gain gradual approval from the community. Canon formation may also involve specialization. "Communities often sanction specialist-performers, sometimes to reinforce the musical canon and at other times to infuse the canon with some aspects from outside traditions."[28] Such great translators as Stefan George or Ezra Pound enlarged the national canon because they regarded it as provincial. Bartók and Kodály, on the other hand, virtually narrowed the Hungarian canon of folk music to

Old and New Style peasant songs, disqualifying the gipsy music which had been considered canonical by Liszt and Brahms. These are two radically different ways of canonizing Hungarian popular music. To take another example, the concert hall, where the orchestra or the virtuoso sits on a stage facing the public, did not emerge before the middle of the eighteenth century. This theatrical convention helped create a fairly static canon. Before the nineteenth century no such canon existed, and in recent years attempts have been made to get away from this model.

Canons are closely tied to communities. That is why canonical paintings are often reproduced, canonical plays and pieces of music belong to the core of the standard repertory, and canonical texts are republished, reread, constantly analyzed, and quoted. Some would also add that those works which constitute the literary canon are often translated. I find this third criterion somewhat more problematic. Such courses as "Major Themes" or "Characters in Western Literatures" – regularly taught in departments of Comparative Literature – are certainly indicative of the ideal of an international canon, but my perception is that the precise boundaries of *Weltliteratur* have not been sufficiently fixed. World literature has certainly more to do with different degrees of translatability than with immanent aesthetic values. Certain translations – such as the Vulgate, Luther's Bible, the Authorized Version, perhaps even Carlyle's *Wilhelm Meister,* Baudelaire's Poe, George's *Les fleurs du mal,* or even Fitzgerald's "translation" of Omar Khayyam – may have attained a canonical status, but it is propably no exaggeration to suggest that the canonicity of translations can be felt on the level of national rather than on that of international culture. To put it another way, the rendering of a text in another language involves not so much a liberation from, as a reconstituting of the rootedness therein. There are great works of literature which resemble wines that do not travel. It is difficult to see how anyone could expect to understand Hölderlin without such an understanding of the German language as can only be acquired by a member of a community of living Germans. My example is almost arbitrary. Hölderlin is not only a very great poet but is also well-known enough to be on the fringe of the international canon. The existence of inaccessible or badly translated works from Central Europe or the Third World could serve as more convincing evidence for showing how questionable the concept of a world literature may be.

4. Canons and Cultural Institutions

Translations may remind us how vulnerable our knowledge of literature is. Few people have an ability to distinguish between the important and the unimportant works in any way other than by the demands of the market. Only accessible works can be enjoyed, and taste is dependent not only on individual talent but also on cultural institutions. Schools and publishers play a major role in stimulating the process of canonization, just as the high regard of the literary establishment for certain works helps define the limits of the repertory. All histories of literature, art, or music are written with tacit assumptions about canons. Both the canonical process and the decanonizing of a work are historical phenomena influenced by institutions that sometimes savour of superstition or at least of prejudice. Accordingly, ideologies, movements, and even individuals may exert pressure on cultural institutions to ascertain exactly what works should be regarded as standard.

The stability of a canon is bound up with the stability of the institutions which confer privilege upon it. The canonical authorities were always attacked by populist or anarchistic heretics. The guilds were undermined by free enterprise, the "schools" – in which the work of the apprentice became indistinguishable from that of the master – were replaced by more dynamic forms of association called "movements." In the Western world no establishment could measure up to the canonical authority of the Imperial Academy of old China, the comparable institutions had much more limited power, yet by the nineteenth century even these were ousted by salons, which, in turn, were challenged by the avant-garde.

The canons of these establishments are usually handed down in oral or written form. These two are often successive stages in the transmission. A highly sophisticated written culture may develop very specific criteria. University curricula, translations, and secondary literature are certainly important factors in the hardening of canons. The departmental structure of the universities implies assumptions about professionalism and specialization which make only some modes of interpretation acceptable. The generic distinctions drawn in works of scholarship determine our very concept of art. The role played by translations is more ambiguous. The original is both canonized and decanonized. On the one hand, translatability means accessability; on the other, the untranslatable may remind us of the interrelation between form and canonical status. "Because of this, poetry is more enduring (dauerhafter) than Prose," says a musicologist.[29]

Translation is a constant reminder that what I experience is not art in general but a corpus strictly limited by institutions. Whole genres have disappeared from the literary canon or the musical repertoire together with the social occasions associated with them. It is probably understandable that the songbooks used by most churches contain old-fashioned material, but it may be less admissible that great museums decide whether to present a painting to their public. The larger an art collection is, the more obvious may be the canonical considerations underlying the selection.

The standard repertoire of the great orchestras is more conservative today than it was in the early decades of the century when a Mengelberg or a Furtwängler often conducted works composed by their contemporaries. With the appearance of compact discs, the availability of contemporary music has become even more difficult. What we have in literature is a vicious circle: while publishers tend to focus on those works which are required books in secondary education or at the university, instructors are forced to teach material widely accessible in paperback edition. To mention one specific case, some novels and short stories by Henry James are constantly in print in several editions, whereas other works by the same writer – *The Sense of the Past* and *The Ivory Tower,* for example – have been out of print for several decades. There is only one aspect from which there may have been an improvement in recent decades: the proliferation of interpretive methods has undermined the ideal of canonical reading or authoritative interpretation. The same music can be performed either on period or on modern instruments, and students can choose among a wide range of interpretive strategies when reading a literary work.

We acknowledge the existence of a canon even when we look for reading matter outside the list of "classic" texts included in a curriculum. Canons are reopened by major works, but in most cases this is the result of a change in perspective brought about by professional interpreters. The test of time is not an impersonal and impartial mechanism, but the functioning of cultural institutions. It is the critic or the interpreter who can press the canon to open itself to works which have no established reputation.

Cultural historians are the custodians of tradition. As Sir Ernst Gombrich wrote in a letter to his colleague Quentin Bell: "our civilisation transmits to us a canon of great poets, composers, artists and [...] we are in fact appointed to pass it on to future generations."[30] Whenever critics theorize about art or literature, describe movements or periods, introduce concepts, or define structural phenomena, they tend to think in terms of canonicity.

Just as ethnomusicologists speak of canonic formulae, the historians of art and literature distinguish between the canonic and noncanonic features of genres and trends. On the one hand, the fixing and ossification of the canon makes generic classification and periodization possible; on the other, the discourse of generic or historical classification may perpetuate old canons but also forge new ones. Not only aesthetic but also ideological principles regulate this process. In most cases, the consolidation of a canon is a gradual process of change; in periods of political and social instability, however, it may occur dramatically to precipitate and then to stabilize a new ideology.

In the visual arts it is especially easy to see the determinist elements affecting canon formation. Collecting habits were always influenced by the ideological commitments of dealers and historians. The revaluation of the Germanic culture of the Middle Ages was closely tied to the nationalism of the German Romantics, the Italian "primitives" were rediscovered by the art historian Seroux d'Agincourt, in the late eighteenth and early nineteenth century, and it was after the gigantic art exhibition organized by the influential dealer Thomas Agnew in Manchester, in 1857, that newly-rich factory owners were persuaded to invest in "modern" pictures. It was "very soon after this that there developed that over-riding enthusiasm for Gainsborough, Reynolds, and other eighteenth-century masters that was to last until the 1920s."[31] The ideology of a despotic society was certainly one of the reasons why public museums were unheard of in pre-modern China; social and moral principles made Ruskin admire that which lay outside the academic canon of his times (landscape versus the nude, an emphasis on colour rather than on line, art in the age before versus after Raphael); and there are obvious political implications both in the alienation of such traditional patrons as the aristocracy, the monarchy, or the church from twentieth-century art, and in the way some contemporary artists create expressly for museums.

Institutional changes obviously affect the criteria of canon formation. Before the nineteenth century artistic genres were based on the interrelations between social function and technique. In poetry each genre was associated with a certain "height" of diction, in music "the *prima prattica* was an ecclesiastical style (ein Stil der Kirchenmusik), the *seconda prattica* an operatic one."[32] In the nineteenth century generic distinctions underwent a radical change, the individual character of the work became emphasized, and finally the conception of the work as a historical document led to a building of repertoires.

Whatever the dangers of cultural manipulation may be, it is inherent in the institution of literature and art. Canons are inseparable from the transmission of culture; they govern education and the study of texts and artifacts. The political implications of these activities are undeniable. A comparative analysis of the syllabi used at universities in different countries would reveal probably more about the political aims of the leaders of those countries than about aesthetic conceptions.

For better or worse, we are all brought up on some canon and accept it on human authority. Later on we may question its legitimacy, but this can happen only after a confrontation with other canons. No canon has the means to criticize itself, so a breaking away from our inheritance is always the result of a conflict between different canons. I am almost tempted to believe that it is impossible to forget the first canon.

Towards the end of the second decade of the twentieth century, György Lukács turned his back on his upbringing, but his later career could be interpreted as representing an imperfect reaction to the canon of his youth. The difficult task is to have a creative relationship with one's heritage and to develop a critical faculty when faced with conflicting traditions.

Education, of crucial importance to culture, can teach us to recognize the demarcation of important works. As the needs of education over the centuries have been varied, and different works have spoken to and answered those needs, one obvious test of authority for a book is its continuous acceptance and usage by schools at large. This would suggest that the role played by canons is full of ambiguity: on the one hand, they are indispensable to education; on the other hand, they can have a disastrous effect on culture because they can be manipulated. In the past, a basic prerequisite for canonicity was conformity to national, religious, and political traditions recognized as normative by certain communities. Consequently, those with political power could decide to what extent a text met the criteria of orthodoxy. There is no reason to believe that such party tyranny cannot happen in the future. Besides, the market economy of Liberal democracy can also have its shortcomings: it is capable of exercising oppression upon minorities. One of the dangers of institutionalization is enslavement to public opinion. I can read only those books which have been sanctioned by authority. It would not be absurd to postulate an interrelation between canonicity and censorship and to argue that canons often restrict the acessibility of culture.

Unfortunately, it is possible to establish a canon on the basis of a wilful misinterpretation of the past. In the decades following World War II, political oppression went hand in hand with the exclusion of many works from the national canon in the European countries occupied by the Soviet Union. This drastic form of censorship resulted in the severing of important historical roots of the nations living in that region. The removal of texts by contemporary authors who decided to live in the West, or by aristocrats, or by authors who had misgivings about Socialism or Russia, led to the impoverishment of cultural heritage. A case in point is Sándor Márai. Born in 1900, this writer established a high reputation in the 1930s. In 1948 he left Hungary and since that time his native country published not a single volume by him until his suicide in San Diego, in 1989. In a culture which had strong gentry, Populistic, and Jewish traditions, Márai stood for a fourth alternative, representing the urban values of the non-Jewish bourgeoisie. His absence from literary life in a period of deep crisis badly hurt Hungarian culture, allowing such Marxists as Lukács to make sweeping generalizations about the backwardness of the Hungarian cultural heritage and the absence of bourgeois tradition.

On most canons there is a signature. They are signed by somebody "in the name" of a community. A canon is meant to be representative, so it is given authority by a continuity-seeking spokesman (*porte-parole, Mundstück,* or *Fürsprecher*). F. R. Leavis and György Lukács established canons, and both claimed that their selection and interpretations had greater authority because they bore the countersignature of an interpretive tradition. Their canons were handed down by institutions. In the case of Leavis, the journal *Scrutiny* as well as *The Pelican Guide to English Literature* played a major role in propagating his views, making T. F. Powys and L. H. Myers better known, while excluding Bloomsbury from the circle of suggested readings. Standard series, collections, and anthologies which have the widest circulation can also contribute to the canonicity of certain texts. Palgrave's *Golden Treasury* was certainly responsible for the influence which the Victorian conception of poetry exerted upon several generations. In the later nineteenth and the early twentieth centuries the German publisher Tauchnitz established a canon of English and American literature for readers in Central Europe, and in the period following World War II Penguin Books became a very influential canon shaper.

The value of a work of art is not given: it is constantly reproduced and contested by acts of evaluation. One measure of the canonicity of a work is its availability. A novel that is not in circulation in a community seems to have no value for it. Besides other extra-literary factors, economic considerations may also help readers have relatively easy access to a text in the form of anthologies or affordable paperbacks. Johnson's *Lives of the English Poets* was based on a canon dictated by booksellers. The conclusion seems inescapable that a canon is a pragmatic concept and not an embodiment of immanent values.

5. Canon and History

Still, it is an oversimplification to assert "that the force of a work of art is directly proportional to its historicity."[33] There are novels which are more interesting as historical documents than as works of art, and the instrinsic excellence of a poem is not necessarily identical with its historical interest or significance. We all know about great changes in taste. There was a time when Orcagna, Luini, Annibale Carracci, Metsu, or Guido Reni may have been more famous than Masaccio, Piero della Francesca, Botticelli, El Greco, or Vermeer. What is probably more surpising is that there were also artists whose reputation never changed in a drastic way – Raphael, Titian, and Rubens come to mind as obvious cases. With more recent periods there may be much uncertainty: Tennyson seems to be far less universal than he was in his lifetime, but today his reputation may be higher than some decades ago; the Pre-Raphaelites are having a partial recovery; and Art Nouveau was definitely rediscovered in the second half of the twentieth century. Some of these changes suggest that accessibility may not be the only precondition for canonical status.

In any case, the rejection of an essentialist or normative view of canons should not obscure their systematic character. The canon shaper "denounces the futility of great stores without orderly distribution."[34] He reminds us that art is a collective enterprise and the canonical works repeatedly acknowledge one another. In most of them there is no ownership, they reveal the self as the undoer of selfhood. That is why "a canon is not a list but a narrative of some intricacy, depending on places and times and opportunities."[35]

As is well-known, no history can do without hypothetical assumptions. Although the change from Classicism to Romanticism brought crucial changes, in one sense continuity was unbroken: the Romantics did not reject the stylistic integrity of the individual work of art as a basic concept. This continuity made it possible to perceive relationships between different works and so create canonical narratives. In music, even the principle of generic classification was preserved.

Yet the concepts of the individual work and the genre could not serve as the only criteria of canon formation in the nineteenth century. The idea of the strong personality hidden behind his creations represented a departure from Classicism. In harmony with the spirit of the industrial progress and evolutionary thinking, innovation and originality became essential goals, and the terms of *Epigonentum, Trivialisierung,* and *Kitsch* were introduced to distinguish the noncanonical from the canonical. This principle implied that canons were based on historical processes leading in specific directions. It proved to have such a decisive influence that we may be tempted to believe it to belong to the permanent legacy of aesthetics. To take random examples from the sphere of music, this principle is at work when the Neoclassical works of Stravinsky are dismissed or when Wagner's canonical status is explained in terms of the destruction of the "Periodenstruktur" and the creation of a "Leitmotivtechnik."[36]

If the canonical work marks the culmination of a historical process, the idea of canonicity has both a dynamic and a static aspect. It affirms but also denies history. "The canon participates in the establishment of consensus as the embodiment of a collective valuation. Hence it is in the interest of canonical reformations to erase the conflictual prehistory of canon-formation or to represent such history as the narrative of error."[37]

Those who establish a canon tend to read the past backward and intend to justify their own position in history by significant omissions. Such a highly biassed interpretation of the past has been ascribed to Hegel and Heidegger, two thinkers whose view of philosophical traditions is strongly canonical: "conflicts, contradictions, struggle among philosophers are ignored or covered up, and the whole history of philosophy is linearized so as to reach its destined result – the closure of metaphysics and its thinker, Heidegger. With Hegel, all philosophies are reduced to the same in the sense that all of them represent merely 'moments' in the process of self-consciousness and self-cognizance of the spirit – and in the sense that all these 'moments' stand convicted as 'moments' of the (hegelian) System. With Heidegger, all philosophers are reduced to the same."[38]

Canons read cultural phenomena in terms of otherness, but they are narratives which are metaphors of the present. The innovations of the present are often projected back on to works created in the past. Bach's cantata *Actus tragicus* ("Gottes Zeit ist die allerbeste Zeit" BWV 106) became a canonical work in the nineteenth century on the basis of a profound revaluation brought about by the Romantics: the composite or fragmented form considered archaic in the 18th century was viewed as modern in the 19th.[39] The emphasis on "les 'cing grands' de la musique contemporaine"[40] in the writings of Boulez, the thesis that there were five major composers in the period between the two world wars is an attempt to give a historical justification for the type of music Boulez himself composed after 1945. With this purpose in mind, he made a clear-cut distinction between the canonical and noncanonical works of even those five masters. For example, Bartók's string quartets, the two sonatas for violin and piano, the *Music for Strings, Percussion, and Celesta,* and the *Sonata for Two Pianos and Percussion* were regarded as canonical because these were the compositions from which Boulez could draw inspiration in his formative years.[41]

Schönberg established his canon in a similar way, several decades before. In an article entitled *Zu: "Nationale Musik,"* dated February 24, 1931, he named primarily Bach and Mozart, and secondarily Beethoven, Brahms, and Wagner as the canonical composers on the basis of what he had learned from them.[42] From Cézanne to Pollock, many visual artists reinterpeted the past, and similar revaluations are well-known in literature: Hölderlin's greatness was established by Nietzsche and George, and Henry James or the French "new novelists" had rewritten the history of narrative fiction published in the Western world.

What all these examples suggest is that major artists may be the most powerful shapers of canons. They create different versions of the past, selecting works which they consider to be of historical significance. Whatever the value of contemporary art may be, it cannot be made responsible for the decline of the ideal of canonicity. What is at stake is the state of historical consciousness in our world.

The justification for the existence of canons is that no literary or artistic work can have its complete meaning alone. The appreciation of any such work involves the understanding of its relation both to earlier and to later works. Since the transmission of meaning is an open process, the history of art and literature must be rewritten at regular intervals. We have seen too many revalutions to uphold the ideal of an international canon of masterpieces selected by some impersonal authority. In view of the profound transvaluations that occurred when one period or movement passed into another, it must be taken for granted that new values are constantly pushing out the old and reconstructing the past. The "Great Books" conviction has been so much undermined by cultural relativism that no field could remain untouched by the tendency to deconstruct canonicity – not even Biblical criticism. "The ecumenical movement has raised our consciousness to see that there is a plurality of canons in the several Christian communions. It is very difficult now to think about canon, either as it was in antiquity or as it is today, in parochial or singular modes. Pluralism is a part of responsible perception of the concept of canon."[43]

If this is true of religious, it must be even more so of secular culture. The historical nature of art and literature makes it impossible to settle, once and for all, what belongs to the canon. Additionally, the number of candidates for possible inclusion is certainly increasing. Still, I would give some thought to the caution that "the fact that there have been different opinions about good and bad in different times and places in no way proves that none is true or superior to others."[44] The canonical status of certain works bespeaks the conservative nature of communities and testifies to the members' respect for the wisdom of others. The very fact that in most societies there are iconoclasts whose aim is to discredit the authority of an example meant to be followed proves that there are people whose attitude is governed by a close conformity to the practice of their predecessors. A community cannot survive without some continuity, which involves the legitimacy of canonized texts. Respecting our spiritual forefathers, we recognize ourselves in the past. Liberalism can breed tolerance, which is indispensable to the development of historical sense, but many people, if not all, are brought up on a canon representing a kind of orthodoxy about the relative value of certain monuments of the past. Those who undermine a canon are likely to establish a counter-canon.

If canonization is a process by which some works come to occupy a unique or at least distinguished status of authority in a given community, it involves evaluation and so is a matter of some perspective. In most cases, a canon is a narrative based on such premises which make it the allegory of the development of some community. Each canonical work represents a decisive stage in this development.

Although the idea that the history of art is comparable to the life of living organisms emerged a long time before the nineteenth century – Vasari's evolutionary views, for example, "had been reinforced by scientific and technological evidence of advance in other fields"[45] – it was Romanticism which viewed the nation as the most legitimate form of community and associated the canon with the self-justification of such a community. The criterion of creating a national style represented a break with the universal spirit of Classicism, suggested the incompatibility of aesthetic and historical values, and thus undermined the credibility of an international canon.

Understandably, the concept of self-regulating national cultures was especially influential in literature. The idea that ethnocentric traditions generate their own canons with no authority above them, together with Ranke's influence and evolutionism, made some literary historians especially sensitive to the distinguishing features of national cultures. Standard editions of national classics were published, fixing a canon for several generations. The selection was justified by prominent literary historians.

The assumption underlying an attempt to construct a national canon is that a decisive moment can be found in the history of each literature when it seems to awaken to itself and comes to self-knowledge. If viewed from this crucial stage of serious self-reflection and critical as well as historical self-consciousness, each national literature can be regarded as a self-constituting system which generates a canon of its own.

It is easy to argue that the Romantic conception of *Volksgeist* and the Liberal idea of national self-determination are at work in such a conception, but the influence of this Romantic heritage is more far-reaching than some may believe. Let me quote from an essay written by one of the most celebrated representatives of Deconstruction criticism. The following words testify the survival of the evolutionary conception of national canons in the second half of the twentieth century: "the impact of Hugo on French nineteenth- and twentieth-century poetry is comparable only to that of Goethe on German poetry of the same period, or of Milton and Spenser combined on English Romanticism. If so-called symbolist and surrealist French poetry has a 'face,' it is that of Hugo."[46]

It is not difficult to see that the conception just described may have a weakness comparable to the one which Hayden White detected in Ranke's work: "He admitted the possibility of genuine transformation, revolution, convulsion only for ages prior to his own; but the future for him was merely an indefinite extension of his own present."[47] The question is whether a similar charge cannot be levelled at all shapers of a canon, especially at those who tried to find a stage in the evolution of their own national culture that would be comparable to the age of Pericles or Augustus.

In retrospect, most canons seem to be dated. This, however, should not make us forget about their heuristic value. The sense of timelessness associated with canonicity is in harmony with the fact that aesthetic value may be not exclusively of historical nature. It is also taken for granted that canon formation exceeds the limits of purely artistic considerations. Still, if pushed to an extreme, the ideal of canonicity may lead to an almost unhistorical conception of culture.

An interesting attempt to create an international canon is the *History of European Literature* (1934–35) by the poet and critic Mihály Babits (1883–1941).[48] This book was written with the idea that there existed a *sui generis* European value. The author was aware that he could not justify his canon with reference to any international consensus, so he rendered spatial what was essentially temporal. For him the canonical works of European literature had become independent of their original context, transcended history, and thus appeared to be timeless. Homer, Dante, Shakespeare, Goethe, and Baudelaire seemed to have lived in the same period.

There is no doubt that this work set an example for those who wish to go beyond the political implications of nineteenth-century nationalism. Still, there may be two dangers inherent in such an approach to literature. First, the selection may be too personal. This is absolutely justified in the case of such a major poet as Babits, but can hardly serve as basis for a generalization. The other possible objection is that the shapers of international canons tend to overemphasize extraliterary considerations at the expense of aesthetic value. When it is suggested that Wordsworth and Hölderlin are greater poets than Byron and Goethe, but the latter are greater Europeans,[49] my comment is that in literature it might be more difficult to go beyond national canons than in music or even in the visual arts. There is no reason to believe that the best works are available in translation, so it is less difficult or at least more possible to make value judgements if we stay inside the limits of those canons which belong to actually existing communities.

Notes

[1] Friedrich Nietzsche, "Über Wahrheit und Lüge in außermoralischen Sinn," in *Werke in drei Bänden*. München: Carl Hanser, 1956. III, 312.

[2] Frank Kermode, *The Classic: Literary Images of Permanence and Change*. Cambridge, Massachusetts: Harvard University Press, 1983, 172.

[3] Bruce M. Metzger, *The Canon of the New Testament: Its Origin, Development, and Significance*. Oxford: Clarendon Press, 1987, 111.

[4] Metzger, *The Canon of the New Testament*, 289–290.

[5] F. R. Leavis, *The Great Tradition: George Eliot – Henry James – Joseph Conrad.* New York: New York University Press, 1969, 9.

[6] Ezra Pound, *Guide to Kulchur.* New York: New Directions, 1970, 312, 317.

[7] T. S. Eliot, *Christianity and Culture.* New York – London: Harcourt, Brace, Jovanovich, 1968, 91.

[8] Edmund Burke, *Reflections on the Revolution in France.* Chicago: Henry Regnery Co., 1955, 140.

[9] Carl Dahlhaus, *Grundlagen der Musikgeschichte.* Köln: Hans Gerig, 1972, 107; *Foundations of Music History.* English translation by J. B. Robinson. Cambridge: Cambridge University Press, 1983, 64.

[10] T. S. Eliot, *After Strange Gods: A Primer of Modern Heresy.* New York: Harcourt, Brace and Co., 1934, 51.

[11] Joseph Kerman, "A Few Canonic Variations," in Robert von Hallberg, ed., *Canons.* Chicago: The University of Chicago Press, 1984, 181.

[12] Charles Altieri, "An Idea and Ideal of a Literary Canon," in Robert von Hallberg, ed., *Canons,* 41.

[13] Burke, *Reflections on the Revolution in France,* 127.

[14] T. S. Eliot, *Selected Essays.* New York: Harcourt, Brace and World, 1960, 5.

[15] Carl Dahlhaus, *Analyse und Werturteil.* Mainz: B. Schott's Söhne, 1970, 47, 148.

[16] Richard Rorty, "Comments on Castoriadis's 'The End of Philosophy'," *Salmagundi* 82–83 (Spring – Summer 1989), 26.

[17] Mihály Szegedy-Maszák, "Teleology in Postmodern Fiction," in Matei Calinescu and Douwe Fokkema, eds., *Exploring Postmodernism.* Amsterdam: John Benjamins, 1987, 56.

[18] Paul de Man, *The Resistance to Theory.* Minneapolis: University of Minesota Press, 1986, 72.

[19] Philippe Lacoue-Labarthe, *La fiction du politique: Heidegger, l'art et la politique.* [Paris:] Christian Bourgois, 1987,71.

[20] Cynthia Ozick, "A Critique at Large : T. S. Eliot at 101," *The New Yorker,* November 20, 1989, 152–153.

[21] Leslie A. Fiedler, "Literature as an Institution: The View from 1980," in Leslie A. Fiedler and Houston A. Baker, Jr., eds., *English Literature. Opening up the Canon.* Baltimore and London: The Johns Hopkins University Press, 1981, 85.

[22] Nelson Goodman, *Of Mind and Other Matters.* Cambridge, Massachusetts: Harvard University Press, 1984, 14.

[23] Henry James, *William Wetmore Story and His Friends: From Letters, Diaries, and Recollections.* New York: Grove Press, n.d., vol. I, 17.

[24] Ludwig Wittgenstein, *On Certainty.* Oxford: Basil Blackwell, 1974, 18.

[25] H. Bruce Franklin, "English as an Institution: The Role of Class," in Leslie A. Fiedler and Houston A. Baker, eds., *English Literature: Opening up the Canon,* 100.

[26] Philip V. Bohlman, *The Study of Folk Music in the Modern World.* Bloomington and Indianapolis: Indiana University Press, 1988, 113–114.

[27] T. S. Eliot, *Christianity and Culture,* 198.

[28] Bohlman, *The Study of Folk Music in the Modern World,* 95.

[29] Alfred Einstein, *Grösse in der Musik.* Zürich – Stuttgart: Pan-Verlag, 1951, 25.

[30] „Sir Ernst Gombrich to Quentin Bell, 13 May 1975," in Quentin Bell, *Bad Art.* Chicago: The University of Chicago Press, 1989, 201.

[31] Francis Haskell, *Rediscoveries in Art: Some Aspects of Taste, Fashion and Collecting in England and France*. London: Phaidon, 1976, 99.

[32] Dahlhaus, *Grundlagen der Musikgeschichte,* 124.

[33] Fredric Jameson, *The Ideologies of Theory: Essays 1971–1986. Volume 1: Situations of Theory.* Minneapolis: University of Minnesota Press, 1988, 136.

[34] Pound, *Guide to Kulchur,* 18.

[35] Hugh Kenner, "The Making of the Modernist Canon," in Robert von Hallberg, ed., *Canons,* 373.

[36] Carl Dahlhaus, *Richard Wagners Musikdramen.* Velber [bei Hannover]: Friedrich Verlag, 1971, 105–106.

[37] John Guillory, "The Ideology of Canon-Formation: T. S. Eliot and Cleanth Brooks," in Robert von Hallberg, ed., *Canons,* 358.

[38] Cornelius Castoriadis, "The 'End of Philosophy'?" *Salmagundi* 82–83 (Spring-Summer 1989), 6.

[39] Dahlhaus, *Analyse und Werturteil,* 70.

[40] Pierre Boulez, *Points de repère.* Textes réunis et présentés par Jean-Jacques Nattiez. Deuxième édition revue et corrigée. [Paris:] Christian Bourgois – Éditions du Seuil, 1985, 384.

[41] Pierre Boulez, *Relevés d'apprenti.* Paris: Editions du Seuil, 1966, 302.

[42] Arnold Schönberg, *Stil und Gedanke: Aufsätze zur Musik.* S. Fischer, 1976, 253.

[43] James A. Sanders, *Canon and Community: A Guide to Canonical Criticism.* Philadelphia: Fortress Press, 1984, 15.

[44] Allan Bloom, *The Closing of the American Mind.* New York: Simon and Schuster, 1987, 39.

[45] Haskell, *Rediscoveries in Art,* 54.

[46] Paul de Man, *The Resistance to Theory,* 52.

[47] Hayden White, *Metahistory: The Historical Imagination in Nineteenth-Century Europe.* Baltimore and London: The Johns Hopkins University Press, 1973, 173.

[48] Mihály Babits, *Geschichte des europäischen Literatur.* Zürich – Wien: Europa, 1949.

[49] T. S. Eliot, *On Poetry and Poets.* New York: Farrar, Straus and Cuhady, 1957, 247.

The Legitimacy of a Western Canon

Harold Bloom's book *The Western Canon*, published in 1994, is by general consent a vulnerable achievement. Its author was over the hill at the time he wrote it, and one may be tempted to say that it contains very little that the reader could not find in the earlier works of this highly prolific, self-repetitive, and overrated critic. Many comparative scholars would go as far as saying that the distinction between a Western canon and what is loosely called world literature cannot hold at the end of the twentieth century.

Although I have grave reservations about the merits of *The Western Canon*, my intention is not to point to its rather obvious weaknesses but to examine the dangers imminent in a canonical view of literature.

All architects of the canon select their material in reaction against their predecessors. As is well-known, Bloom's ambition was to undermine the conception of T. S. Eliot and the New Critics. There are surprisingly few references to them in the pages of *The Western Canon*. One of the exceptions is a statement suggesting Bloom's awareness that the value of his outline history of Western literature could be questioned from the perspective of New Criticism. "My late teacher, William K. Wimsatt, used to take grim pleasure in my accounts of my Dickinson seminars, which confirmed (he said) my status as a monument to what he had termed the Affective Fallacy" (296).

Bloom's position is in contradiction with the legacy of New Criticism at least in four aspects. He seems to value Romanticism more than any other literary current; he often translates verse into prose; he is fond of relying on biography, which he regards as indistinguishable from interpretation; and he never refrains from using his individual and strongly emotional response to literary works as a point of reference. The last among these factors is the main reason why his selection seems vulnerable. His value-judgements tend to be arbitrary, because his arguments are either cryptic or insufficient. On some occasions he talks pure sentiment (or rather, impure sentiment), like an amateur. One of the numerous examples of this is his statement that "the rhapsodic fiction of *Thus Spake Zarathustra* is now unreadable" (454).

The analysis of the principles underlying his selection reveals an obvious self-contradiction. In the chapter on *Middlemarch* it is admitted that George Eliot "is not a great stylist" (320), and a similar ambiguity can be detected in the following generalization about twentieth-century literature: "Except for Neruda and Pessoa, the poets of the era are not here: Yeats, Rilke, Valéry, Trakl, Stevens, Eliot, Montale, Mandelstam, Lorca, Vallejo, Hart Crane, and so many others. I myself would rather read poems than novels or plays, yet it seems clear that even Yeats, Rilke, and Stevens are less fully expressive of the age rather than are Proust, Joyce, and Kafka" (447). The point I wish to make is not that Bloom is using a double standard. It is more important to realize that by abandoning the aesthetic standpoint, he comes close to the attitude of the middle-aged T. S. Eliot, which Bloom rejects as conservative. In 1935 the American-born poet-critic gave a definition of the canonical status that is in harmony with the main hypothesis of *The Western Canon*: "The 'greatness' of literature cannot be determined solely by literary standards, though we must remember that whether it is literature or not can be determined only by literary standards" (Eliot 1962: 617).

All canons are defined from the defensive perspective of preserving values. The architect of the canon cannot help opposing his/her own age. That explains Bloom's attack on trends influential at the end of the twentieth century. Paradoxically, Bloom finds himself in a situation similar to that of the New Critics: he is defending the autonomy of literature against the spokesmen of social utopia. New historicism and the psychoanalytic approach to literature are harshly criticized: "'Shakespeare makes history' seems to me a more useful formula than 'history makes Shakespeare.' [...] A political reading of Shakespeare is bound to be less interesting than a Shakespearean reading of politics, just as a Shakespearean reading of Freud is more productive than Freudian reductions of Shakespeare" (283). No less clear is Bloom's distrust of feminism: "Half a century after Woolf's death, she has no rivals among women novelists or critics, though they enjoy the liberations she prophesied" (436). Any skepticism concerning the legitimacy of a Western canon is condemned as destructive, since it is taken for granted that axiological relativism is dangerous. "The movement misnamed 'multiculturalism,' which is altogether anti-intellectual and anti-literary, is removing from the curriculum most works which present imaginative and cognitive difficulties, which means most of the canonical books" (422). The tone of the final chapter, characteristically called "Elegiac Conclusion," is defensive. Emerson, Walter Pater, and Wilde are praised and some German and French critics rejected. Only one of those criticized is mentioned by name. Although the reference to Paul de Man could be explained in terms of the political scandal caused by the publication of the Flemish-born author's war-time journalism, for our purposes it is more relevant to remind ourselves of de Man's insistence on the necessity of de(con)structing cultural canons. "Despite its irresistible tendency toward canon formation," he wrote, "literature is noncanonical, the critique or, if you wish, the deconstruction of canonical models" (de Man 1993: 191).

The defensive tone is perceptible from the very beginning in Bloom's work. "I wish to explain the organization of this book," he writes in the "Preface and Prelude," "and to account for my choice of these twenty-six writers from among the several hundreds in what once was considered to be the Western Canon" (1). The value judgement which serves as the basis for the selection is not made from some international perspective but from the perspective of national cultures, which is tentatively supplemented by generic considerations: "I have tried to represent national canons by their crucial figures: Chaucer, Shakespeare, Milton, Wordsworth, Dickens for England; Montaigne and Molière for France; Dante for Italy; Cervantes for Spain; Tolstoy for Russia; Goethe for Germany; Borges and Neruda for Hispanic America; Whitman and Dickinson for the United States. The sequence of major dramatists is here: Shakespeare, Molière, and Beckett; and of novelists: Austen, Dickens, George Eliot, Tolstoy, Proust, Joyce, and Woolf. Dr. Johnson is here as the greatest of Western literary critics; it would be difficult to find his rival" (2).

Few would quarrel with Bloom's assumption that Shakespeare is the central author of the canon, but the treatment of most national literatures is coloured by the fact that at the end of the twentieth century English has the status of the language of international communication. Bloom seems to regard French as the second most important national literature. In his view its relative inferiority is caused by the lack of a central figure. "There appears to be no single figure in French literature who is at the center of the national canon: no Shakespeare, no Dante, Goethe, Cervantes, Pushkin, Whitman" (146). Even more puzzling is the handling of German letters. Chapter 9 starts with the following reservation: "Of all the strongest Western writers, Goethe now seems the least available to our sensibility. I suspect that this distance has little to do with how badly his poetry translates into English. Hölderlin translates poorly also, but his appeal to most of us dwarfs Goethe's" (203). After such an unfavourable remark the reader may find somewhat surprising not only the statement that "*Faust, Part Two* is the central work of European Romanticism" (220), but also the exclusion of Hölderlin from the Western canon.

Similar inconsistencies abound in the rest of the book. In the Appendices long texts of the ancient Near East and India are included, while the justification of the absence of Chinese literature from the list of recommended readings is rather questionable: "The immense wealth of ancient Chinese literature is mostly a sphere apart from Western literary tradition and is rarely conveyed adequately in the translations available to us" (531). The provincialism of such a conception becomes apparent if we remember that *The March of Literature*, a book by Ford Madox Ford, comparable in scope and length to *The Western Canon*, published in 1938, gives a respectful analysis of the texts associated with the names of Lao-Tsze and Confucius, the poetry of Chu-Yuan, Li-(T'ai)-Po, and Po-Chu-I, with the help of translations by Arthur Waley and Ezra Pound. It is difficult to understand why Bloom failed to acknowledge the influence of Chinese and Japanese culture on the literary avant-garde.

This last example is of special importance in view of the critic's insistence that canonicity depends on influence, an argument made in such earlier books by the same critic as *The Anxiety of Influence* (1973), *A Map of Misreading* (1975), *The Strong Light of the Canonical* (1987), and *Poetics of Influence* (1988). The statement that "really strong poets can read only themselves" (Bloom 1972: 19) is repeated in the opening section of *The Western Canon*: "There can be no strong, canonical writing without the process of literary influence [...]. Any strong literary work creatively misreads and therefore misinterprets a precursor text or texts. [...] Strong writers do not choose their prime precursors, they are chosen by them" (8, 11).

Among the manifestations of canonicity is the impact of Dante on Chaucer, the influence of Chaucer on Shakespeare, and the interest taken by Dostoevsky in Shakespeare. *The Borderers* and *The Prelude* are interpreted as rewritings of *Othello* and Milton. George Eliot's canonical status is explained in terms of intertextuality: "*Silas Marner* returns us to *The Ruined Cottage*, 'Michael,' 'The Old Cumberland Beggar' – to the vision of pastoral man and woman as a primordial good" (321). The same criterion is used in the selection of twentieth-century works: Kafka relies on Dickens, *Ulysses* gives an interpretation of the *Odyssey* and *Hamlet*, and *Finnegans Wake* is viewed as a recreation of works by Shakespeare, Lewis Carroll, Swift, and Richard Wagner. Quotation goes together with anticipation: Dickinson's forty-one-word-long text *From Blank to Blank...* borrows from Milton's sonnet on blindness and Coleridge's *Dejection: An Ode* and foreshadows poems by Stevens and Celan. Inspiration also involves alienation: Beckett decided to write in French to escape from the influence of Joyce. Parody is regarded as a possible constitutive rule of canon formation: the first part of *Faust* parodies Shakespeare, the final choruses of the second part of the same tragedy represent an ironical reading of Dante's *Paradiso*, whereas *Peer Gynt* is a rewriting of *Henry IV* and a parody of *Faust II*.

The emphasis on intertextuality involves a focus on translation. All texts are quoted in English, but translators are always mentioned by name. No text written in other languages can belong to the canon which has not found a significant English translator. Such poets as Shelley, Celan, Borges, and Neruda are given special attention because of their translations of Dante, Dickinson, and Whitman.

One of the remarkable features of *The Western Canon* is Bloom's reluctance to restrict the definition of influence to a literal sense. "Molière evidently knew nothing of Shakespeare, yet Alceste in *The Misanthrope* evokes Hamlet. Ibsen most certainly knew Shakespeare, and Hedda Gabler is a worthy descendant of Iago" (187). This observation suggests that the canon is considered to be an institution of historical nature. A similar flexibility characterizes the following observation: "There is a sense in which 'the canonical' is always the 'intercanonical,' because the Canon not only results from a contest but is itself an ongoing contest" (54). The problem is that this principle is not observed consistently. Whenever Bloom draws inspiration from such critics of international perspective as Auerbach, Curtius, Hugo Friedrich, Ortega y Gasset, Spitzer, Ramón Fernandez, or such Anglo-American scholars as Kenneth Burke, Empson, Northrop Frye, and Wilson Knight, he succeeds in making valuable comparative remarks. On other occasions, however, he seems to give up the ideal formulated in the title of his book and resorts to a double standard. The assessment of the significance of Whitman can be taken as an example: "I suspect that to center a national canon is to guarantee a perpetual currency within a language, but that an eminence beyond a particular language is very rare as a permanent phenomenon. Whitman may yet fade abroad, though never, I think, in these states" (284). A similar inconsistency can be felt in the overall assessment of the American legacy; the ambition to establish an international canon is thwarted by parochialism: "there is no question who has had the largest influence, at home and abroad. Eliot and Faulkner may be Whitman's nearest rivals in their effect upon other writers, but they are not of his almost worldwide significance. Dickinson and James may have an aesthetic eminence equal to Whitman's, but they cannot compete with his universality. American literature abroad is always, in the first place, Whitman, whether it be in Spanish-speaking America, Japan, Russia, Germany, or Africa. Here I want only to note Whitman's influence on two poets, D. H. Lawrence and Pablo Neruda" (288).

There is a fundamental contradiction in Bloom's approach: on the one hand, he views all other literatures from the angle of the English-speaking community, on the other hand, he tries to look at his own culture from the outside. The two perspectives undermine the teleology borrowed from Vico.

There are two conclusions one can draw from the failure of the American critic. First, it is almost certain that no architect of the canon can escape from the spatial limitations of his situation. For Bloom those works are of lasting value which are available in some English translation that he believes to be acceptable. It is highly improbable that the linguistic division of the world can be ignored in such a simple manner. The other reason for the questionable legitimacy of a Western canon is the constant revaluation of works. The defender of the canon intends to raise his present to the rank of the eternal. The mutability of values belongs to the mode of existence of all arts. It affects even fields which lack the diversity of languages. One of the versions of *Christ Before Pilate*, painted by Mihály Munkácsy in 1881, was bought by John Wanamaker for 150,000 U. S. Dollars, the equivalent of nearly 2 million one hundred years later. In 1988 the same painting was sold for 60,000 (Lukacs 1988: 6–7). Within less than half a century the painter(s) known as Van Eyck has/have been the cheapest old master(s) and very nearly the dearest. In 1872 the price of *The Three Mairies At the Sepulchre* was 336 British pounds, in 1940 it was 225,000 pounds (Reitlinger 1982: 306). Numerous other examples could show that it is a misconception to believe in the constancy of aesthetic values.

All canons lose their legitimacy at the moment they are established. Although the reception of works of art is inseparable from canonicity, understanding means the destruction of the existing canons. This ambiguity is closely tied to the historical nature of art and literature. Reading involves the rejection of the canons we have inherited from our predecessors. That is why literary history has to be constantly rewritten. As a Portuguese critic wrote in a recent article, "Nations, history, and literature alike appear, like ghosts, literally *by mistake*, that is, through revision" (Tamen 1998: 304).

The fundamental weakness of *The Western Canon* resides in Bloom's outmoded approach to history: his chronological, linear, and Eurocentric concept of progress fails to do justice to the heterogeneity and discontinuity of cultures. The long list of works, presented as an appendix, has a hit-or-miss appearance, because the criterion underlying the selection, the accessibility of English translations, is insufficient if we have not a source- but a target-oriented view of intertextuality. Bloom seems to ignore the difficult yet fundamental questions whether national literatures are equivalent, and whether the classifying concepts (those of genres and periods or movements) used by Western scholars are applicable to non-Western cultures. These two questions have to be answered by comparative scholars in the future.

References

Bloom, H. 1973. *The Anxiety of Influence: A Theory of Poetry.* New York: Oxford University Press.

de Man, P. 1993. *Romanticism and Contemporary Criticism: The Gauss Seminar and Other Papers.* Baltimore and London: The Johns Hopkins University Press.

Eliot, T. S. 1962. "Religion and Literature," in Morton Dauwen Zabel (ed.) *Literary Opinion in America: Essays Illustrating the Status, Methods, and Problems of Criticism in the United States in the Twentieth Century.* Third edition, revised. New York/Evanston: Harper and Row.

Lukacs, J. 1988. *Budapest 1900: A Historical Portrait of a City and Its Culture.* New York: Weidenfeld and Nicolson.

Reitlinger, G. 1982. *The Economics of Taste: The Rise and Fall of Picture Prices 1760–1960.* Volume I (1960). New York: Hacker Art Books.

Tamen, M. 1998. "Phenomenology of the Ghost: Revision in Literary History." *New Literary History* 29: 295–304.

National Canons

1. Canon and Identity

No treatment of canonicity can ignore that in the Old Testament plurality often means dissonance, whereas unity stands for harmony and strength. The story of Babel suggests that human pride dispersed languages. The Holy Spirit speaks one language, and the emergence of the ideal of the canon was inseparable from the ideal of one God, one church, and one book. Protestantism represented a departure from this "Catholic" assumption. When Latin was replaced by a proliferation of local dialects, the concept of canonicity was brought into question. Mihály Babits was not entirely wrong to insist in his *History of European Literature* (published in Hungarian in 1934-35 and in German in 1949) that a national canon is in a sense a self-contradiction, the result of a conflict between imitation and isolation, other and self.[1]

The origins of the concept of a supranational canon can be traced back to the idea of an unchanging, uncorrupted, and privileged "original" language. In the Western world it was in the age of the Reformation that the diversity of languages was transformed from a punishment into a grace. The conventionality of all languages served as a starting point for translations of the Bible into the vernacular.

While in the seventeenth and eighteenth centuries the uniformity of human reason led to speculations about a universal grammar, the Romantics returned to the relativist legacy. Although the origins of this paradigm shift can be traced back to the works of Jean-Jacques Rousseau, its most influential spokesmen were among the opponents of the 1789 French revolution. "J'ai vu, dans ma vie, des François, des Italiens, des Russes. etc.: je sais même, grâces à Montesquieu, *qu'on pet être Persan:* mais quant à l'*homme*, je déclare ne l'avoir rencontré de ma vie." This statement from *Consirédations sur la France* by Joseph de Maistre, first published in 1796 or 1797,[2] may be taken as a critique of the *Déclaration des droits de l'homme et du citoyen*, proclaimed by the Assemblé nationale at the end of 1789. Another well-known response to the same document is Edmund Burke's *Reflections on the Revolution in France*, a letter "intended to have been sent to a gentleman in Paris" in 1790, a defence of local habits, conventions, "untaught feelings," "old prejudices."[3] The Romantic cult of the "couleur locale" developed simultaneously with a study of linguistic diversity. Wilhelm von Humboldt's *Über die Verschiedenheit des menschlichen Sprachbaues und ihren Einfluß auf die geistliche Entwickelung des Menschengeschlechts*, published posthumously in 1836, emphasized the close link between cultural relativism and the Liberal idea of free self-development ("Bildung").

The rise of the national canons represented a movement towards shared consciousness. They can be characterized as a) structures of meanings extending behind habitual practices that may not have relevance beyond the limits of certain ethnic and/or linguistic communities, b) constitutive components of national identity, and c) institutionalized forms of memory by which regional and/or linguistic communities attempted to stabilize themselves. Standing for normative self-definitions, institutionalized fictions with "as if" qualities to fill out, they were meant to provide a sense of security and belonging. Retrospectively it has to be admitted that as assertions of identity and difference sometimes they involved violent overreactions.

As there is no selfhood without some other, a national canon – whether attached to land or language – is constituted in such a way that its identity has both intra- and intercultural aspects. In other words, it is mediated by the memory of the other and its development always involves at least two cultures. The court of Louis XIV, English Classicism, or the Weimar Klassik defined itself with reference to Graeco-Roman Antiquity. Thus, it is possible to argue that national canons reveal an interacting with other creeds. They are intercultural manifestations, conflictual as well as mutually complementary, configurations that are, in relation to each other, not only powerfully reciprocal but also strongly oppositional. In English culture a period is often called the "Augustan Age," and several cities claim to the status of "the Venice of the North" or "the Paris of the East." The historians of less well-known literatures are inclined to define their topic with the help of internationally accepted terms and celebrated names. In Russia Symbolism and Futurism developed as reactions to French and Italian movements, in Hungarian literary history Miklós Jósika was often mentioned as "the Hungarian Walter Scott" and Zsigmond Kemény "the Hungarian Balzac."[4]

From the late phase of the Enlightenment to the twentieth century, in some parts of Central Europe there was a strong desire to build up a deliberate "counteridentity" against some dominating culture. Under the conditions of resistance to cultural colonization national canons emerged inspired by the idea that cultures defied translatability. The political implications of negative self-definitions were as obvious during the reign of Joseph II (1780–1790), an enlightened Habsburg who wished to replace Latin with German as the language of administration in his empire, as around the 1848 revolutions, or in the period in which the army of the Third Reich invaded some countries of the region.

The danger inherent in the development of national canons was that it was often forgotten that the complementarities and contradictions of the dialogue of national cultures had been chiastically structured. Total orderedness usually terminated in ossification. A national tradition can survive only if it is always in the making. The idea of a constant, unchanged national character, a cultural stereotype – often coupled with the (mis)conception that national identity has to be discovered in the distant past – can be called conservative, in contrast to the liberal tradition based on the assumption that "se trouve autant de différence de nous à nous mesmes, que de nous à aultruy."[5]

2. Translatability

The interaction between national canons inevitably raises the question of translatability. As is well-known, the word "translation" means displacement, recontextualization. Accordingly, the success of a translation depends on the target and not on the source culture. "Translation" has a much wider semantic field than "traduction;" it covers a wide range of intertextuality, from adaptation through appropriation to interpretation. The analogy is not with repetition but with transposition, orchestration, imitation, pastiche, paraphrase, variation, or parody.

Can divine names be translated? How are Zeus, Demeter, and Persephone related to Jupiter, Ceres, and Proserpina? Can a pagan or a Buddhist text have a Christian interpretation? Such are the questions the scholar comparing various national canons has to ask. The works of Racine, Hölderlin, or Wordsworth translate poorly, and the same is true of the long epic poems written in languages of more limited distribution. Such verse narratives as *The Flight of Zalán* (1825) or *The Death of Buda* (1863) are barely translatable. Their authors (Mihály Vörösmarty and János Arany) are great Hungarian poets, and these works about the 896 conquest of the Carpathian Basin and the alleged continuity between Huns and Hungarians have made a decisive contribution to Hungarian national identity. Although it would be risky to speculate about the future, it is possible to argue that while these works belong to the core of a national canon, they cannot hope to gain international relevance, so they may lose their status after the restructuring of national canons. Such revaluations have occurred even in internationally well-known literatures. Pierre-Jean Béranger's poetry was given a detailed analysis in Johannes Scherr's *Allgemeine Geschichte der Literatur*, one of the most influential early histories of "Weltliteratur," first published in 1850. One hundred and forty years later the editor (David Hollier) and many authors of the eleven-hundred-page-long work entitled *A New History of French Literature* and published by Harvard University Press did not even mention the name of the once celebrated versifier.

Such examples may suggest that it is not misleading to emphasize the self-contradictory nature of the subject of our discussion. On the one hand, national canons were created with the idea that they should serve as a source of inspiration to resist assimilation. The Romanian, Czech, Slovak, or Hungarian nationalists who introduced language reforms, collected folk poetry, started periodicals, founded public libraries, publishing houses, academies, and schools in the late phase of the Enlightenment were reluctant to give up a cultural identity in favour of a dominant culture. On the other hand, Liberals maintained that tolerance depended on translatability. The translation of the "classics" into the vernacular confirmed the nationalist agenda by permitting the easy appropriations of texts originally written in foreign languages. "As long as there is the possibility of translation there is no need of conversion," an Egyptologist writes, but he also admits the limited relevance of his statement by adding that "translatability rests upon experience and reason, unstranslatability on belief which in itself proves to be an untranslatable concept."[6]

Most national canons include works which ridicule some other community. *The Life of Henry the Fifth*, *The Merchant of Venice*, and *The Tragedy of Othello the Moor of Venice* belong to a large group of texts that may remind us that a lack of tolerance is not an exclusive characteristic of the cultures of the eastern half of Europe. The alien is frequently presented as standing for extra- or nonculture in nineteenth-century historical paintings or novels, not to mention works of historiography. In *Toldi* (1846), a verse narrative taught in Hungarian primary schools, the title-hero's opponent is a Czech warrior. In *War and Peace* (1863–9) Napoleon is portrayed in a way that is still not acceptable to most French readers.

There are so many significant works containing unfavourable portraits of the alien that it would be impossible to exclude them from the European tradition. In a highly provocative essay, the Slovak historian Lubomír Lipták argued against the demolition of monuments, which always played a major role in canon formation. "Memorial and monument are both related to commemoration, and this also applies to things about which we might want to, but should not forget."[7] This statement may deserve some attention. If the French can cope with the works of their collaborationist writers, other nations may also be expected to resolve the historical problems of their identity. Hungarian children are brought up on historical novels describing places which no longer belong to Hungary. Historical discontinuities always affect national identity and may disturb the translatability of cultures.

In view of the incompatible versions of history one may find in textbooks widely used, it is not easy to see how national canons can play upon each other, intersect, or merge. There have been relatively few attempts to create models of mutual understanding. The very term dialogue has been used somewhat irresponsibly, or at least it has lost its outlines. Religion and cross-national economy appear to have been promoters of international communication. Translation culture may also lead to greater tolerance. An individual able to change from one language to another may be more tolerant than monolingual people.

There have been relatively few successful attempts at construing a cross-cultural discourse. Paradigmatic examples are Goethe's *Torquato Tasso* (1789), a verse play containing many creative translations of passages from the Italian poet's *Gerusalemme liberata*, Madame de Staël's *De l'Allemagne* (1813), a book-length essay that popularized the idea that literature was an expression of "Volksgeist," and Carlyle's *Sartor Resartus* (1836), in which the "concept-oriented philosophical culture of German idealism is to be transposed into the experience-oriented culture of British empiricism," so that it epitomizes "the telescoping of transcendentalism and empiricism."[8] The English author's Menippean satire may remind us that translation always defamiliarizes: the other culture is "clothed," disguised, and de(con)structed.

In literature most of the national cultures are ignored by international scholarship. It is symptomatic that the list of recommended readings at the end of Harold Bloom's *The Western Canon: The Books and School of the Ages* (1994) does not include a single work that is not available in English translation. "On peut acquérir dans une vie deux cultures, peut-être trois – pas davantage," writes Tzvetan Todorov,[9] who was born in Bulgaria and did his best to leave his native culture behind and become a French intellectual.

3. Globalization

The Enlightenment project of modernity implied a progress toward globalization. This goal, however, may be leading to a kind of uniformity. Those who see a danger in this, following the lead of Alexis de Tocqueville, argue that the cultural imperatives today point to regionalism and necessitate the preservation of national canons which stand for otherness. In the early nineteenth century it was asserted that national canons evolved and declined in the same way as human individuals. It is easy to dismiss such an organicist conception in the name of some universal humanity – as Thomas Mann did in his 1924 review of *Der Untergang des Abendlandes*, calling Spengler "geistfeindlich" and "ein Snob."[10] More difficult is to put up an alternative conception against the sophisticated critique of cultural translatability represented by Heidegger or the later Wittgenstein.

In the Hellenistic world Greek and in the Middle Ages Latin was the most important mode of transmission, although in some Western countries French was used in the discourse of "co(u)rtoisie," a form of high culture tied to knightly qualities. Later French served as the language of diplomacy, and in the nineteenth century German became the language of communication in Central Europe. Today there is a chance that English will emerge as a lingua franca of the mutual translation of culture, a common denominator for a multitude of local differences. All these examples suggest that a lingua franca is never a neutral medium. It conditions the transformation of the message.

The dilemma is between the hermeneutic necessity, "das elementare Bedürfnis, in der Situation der Rede den Andern zu verstehen und selbst verstanden zu werden"[11] and the sustained resistance of the other. The dangers are colonization and lack of communication. More specifically, one of the characteristics of the postmodern condition may be a constant exposure to cultural interpenetration that may involve a loss of identity. The more works we read in translation, the more we may feel that the dividing line between the familiar and the unfamiliar becomes blurred. Projecting one's own frame of reference onto an alien culture may lead to the suppression of alterity.

There are different modes of assimilation, incorporation, and appropriation. Does it lead to the destruction of otherness if an art historian views the national canon of nineteenth-century historical paintings from the perspective of French Impressionism? Currently there is an exhibition of the works of Bertalan Székely (1835–1910), arguably the most important Hungarian representative of historical painting in the National Gallery of Budapest. The lack of attention this presentation has met with suggests a radical devaluation of what used to be regarded as belonging to the core of Hungarian culture. In the past scenes from Hungarian history painted by Székely and his contemporaries (Viktor Madarász, Károly Lotz, Gyula Benczúr, Mór Than, Jenő Gyárfás, Sándor Wagner, and others) constituted a kind of illustrated history which played a major role in the creation of national identity. The decline in the reputation of these works, comparable to the loss of popularity of historical fiction and drama may cause radical changes in the self-perception of Hungarians as a nation.

To have an inside knowledge of a national canon is far from easy. To have and convey a sense of cultural difference when approaching a foreign canon is even more difficult. Instead of studying national canons as self-sufficient entities, it is more appropriate to expose ourselves to their influence. Several recordings of *Jenůfa* and *Duke Bluebeard's Castle* suggest that the mispronunciation of the text distorts the musical structure, a native speaker's reading of a poem may be radically different from the interpretation of someone reading in a language s/he has learned, and even Székely's 1860 canvas *The Corpse of Louis II in the Csele Brook* may be seen in very different ways, depending on the viewer's attitude to the battle of Mohács, a paradigmatic event in Hungarian history.

54

The value of a cultural product may vary according to its central or marginal position in a national canon and the interpreter's distance from that canon. It happens that some elements of a national canon become alienated from the community. They may recede into the past as lifeless monuments. If the inherited frame of reference has been invalidated and the gap between past and present become too wide, a reinterpretation of the canon is imminent. The experience of a crisis will issue into a critique of one's culture. The revitalization of what has become defunct may be difficult.

One of the assumptions of the Romantics was an estrangement from old traditions. In the works of such Hungarian authors as István Széchenyi, Ferenc Kölcsey, Mihály Vörösmarty, and others there is the awareness of the otherness of the surrounding culture. These two factors, together with the lesson taught by history suggesting the possible death of certain civilizations (Egypt, Assyria, Babylon), led to the conclusion that new interpretations may supplant old meanings in such a way that continuity is broken.

"The iron fist of centuries finishes
but all that man has built: gone is noble Troy;
   gone are the might and pride of Carthage,
      Babylon, Rome – they have all gone under."

These words, written by Dániel Berzsenyi around 1796,[12] in an ode addressed "To the Hungarians," indicate that the organicist view of national character developed in an age marked by a growing awareness of historical discontinuity.

Sometimes the same writers made a prediction about the death of the nation and expressed a strong desire to preserve or rather revitalize at least something of an ancient heritage. This idea was largely responsible for the rise of folklore. From Thomas Percy's *Reliques of Ancient English Poetry* (1765) to Kölcsey's *National Traditions* (1826) many collections and essays were published to prove the close link between the legacy of the distant past and the traditional culture of the peasantry.

One's own past may be seen as a foreign otherness. Most Germans would dissociate themselves from the Third Reich. Modern Greeks view Hellas and Sparta both as part and not as part of their identity. More uncertain is the relation between Dacia and Romania, Magna Moravia and Slovakia, Huns and Hungarians, or ancient and modern Egypt. In the past Franz Joseph was viewed by most Hungarians as alien. Today the 1848 revolution and the 1867 Ausgleich are generally accepted as canonical events of

Hungarian history, in the same way as both Saxons and Normans are regarded as the ancestors of the English. More recent attempts to combine African and native American heritage with that of the white population of the New World may need some time. Cultural canons may require a choice of a past and a selection of one's parents and enemies. Sometimes traditions that appeared to be incompatible in the past are integrated.

The situation in which relatively small nations, especially those which belonged to Communist states in the decades following World War II, seek to explain themselves to others, and in doing so first create these others, needs further exploration. The use of languages spoken by others, taking language in a very broad sense, is usually imperfect. To take one example, many Hungarians believe that their poetry is of universal value, yet the international reputation of Hungarian poetry is not too high. By general consent, the quality of the translations is made responsible for this discrepancy. The fact that the native speakers of other languages find most translations unreadable means that what we have here is a lack of mutual understanding. Those who are convinced that runic script is a crucial element of the Hungarian national canon, upholding the anachronistic view that the outlines of national identity have to be discovered in early history, and those who select and translate Hungarian verse into other languages often have misconceptions about the other. Some of these may be Hungarians who lived in exile during the Communist period and may have become alienated from their original culture in the sense that they have lost contact with the specific experience of those who did not leave their country. For those who went abroad after World War II or the revolution of 1956 Communism represented the other that could never be integrated into the identity of the nation, whereas for those who lived in the Eastern Bloc Communism represented a historical situation they could not ignore.

To avoid possible misunderstandings, I do not wish to suggest that people who lived under Soviet rule could develop a more authentic interpretation of the recent past. To my knowledge Ignác Romsics was the first Hungarian scholar who made a serious attempt to analyze Communist Hungary from a Postcommunist perspective. His book, published in English under the title *Hungary in the Twentieth Century* for the 1999 Frankfurt Book Fair, is a highly successful synthesis. Understandably, its task was not to solve the problems of cultural historians. In the case of 1848 and 1867, a revolution fought against and a compromise made with the Habsburg dynasty, memory has made self and other part of the same identity. It remains to be seen how the bridge between the different, sometimes even warring, memories of the twentieth century can be bridged. The fragmentation of the national canon is the result of the Hungarians' inability to integrate traumatic events in the collective consciousness.

It would be unhistorical to assume that if the Communist other is rejected, Hungarians can define their identity by restoring continuity with the culture that was broken after 1945. My suspicion is that in the twenty-first century national canons have to be reorganized. The former Eastern Bloc may present special difficulties. While it is true that the mediation of memory through publications and censorship created a gap for the generations educated in Communism, it is not possible to return to the interpetation of the past generally accepted before World War II.

Since the late eighteenth century the forgotten, repressed, or foreign as the noncanonical has undergone such radical reinterpretations that it will not be easy to reestablish national canons. The representatives of the polysystem theory suggest that canons belonging to the "core" of universal culture may have a better chance than "marginal" ones in a world gravitating towards homogeneity. This would mean that continuities linked to relatively small communities are threatened and the fundamental principles of cultural history have to be reformulated. It will be impossible not to take part in the debate about the cultural consequences of joining the European Union. Provided the memory of this Union is to be created, nations entering this community must mediate between their own particular memories and their participation in the new European retrospection. As cultural and aesthetic value, in contrast to exchange and similarly to use value, is not quantifiable, a cultural product that is part of a national canon may lose its relevance for an international public. The establishment of an economy that knows no national boundaries will require that we solve the problem of the relation between the economic and the cultural.

My conclusion cannot be other than tentative. The rise of most national canons was simultaneous with the relativist reaction against the universalistic aspects of the Enlightenment. In a more distant future they may lose some part of their legitimacy for the simple reason that in the human sphere there are no permanent values. "So our virtues / Lie in the interpretation of the time," as Affidius says in the last scene of Act IV of *The Tragedy of Coriolanus*, a play that gives a subtle analysis of man's alienation from his own community.

Notes

[1] See my essay "The Permanence and Mutability of Aesthetic Values (Mihály Babits: The History of European Literature)," *Hungarian Studies* 12 (1997), 93–105.

[2] Joseph de Maistre, *Considérations sur la France*. Genève: Slatkine, 1980, 123–124.

[3] Edmund Burke, *Selections from His Political Writings and Speeches*. Paris: T. Nelson, n. d., 295–296.

[4] Sándor Endrődi, *Századunk magyar irodalma képekben (Széchenyi föllépésétől a kiegyezésig)*. Budapest: Athenaeum, 1900, 143, 166–186.

[5] Michel Montaigne, "De l'inconstance de nos actions," in *Essais*. Paris: Hachette, 1868, tome premier, 209.

[6] Jan Assmann, "Translating Gods," in Sanford Budick and Wolfgang Iser, eds., *The Translatability of Cultures: Figurations of the Space Between*. Stanford, CA: Stanford University Press, 1996, 31, 33.

[7] Lubomír Lipták, "Monuments of Political Changes and Political Changes of Monuments," in Miro Kollar, ed., *Scepticism and Hope: Sixteen Contemporary Slovak Essays*. Bratislava: Kalligram, 1999, 142.

[8] Wolfgang Iser, "The Emergence of a Cross-Cultural Discourse," in Sanford Budick and Wolfgang Iser, eds., Op. cit., 248–249.

[9] Tzvetan Todorov, *Nous et les autres: La réflexion française sur la diversité humaine* (1989). Paris: Seuil, 1992, 338.

[10] Thomas Mann, "Über die Lehre Spenglers," *Reden und Aufsätze*. Frankfurt am Main: Fischer, 1990, Vabd 2, 179.

[11] Hans Robert Jauß, *Wege des Verstehens*. München: Wilhelm Fink, 1994, 7.

[12] The translation is by Adam Makkai. See his anthology *In Quest of the 'Miracle Stag'; The Poetry of Hungary*. Budapest – Chicago: Atlantis-Centaur – M. Szivárvány – Corvina, 1996.

Translation and Canon Formation

"Die toten Meister heben ihre Hände,
Sie rufen aus dem Grabe: 'Rette, rette,
Ach, wer errettet unsere Musik?!"
(Hans Pfitzner: *Palestrina*, Erster Akt. Dritte Szene)

"[...] how much I feel that in a literary work of the least complexity the
very form and texture are the substance itself and that the flesh is in-
detachable from the bones! Translation is an effort – though a most flatter-
ing one! – to *tear* the hapless flesh, and in fact to get rid of so much of it
that the living thing bleeds and faints away!"
(Henry James: Letter to August Monod)[1]

Is translation resurrection or death? Pfitzner seems to suggest that works
are dead unless they are translated, whereas James insists that texts are
mutilated in translation.

How can we describe the relations between transaction in the ordinary
sense and so-called literary translation? In the heyday of Structuralism,
when poetics was cultivated as an integral part of applied linguistics, the
answer seemed rather simple. Nowadays different scholars may give different definitions of literary translation, depending on their awareness of
the complexity of the historical implications. If our starting-point is the
"target text" ("texte-arrivée") rather than the "source text" ("texte-départ"),
it becomes perfectly understandable why "originals" of great artistic merit
can have bad translations and mediocre texts can be transformed into works
of great beauty by imaginative translators. Although no culture can do
without translations, the approach to them will differ according to the preconceptions of the translator. S/he may either believe in a universal grammar of all cultures or insist on their diversity. A universalistic interpreter of
culture may view literature as an international canon of great works of
everlasting aesthetic value, whereas a relativist will emphasize the mutability of artistic values. For the former the distinction between "adequate,"
"faithful," or "close" and "inadequate," "unfaithful," or "false" translation
is crucial; for the latter the legitimacy of translation cannot be considered
in terms of equivalence between source and target text, since its credibility
is bound up with a historical process leading to the successful reception of
the translated text in the target culture. The opposition between these two
ideal types can also be rephrased as one between a logocentric conception,

suggesting that the source text has an unquestionable and easily accessible identity, and a hermeneutic or de(con)structive interpretation highlighting the historical nature of the cultural distance between "original" and "translation," the same and the other, identity and difference.

The representatives of the source-oriented approach may focus on interlingual relations, assert that "we can and should do both measure and describe the degree of achieved equivalence,"[2] and assume that retranslating is necessary because old translations become dated. By contrast, a target-oriented conception suggests that interlingual relations imply intercultural dialogues, encounters, and even conflicts, a distance between different traditions and interpretive communities. A translation may change its status and meaning in the same way as any literary work does. My assumption is that at the very end of the twentieth century, a period of growing awareness of multiculturalism, it seems difficult to insist on a clear-cut distinction between poet and translator, in the manner of Walter Benjamin, who in his essay on the task of the translator, written around 1923-24, made the following remark: "Wie nämlich die Übersetzung eine eigene Form ist, so läßt sich auch die Aufgabe des Übersetzers als eine eigene fassen und genau von der des Dichters unterscheiden."[3] This statement deserves special attention because it contradicts the general belief that an adherence to canonicity involves ideological conservatism. Benjamin's distinction between creation and adaptation, in the same way as the opposition between Realism and decadence or progressive and retrograde formulated by György Lukács in his Marxist works, would suggest that the canonical view of literature may also be tied to a belief in some social and political Utopia. A liberal pluralist critique of the canon is opposed not only to conservatism but also to messianic interpretations of history or at least to the Enlightenment idea of "une unique humanité sous l'angle du progrès."[4]

Canons are inseparable from discourses of value based on ideology, which is characterized by Wlad Godzich as "the arrogance of the finite subject who speaks as if he were the ultimate legislator, as if he had been appointed the final judge."[5] These words occur in an essay on Paul de Man, suggesting that one of the self-contradictions of deconstruction theory was its failure to break with the ideal of canonicity. In one respect de Man and Derrida continued the tradition of prominent Marxists and New Critics by focusing on a limited corpus of texts viewed as crucial. One of the phenomena indicating the source-oriented nature of their approach is that some of their basic principles have proved to be inapplicable to literatures outside their sphere of interest. To translate Derrida into some languages is not much easier than to recreate a poetic text. If Shakespeare is transformed by a major artist, the result can be remarkable poetry. What happens to Derrida (see the Hungarian translation of *La Dissémination*) in translation is a topic that would deserve investigation. It is easy to believe in an international canon of literary theory; it would be much more difficult to analyze the reception of certain theoretical texts in communities with languages that do not belong to the Indo-European family.

Whether speaking of imaginative literature or theoretical works (the distinction itself is rather questionable), it seems that the emphasis on the primary significance of the source text often goes together with a distinction between central and marginal literatures. Marginal literatures, the main representative of polysystem theory argues, desperately need translations, while central literatures may do without them, for the simple reason that they constitute the core of an international canon.[6] Although such discrimination may owe something to the rise of the ideal of "Weltliteratur," its origin can be traced back to earlier periods. Some writers involved in the "Quer(r)elle des Anciens et des Modernes" maintained that this core was represented by the legacy of Classical Antiquity. Swift compared the Ancients to bees and the Moderns to spiders, using the opposition between productive and parasitic beings to suggest a distinction between creative originality and derivativeness, and went as far as emphasizing that "the Moderns were much the more ancient of the two," in a work published in 1704 and entitled "A Full and True Account of the Battel Fought last Friday, Between the Ancient and the Modern Books in St. James's Library."[7] A similar position is taken by some twentieth-century scholars influenced by hermeneutics and "Rezeptionsgeschichte" who suggest that a reader can continue a more meaningful dialogue with a work that has the status of a Classic than with more recent literature. "Mit Texten wie Homer und Herodot, Hiob und Paulus," the editors of a representative collection of essays on canon and censorship write, "können wir in direkter Zwiesprache leben. Sie sind uns in höherem Maße *präsent* als Heiner Müller und Botho Strauss."[8] Of course, it would be a gross mistake to condemn a convinced adept of the significance of the reinterpretation of great works composed in the past. The rereadability of the Greek epics and the different performances of Greek tragedies prove the ambiguity of cultural distance.

"Was ich besitze, seh ich wie im Weiten,
Und was verschwand, wird mir
zur Wirklichkeiten,"

as Goethe says at the beginning of *Faust*. There is something to be said for the idea formulated by Wilhelm Furtwängler, one of the most powerful canon builders, that true universality may derive from the profound understanding of one work rather than from a superficial acquaintance with many works: "Die wahre Universalität stammt aus dem völligen Beherrschen und Verstehen des *Einen*, nicht aus dem halben Verstehen des Vielen."[9]

I quote a musician because the spokesmen of international canons often rely on the other arts: the great masterpieces in the outstanding museums or the repertoire of celebrated conductors, instrumentalists, and singers. While it is certainly true that both the visual arts and music are familiar with phenomena that are comparable to translations in certain respects – one may think of transposition, transcription, and (re)orchestration, not to speak of variation, paraphrase, and adaptation –, translation in a strict sense is inseparable from the diversity of natural languages. One of the points made by Benjamin in the above-mentioned essay is about untranslatability. The Hungarian poet and prose writer Dezső Kosztolányi (1885–1936) spoke of the untranslatability of literature as early as 1913, in his essay on the translation of Poe's poem *The Raven*, as well as in the Preface to his collection of verse translations *Modern Poets*.[10] Like Kosztolányi, Gadamer discussed translation as a form of interpretation in his essay "Lesen ist wie Übersetzen," written in 1989. The views of these three authors were anticipated by some German Romantics. Friedrich Schlegel, for instance, argued that "Was in gewöhnlichen guten oder votrefflichen Übersetzungen verlorengeht, ist grade das Beste."[11]

What constituents of an "original" can be preserved in a "translation"? For Kosztolányi this question seemed inappropriate. The fundamental weakness he saw in most translations was the emphasis on the signified at the expense of the signifier. In 1917 he compared the translation of Baudelaire to that of proverbs, reminding his readers that in literature words had the status of proper nouns with an identifying reference that was recognizable within a specific interpretive community defined by language taken in a broad sense (meaning cultural memory).[12] The literal translation of a poem is not poetry, just as the literal translation of a proverb is not a proverb. If this is true, a work can realize its aesthetic potential within an interpretive community that shares its mother tongue with that work, taking the term mother tongue in a broad cultural and historical sense and granting that communities are temporary, shifting, constantly embattled, disintegrating, multiple, and intersecting. Translation means that the canonicity of a work has been de(con)structed. This is what Henry James called "tearing the hapless flesh," in the letter showing his great satisfaction when told about the untranslatability of his works. In the course of intercultural appropriation a new text is created which may or may not acquire a canonical status in a different tradition. In short, the value of a translation depends on how it has been received by a second community. As John Guillory argued in his book on canon formation: "The translation of the 'classics' into one's vernacular is a powerful institutional buttress of imaginary cultural continuities, it confirms the nationalist agenda by permitting the easy appropriation of texts in foreign languages."[13] Instructors teaching general courses on what they call the "great books" often ignore the historical context of the translation. The same could be said about most teleological interpretations of "world literature."

The case of Kosztolányi suggests that a deep historical awareness may involve a distrust of international histories of literature. Unlike Benjamin, Kosztolányi was not attracted to messianism. Since he was convinced that the poet had no control over his language, which was the embodiment of historical memory, he developed a target-oriented approach to translation and a reader-response theory of literature. His distrust of international canons was the result not only of his cultural relativism but also of his rejection of the production-oriented aesthetics implicit in the first sentence of Benjamin's essay: "Nirgends erweist sich einem Kunstwerk oder einer Kunstform gegenüber die Rücksicht auf den Aufnehmenden für deren Erkenntnis fruchtbar."[14]

Belonging to a small community with a relatively inaccessible language, Kosztolányi had strong reservations about the legitimacy of any international canon. Viewing translation as one of the many possible manifestations of intertextuality, he rejected the dichotomies creative writing versus translation, originality versus derivativeness, canonical versus non-canonical, correct versus incorrect interpretation. Convinced that all works of literature contained quotations that cannot be recognized outside a specific interpretive community, he dismissed the idea that equivalence was a valid criterion for judging translations. His theory and practice had striking similarities with those of Ezra Pound, who undermined the distinction between translation and original verse, Vladimir Nabokov, whose translation of *Evgeny Onegin* has to be read as part of his textual commentary, and Samuel Beckett, who transformed Chamfort's prose maxims into English verse and created very free adaptations of his own French texts. The gap between *Zashchita Luzhina*, an avant-garde novel rich in metafictional puns, published in Berlin in 1930, and *The Defense, a* Postmodern fiction "translated by Michael Scammell in collaboration with the author" and published in New York in 1964, is as wide as between the deliberately sentimental *Oh les beaux jours* and the prosaic *Happy Days.* The activity of these writers suggests that translation is of inherently historical nature. If there is any equivalence between two texts, its criteria can be defined by a reader who takes one text as the translation, adaptation, or interpretation of another text. The history of reception shows that the "same" text can be viewed as an original work and a translation from two different historical perspectives. If there is no final interpretation, there can be no correct, accurate, faithful, close, error-free, adequate, or even literal translation. Retranslating is a form of rereading and as such is an inherent quality of the mode of existence and functioning of literature. The relations between translation and canon formation are governed by one principle: on the one hand, literature by its very nature is untranslatable, on the other, no literary work exists that cannot be read as translation.

Notes

[1] Leon Edel, ed., *The Selected Letters of Henry James.* New York: Farrar, Straus and Cudary, 1955, 107.

[2] Willis Barnstone, *The Poetics of Translation: History, Theory, Practice.* New Haven and London: Yale University Press, 1993, 12.

[3] Walter Benjamin, *Illuminationen: Ausgewählte Schriften.* Frankfurt am Main: Suhrkamp, 1961, 63.

[4] Paul Ricoeur, *Histoire et vérité.* Troisième édition augmentée de quelques textes. Paris: Seuil, 1964, 87.

[5] Wlad Godzich, *The Culture of Literacy.* Cambridge, MA: Harvard University Press, 1994, 143.

[6] Itamar Even-Zohar, "Translated Literature within the Literary Polysystem," *Poetics Today,* Vol 11, No. 1, Spring 1990, 48.

[7] Jonathan Swift, *Gulliver's Travels and Other Writings*. New York: Bantam Books, 1962, 403.

[8] Aleida und Jan Assmann, "Kanon und Zensur," in Aleida und Jan Assmann (Hrsg.), *Kanon und Zensur: Beiträge zur Archäologie der literarischen Komunikation II*. München: Wilhelm Fink, 1987, 7.

[9] Wilhelm Furtwängler, "An Karl Straube, 5. II. 45," in *Briefe*. Zweite Auflage. Wiesbaden: E. A. Brockhaus, 1965, 113.

[10] See my essay "Fordítás és kánon," in *Irodalmi kánonok*. Debrecen: Csokonai, 1998, 47–71.

[11] Friedrich Schlegel, "Fragmente 73," in *Werke in zwei Bänden*. Berlin und Weimar: Aufbau, 1980, I. 176.

[12] Dezső Kosztolányi, *Ércnél maradóbb*. Budapest: Szépirodalmi, 1975, 492–493.

[13] John Guillory, *Cultural Capital: The Problem of Literary Canon Formation*. Chicago and London: The University of Chicago Press, 1993, 43.

[14] Benjamin, ibid., 56.

Unheard Melodies and Unseen Paintings
(The Sister Arts in Romantic Fiction)

1. Use and Mention

How can the sister arts "appear" in a work of literature? At the outset, a distinction can be introduced between the ideal types of "use" and "mention." Genette gives the following examples: "In the sentence '*Paris* is a great city,' the word *Paris* is *used* transitively [...]; in 'Paris consists of two syllables,' the name of the city is *mentioned* (cited)" (Genette 1999, 235–36).[1] The actual presence of the sister arts in a literary work can never be a clear-cut case of use or mention. To take specific examples, in chapter 3 of *Notre-Dame de Paris* we are closer to the second of the two ideal types when those characters around the Flemish ambassador are compared to some figures in a painting by Rembrandt.[2] By contrast, the cathedral known as "Notre-Dame de Paris" plays a decisive role in the novel and thus represents the first rather than the second of the two possibilities.

What follows is a brief comparative analysis of some of the basic options for the literary treatment of nonliterary art. The assumption is that music and painting were given a prominent role in the fiction written in the era that was tempted by the ideal of a "Gesamtkunstwerk." Hoffmann's *Ritter Gluck* (1809) and *Don Juan* (1813), Balzac's *Le chef-d'oeuvre inconnu* (The unknown masterpiece, 1831–37?), Mérimée's *La Vénus d'Ille* (1837), Poe's *The Oval Portrait* (1842), and Nerval's *Sylvie* (1853) will represent short fiction, whereas Stendhal's *Le rouge et le noir* (1831), Hugo's *Notre-Dame de Paris* (1831), and *Gyulai Pál* (Pál Gyulai, 1847) by the Transylvanian-born Zsigmond Kemény will serve as examples of novel writing in which music or the visual arts function as structural principles. Interarts studies are an attractive field, but they have one pitfall: since few scholars can have the same competence in literature and the other arts, the literary critic may be inclined to develop literary interpretations of painting or music. This type of distortion is especially frequent in the comparative analysis of opera and literature. Kierkegaard's brilliant interpretation of *Don Giovanni* in *Enten-Eller* (1843), for instance, is based on the analysis of the libretto rather than on that of the music.

2. Ut Musica Poesis

An allusion to some opera may serve two purposes: the behaviour of a character during a performance may provide information about his/her personality, and the plot of the work performed can function as a "mise-en-abyme." Both can be seen in *Le rouge et le noir*. In part II, chapter XXX Julien Sorel goes to the opera. He appears in the box of Madame de Fervaques with the explicit purpose of making Mathilde de La Mole jealous and urging her to marry him. The allusion to the "opera buffa" performed – Cimarosa's *Il matrimonio segreto* (The secret marriage, 1792) – serves to underscore the hero's hypocrisy: the sadness of the heroine makes him cry.[3] The episode may also illustrate Julien's lack of understanding of opera. In this respect this chapter is comparable to chapter XV in part II of *Madame Bovary*, in which Emma identifies herself with Lucia di Lammermoor. In a more obvious way, the plot of Cimarosa's work can be taken as an ironic anticipation of an event that follows the scene in the opera: the secret marriage of Mathilde de La Mole and Julien Sorel announced by Mathilde in a letter addressed to her father in chapter XXXI.

Unlike Stendhal, Hoffmann was a practicing musician. This may explain why "cross-system quotation" (term borrowed from Goodman 1978, 52–55) is more functional in the literary works of the German Romantic. The crucial section of *Ritter Gluck* describes a stranger's response to the overture of *Iphigenia in Aulis*. The structure of the music is reflected in gestures and facial expressions described by the story teller. The musical events are partly narrated with the help of musical terms, and partly translated into visual phenomena, which, in turn, are conveyed with the help of language. This technique has been described by one critic as a "verbal pantomime" (Scher 1968, 62, 77). There is, however, another level at which the story can be read. The stranger is not satisfied with the performance of the overture. He has a different interpretation in mind. The final words of the text – "I am Ritter Gluck!" – may suggest not only that the stranger is insane – the events of the tale take place in 1809, whereas Gluck died in 1787 – but also the absurdity of an "authorial interpretation."

"The narrator's love for music takes him into the sphere of the miraculous" (Nehring 1981, 71). This comparative remark underlines what is common in the structures of *Ritter Gluck* and *Don Juan*: the narrator attends a performance. In the later tale fragments of the Italian libretto are quoted and references to the music are made with the help of musical terminology. The presentation of the finale of Act I is heightened by an allusion to Ariosto.[4] While watching the performance, the narrator develops an interpretation with a focus on the title hero's attitude to Donna Anna. In contrast to the "relations with the cold, weak, and ordinary Don Ottavio," the contact between the title hero and Donna Anna is associated with Don Giovanni's nostalgia for the supernatural. During the intermission the narrator is visited by the woman who is singing Donna Anna, and the last words of the supplement to the story are about the nervous breakdown of the singer in the second act. To the narrator's question: "can we hear the Signora soon?" someone gives the following answer: "the Signora died this morning at two o'clock." Don Giovanni is portrayed as a tragic hero, and Mozart's opera is interpreted as a Romantic work. Life and art are viewed as interrelated, art having the upper hand.

Both *Ritter Gluck* and *Don Juan* contain autobiographical and discursive components. Narrative is more or less subordinated to confession and essay in the series known as *Kreisleriana*. This is true not only of *Der Musikfeind* (1814), a tale based on childhood reminiscences, in which the numerous musical references are coupled with the fanciful idea that cats have a musical talent, whereas dogs are unable to understand music, but also of *Johannes Kreislers, des Kappelmeisters, musikalische Leiden* (The sorrows of Johannes Kreisler 1810), an account of the narrator's performance of the *Goldberg Variations*.

"All art constantly aspires towards the condition of music" (Pater 1986. 95). This well-known dictum is anticipated by Hoffmann. The interpretations of various works of music given in his tales point towards the thesis formulated most consistently in *Gedanken über den hohen Wert der Musik* (Thoughts on the high value of music 1812), an ironic presentation, partly in the form of a dialogue, of the role of art in bourgeois life. The ambiguity of the link between aesthetic and bourgeois values is intensified by the argument about the superiority of music to literature and the visual arts. A characteristically Romantic prejudice underlies the claim that the response to a painting is a shorter process than the understanding of a piece of music, because the meaning of a painting can be discovered, whereas the interpretation of music can never be definitive.

3. Imaginary Works of Art

Although the visual arts are less suited for suggesting the immanence of meaning, they may provide a starting point for an emphasis on the self-referentiality of art. In Poe's "Ich-Erzählung" *The Oval Portrait* the background sets the tone for such an orientation. An "unusually great number of very spirited modern paintings in frames of rich golden arabesque" were "in a remote turret" of a château which is described as an example of "bizarre architecture." The building reminds the narrator of "the fancy of Mrs. Radcliffe." The crucial part of the text is about the "effect" of the portrait of a young woman on the narrator. No painter is named, although the story teller is reminded of the "style" of Thomas Sully (1783–1872), an American artist of English birth. Fascinated by "the secret of its effect," the narrator "sought eagerly the volume which discussed the oval portrait." The last and fairly long paragraph pretends to be a quotation from a book. This story within the story is about an artist painting a portrait of his young bride. While working on this portrait, the artist "had grown wild with the ardor of his work, and turned his eyes from the canvas rarely." By the time the work is completed, the model is dead. The contrast between the artwork and its model is reminiscent of the "real" Gilberte and the "imaginary" woman painted by Frenhofer, the hero of *Le chef-d'oeuvre inconnu*, and foreshadows both *The Real Thing* (1892) by Henry James and *The Picture of Dorian Gray* (1890) by Oscar Wilde. On the one hand, it is a variation on and a distortion of the story of Pygmalion, suggesting that art is an imaginative activity rather than representation, on the other hand, it belongs to what Derrida calls the "literature of murderous works" (Derrida 1990, 41). The irony is heightened by the fact that the message of the fictitious nonverbal artwork is tied to a fictitious text.

The Oval Portrait resembles Hoffmann's tales in so far as it transforms the nonliterary into a self-interpretive device. In other works visual art is given functions radically different from the one that musical compositions have in prose narratives. In *Pál Gyulai*, a historical novel by Zsigmond Kemény, a portrait is used as a starting point for the plot.

This work is an epitome of Friedrich Schlegel's Romantic ideal of the novel as an encyclopedic genre: some sections are in dramatic form, others incorporate letters, diary entries, and lyric verse. Chapter one starts with the death of Kristóf Báthory, Prince of Transylvania, in 1581. The brother of the deceased ruler, István Báthory, King of Poland, has commissioned a Florentine artist to make a portrait of the heir apparent. The painting is taken to the Polish court by the title hero, a young poet. The old king and the young Transylvanian nobleman differ in their readings of the portrait. István Báthory's conclusion is that the character of the model of the portrait, Zsigmond Báthory is full of flaws. Pál Gyulai's radically different interpretation is based on the idea that painters create rather than imitate. Both attempt to verbalize the nonverbal. Their efforts to formulate the semantic vacuum point in opposite directions: the old monarch seeks a definitive, authoritative explanation; the young page views interpretation as open-ended. Two modes of "explication d'image" are contrasted, and the narrator's remarks on the fundamental difference between Italian and Dutch painting further emphasize the dependence of the understanding of art on different conventions. The disagreement between the two characters is also due to the fact that the old monarch stands for political pragmatism, whereas the title hero lives in the autonomous world of creative imagination. The ambiguity of this opening scene is fully developed in the novel. The language is so self-reflexive that the mimetic view of art is constantly undermined. At the same time, the character of Zsigmond Báthory develops in the direction foreseen by his uncle, the old king, who dies shortly after the opening scene. Although the tension between imitation and creation remains unresolved, painting is used as a means of characterization.

Another function is given to the visual arts in Mérimée's nouvelle *La Vénus d'Ille*. In the early nineteenth century most of the music performed was contemporary music. In the visual arts, however, the legacy of the past constantly reminded the public of the age of works of art. The son of two artists, Mérimée was one of those who developed a historical awareness during his extensive travels in the Mediterranean world. *La Vénus d'Ille* manifests not only the Romantic emphasis on "couleur locale" but also on the claim that Classical Antiquity had been misinterpreted by the previous generations. The mutability of values is suggested, in a temporal and spatial sense.

The story is about the close link between the work of archeologists and the activity of art historians. The larger context is constituted by a succession of discoveries in the territory of the Catalan-speaking community, a region known for its rich legacy. "You will see everything; Phoenician, Celtic, Roman, Arabic, and Byzantine monuments," says M. de Peyrehorade, a local connoisseur, to the narrator, who is initiated into the gradual discovery of the monuments of the distant past. The focus is on how a piece of sculpture is found and transformed into a work of art. Ironically, the statue is recovered unbroken but a man is hurt during its transportation. The living body proves to be weaker, more vulnerable and less enduring than the artwork.

It is significant that the statue is of a goddess. The story – "a version of the old legend of a love-pledge between a mortal and effigy of a goddess" (James 1957, 171) – is about the transformation of a religious "idol" into an object for contemplation. The temporality of the life of the work of art is signaled by the patina given to the statue by time. As in the Hungarian novel, the object is offered as a starting-point for a discussion of the meaning of the work of art. The author of *The Figure in the Carpet* paid a special attention to this tale by Mérimée and translated it into English. His interpretation has become an integral part of the history of the reception of the French story. Reading it from the perspective of the numerous self-reflexive tales by James, it is possible to argue that what Mérimée's work highlights is the dilemma of illusion and fiction. The Romantic writer rejects the Classicist idea of imitation; his interest is in the viewer rather than in the creative activity of the artist. Illusion is a matter of effect rather than one of intention. "These brilliant eyes produced a certain illusion that reminded one of reality and life."[5] This statement by the narrator is accompanied by a remark by his guide, questioning the existence of the artist's model: "I doubt that Heaven has ever created such a woman."[6] The suggestion is that understanding art is not a finite process. "I myself was not satisfied with my own interpretation,"[7] the narrator admits after having considered the two inscriptions. M. de Peyrehorade relies on Phoenician etymology, but the narrator is either doubtful of his explanation or questions the idea that a statue can be understood with the help of its inscription. Instead, he tries to make a drawing. Having made twenty sketches, he confesses his failure.

The rest of the story can be read as a manifestation of the Romantic interest in the supernatural and in the disturbed mind. While playing tennis, Alphonse, the son of M. de Peyrehorade, puts the ring he is about to give his future wife on the finger of the statue. When he tries to recover it, on the day of his wedding, he cannot detach it from the finger of the statue. At night the young woman has a vision of the statue visiting and killing Alphonse. Is it possible to suggest that "la Vénus d'Ille" takes vengeance on someone who is unwilling to have the proper respect for her? Is the tale a self-referential parable about the relations between life and art, reality and fiction? Alphonse certainly fails to contemplate the statue as a piece of art. The ironic "Post Scriptum" informs the reader about the aborted attempt by those who lacked understanding of art to transform the statue into a useful object.[8]

4. "Real" Paintings

Unlike Mérimée's nouvelle, *Sylvie* contains references to actual buildings, paintings, and pieces of music dating from various periods. Together with the literary allusions, they are functional rather than merely decorative. The most important among them occurs in chapter IV entitled "Un voyage à Cythère." The narrator recalls a meeting with the title heroine. The participants of the banquet set out for an excursion. The goal is to visit an island on a lake, "perhaps" in memory of Watteau's painting.[9] The subtitle of the tale – "Souvenirs de Valois" – and the larger context makes it difficult to decide to what extent retrospection is responsible for the "mise-en-scène." The significance of the desire to reproduce the image of the festivities of the past increases during the story. The eighteenth century is again remembered in chapter VI, when Sylvie and the narrator put on clothes that the girl's aunt and her bridegroom had worn on the day of their wedding.

Watteau's *Le Pélerinage à l'isle de Cythère* (1717, Musée du Louvre) – a painting that has also a somewhat later version known as *L'Embarquement pour Cythère* (c. 1718–19, Schloss Charlottenburg, Berlin) – serves as a point of departure for hints questioning the identity of the self; "I found her different from herself,"[10] the narrator says about Sylvie, in the chapter relating the excursion to the island. During the narrative the island becomes an emblem of the world of the imagination.

The story is about a loss of illusions. Temporality is emphasized in a way that makes it perfectly understandable why Proust was to take a serious interest in *Sylvie*. "We would have liked to have written these pages of *Sylvie*."

This remark about the "dream-world in which Gérard walked"[11] (Proust 1965, 190) may remind us that today it is virtually impossible not to read *Sylvie* from the perspective of *A la recherche du temps perdu*. Just as *La Vénus d'Ille*, so *Sylvie* proves the influence of rewriting on interpretation.

Watteau's work has been described as a picture that "is imbued with a poignant sense of the losing battle against the reality of time" (Levey 1992, 63). In Nerval's tale the painting is a "mise-en-abyme" suggesting that the narrator's return to the past is a visit to a world created by his imagination. As in Kemény's novel, the certainty of denotation is contrasted with an open field of possible connotations. Some of these call for interarts comparisons. The arrangement of the group painted by Watteau reminds the viewer of theatre and ballet, and the participants in the festivity are absorbed in conversation, suggesting the inferiority, perhaps even inadequacy of writing in comparison with speaking, yet the substance of the conversation remains unknown. Several couples are involved in intimate "tête-à-tête": the man's pose answers that of the woman and makes eye contact with his partner. The couple in the middle seems an exception: the woman's eyes send us to the two couples on the right side of the painting. Yet even this case may confirm that the painting is an image of the celebration of talk. The difference is that the tall lady seems to ignore the words uttered by the man whose face we cannot see since he is standing with his back to us. In his left hand he is holding a stick, while with his right hand he is trying to touch his partner. She turns her face towards others, in striking contrast to the other females, who show an absorption in the speech of the other. Yet we cannot be sure of our interpretation, for in the silent medium of painting legible gestures are the only means of suggesting talk. In contrast to allegorical painting, where the figures' gestures can be read on the basis of some well-known text, Watteau's work is not illustrative or even narrative. The indeterminacy in the word-image relationship characteristic of this painting becomes an important component of self-commentary in Nerval's tale.

On his return to Loisy the narrator tries to find his past in vain. Coming from Paris, he looks for old songs. When he asks Sylvie to sing one of them, she informs him that they are no longer popular. Instead of singing one of them, she praises an aria from an opera by Porpora. While he tries to forget the books he has read, she looks upon the landscape around them through the eyes of Walter Scott. The narrator takes Watteau's conversation painting as a likeness of his own story, the gradual loss of his illusions.[12] That the story teller himself is one of the principal actors of the "fête galante" may remind the reader that s/he not only receives a vision but seems him/herself part of a vision.

There are three young women who attract the narrator's attention: Adrienne, "la religieuse," Sylvie, and Aurélie, the actress. All three loves remain unfulfilled. Sensuality is displaced and deferred. The narrator's position is similar in all the three cases: a figure assumes clothes for a part. Ironically, it is the actress who draws this conclusion: "you look for a drama, and the climax seems to escape you."[13] The reader may remember the function of the statue in the right foreground of Watteau's painting, aptly described by an art historian in the following manner: "Venus, however much she looks like a nude woman, remains a statue. As a symbolic representation of sensual love, she stands not for what is *present* in the painting but for what is *absent* from it" (Vidal 1992, 36).

5. The "Real" and the "Imaginary"; Line vs. Colour

"There are two writers in Balzac – the spontaneous and the reflective one," wrote Henry James less than three decades after the death of the author of *La Comédie humaine* (James 1878, 109). His assessment anticipated those later interpretations that focused on the self-reflexive at the cost of the more descriptive works. The shift of emphasis can be felt in the two longer essays which the American-born writer devoted to the works of the French author. In the late 1870s he characterized Balzac as a "realistic novelist," whereas in 1902 he emphasized "the romantic side of him" and made a comparison between his prose and the paintings of Turner (James 1978, 95-96 and James 1963, 210, 196).

One of the consequences of this reinterpretation was a growing interest in works that focus on the mode of existence of the work of art. Among these are three tales. *Gambara* (1838) is about the creation, and *Massimilla Doni* (1839) about the interpretation of music. The somewhat earlier *The unknown masterpiece* – which Poe and Nerval may have read – is more enigmatic than either of the other two works. The complexity is inseparable from two factors. There are three painters among the characters: the young Poussin, Porbus, and the old Frenhofer, who claims to have been the only pupil of Mabuse. Critics have called attention to the somewhat superficial analogy with *Der Baron von B.* (1819), Hoffmann's tale about three fictitious musicians, as well as with those works by the German author which touch upon the activity of the painter: *Die Elixiere des Teufels* (The devil's elixirs, 1813–1816), a novel that contains a recreation of the legend of Pygmalion, and such stories in the collection *Die Serapions-Brüder* (1821) as *Der Artushof*, a tale about an old painter who presents an empty canvas as his masterpiece to a younger colleague, and *Die Fermate* (The fermata), a highly original text that transforms *Die Fermate* (Bayerische Staatsgemäldesammlungen. München) – a painting exhibited in 1814 by Erdmann Hummel (1769–1852) – into a narrative. The picture shows two musicians, a conductor, and their audience, so Hoffmann's tale can be read as the translation of a translation.

Balzac may have read most of these works by Hoffmann. The first translation of *Der Baron von B.* was published in 1828, in *Le Gymnase*, a periodical for which the French writer worked as printer. The second French version appeared in *L'Artiste* – a "revue" started in 1831 with the explicit purpose of defending the Romantics' emphasis on colour, in sharp contrast to David's insistence on the primacy of line – in April 1831, a couple of months before the first version of *The unknown masterpiece* was published in the same periodical.

In comparison with Hoffmann's tales, the originality of Balzac's "conte" lies in the combination of the "real" and the "imaginary." The "real" names of Nicolas Poussin and Franz Porbus (1570–1622), a Flemish artist known chiefly as the painter of a large portrait of Catherine de Médicis, are supplemented by a name created by the author.

Even more important is that there is no definitive text: both the identity of the painting in the story and that of the text may be questioned. This is the second reason for the complexity of the meaning of *The unknown masterpiece*. The tale of the effects of revision exists in at least four different versions. The first, subtitled "Conte fantastique" and published in two installments (31 July and 7 August) in the periodical *L'Artiste* in 1831, is not radically different from the second, which appeared in book form in the third volume of *Romans et contes philosophiques* in September of the same year. The third, however, part of the seventeenth volume of the author's *Etudes philosophiques* (July 1837), is considerably enlarged and has a different ending. Some philologists believe that this third version is partly the work of Théophile Gautier, who also made a contribution to several other works by Balzac. René Guise, the editor of the text for the Pléiade version of *La Comédie humaine* is one of those who believe that Gautier's contribution was minimal (Balzac 1979, 1406–1407). The text published in volume II of *Le Provincial à Paris* (1847) is slightly different from the previous version and the author's own copy of *La Comédie humaine* has further corrections, so it is possible to assume that he never stopped working on the text.

In the early stage of composition the alterations were hardly perceptible. In the first version Poussin makes the following remark to his mistress: "He will not see the woman in you, he will see beauty: you are perfect!"[14] In the second version, published a month later, the original sentence is transformed into two units: "He won't be able to see the woman in you. You are so perfect!"[15] Charles Rosen's interpretation of the change is somewhat comparable to Wordsworth's line of argument, starting from the idea of "the spontaneous overflow of powerful feelings" and pointing towards "emotion recollected in tranquillity" (Wordsworth 1988, 297): "In the first version 'woman' is physical, sexual, and vulnerable […]. In the second, woman has become a concept, abstract and general. This suggests the way revision in Romantic art moves away from direct experience to a mediated reflection" (Rosen 1998, 7).

The different variant states of the tale suggest that Romanticism undermined the Classicist ideal of the finished work of art. Some of the great achievements of Romantic literature – from Hölderlin's *Empedocles* to Wordsworth's autobiographical poem *The Prelude* or Keats's *Hyperion* – exist in several versions, others have a fragmentary character. The canonical view of the artwork as an object with clear-cut outlines had been replaced by an emphasis on indeterminacy. Balzac's tale can be read as a parable showing the questionableness, vulnerability, and perhaps even irrelevance of the concept of the masterpiece, its dependence on reception.

In the same way that Nerval viewed Watteau with the eyes of a Romantic, Balzac ascribed to his seventeenth-century artists the ideas current in the age of Turner, such as the superiority of colour to line (drawing). This is much more evident in the 1837 version than in the earlier versions. Henri Evans attributes these reflections to Balzac's collaborator (Balzac 1964, XI). The other major difference is the ending: the old painter, seeing the hostile response of the two young artists, throws them out.

Fiction and fact have become inseparable. Frenhofer's explicit allusion to Pygmalion suggests self-referentiality, and the 1837 conclusion of the story moves into the realm of dissemination. What the "fictive" painter Frenhofer calls his masterpiece the "real" artist Poussin cannot see at all. His complaint about a chaos of colours resembles the characterization made by conservative viewers of the later works of Turner. During his stay in London, the Transylvanian-born Miklós Barabás (1810–1898), one of the leading representatives of Central European Biedermeier art, called one of Turner's paintings "a piece of canvas coloured without reason, meaning, and sense" (Márkosfalvi Barabás 1944, 180).[16]

One other revision may suggest that there is also another possible meaning of the story. The canvas by Frenhofer may remind us of the gap between model and artwork or of the tension between the material and ideal, immanent and transcendental aspects of the work of art. This is the way we may understand why one sentence in Frenhofer's monologue was changed by the author in 1837. "This woman is not a creation but a creature." The alteration is simple but not negligible: "This woman is not a creature but a creation." Art as a finished product is contrasted with art as an open-ended process.

6. Architecture: the Romantic Interpretation of the Past

Although *Notre-Dame de Paris* has none of the complexities of *Sylvie* or *The unknown masterpiece*, its multiple reliance on monuments of non-verbal art deserves attention. Cross-system quotations have at least three distinct functions in this novel. The first is similar to what we have seen in several other works: nonverbal art plays an interpretive role. In the opening chapter of Book VII Captain Phoebus de Châteaupers turns to Damoiselle Fleur-de-Lys, asking her about the subject of the "ouvrage de tapisserie" she is working on. "This is grotto of Neptunus," she replies. The captain seems to remember this when later (in chapter 8 of the same book) he makes a confession to la Esmeralda.[17] The appropriation of "the figure in the carpet" suggests the captain's insincerity. The irony is reinforced by the plot: shortly after his insincere confession Phoebus is killed by Frollo.

On other occasions cross-system quotation is a mode of characterization. The solitary cell in which Claude Frollo spends his long hours of meditation is not described. Instead, an etching by Rembrandt is presented, a "horrible and beautiful" portrait of Doctor Faustus and his cell.[18]

Although both the pictorial "mise-en-abyme" and the substitution of the description of a picture for the description of a site play a structural role, this role is much more apparent in those passages of Hugo's novel which portray the destruction of fine buildings. In the Preface the fate of old churches is lamented, and the opening chapter starts with a description of the partly gothic, partly Renaissance Palais de Justice that was destroyed by fire in 1618. A substantial part of the first chapter of Book III – an essay entitled "Notre-Dame" – contains an analysis of the violation of the integrity of the cathedral. The reader is constantly reminded of paintings and etchings dating from periods that succeeded the 15th century and of buildings in Paris that either disappeared or were transformed between the 15th and 19th centuries. No one reading the novel 170 years after its composition can forget continuity and discontinuity between the Paris of 1830 and the early 21st century.

Throughout the novel the preservation of the past is regarded as an unquestionable value. In harmony with many earlier works of Romantic literature, continuity is said to be guaranteed by organic growth. Book III as a whole is discursive in character. Chapter 2 – "Paris from a bird's-eye view" – contains a history of the old districts – "la Cité," "l'Université," and "la Ville" – with special emphasis on their architecture and with multiple references to the Paris of the narrator and "the reader." The cathedral is presented as inseparable from the hero. Archdeacon Claude Frolle is a man of learning. His cell is full of inscriptions. When his brother Jehan visits him (Book VII, chapter 4), he finds him studying a huge manuscript decorated with strange paintings. In the first chapter of Book V the archdeacon makes the following declaration: "The book will put an end to building,"[19] i. e. printing will put an end to architecture. What follows is an interpretive essay entitled "One will kill the other."[20] The opening statement is more complex than it seems at first sight. The decline of architecture is foreseen as a consequence of the diminishing power of the church. This change is linked to another shift: oral culture is replaced by literature. A fundamental change in the forms of memory will lead to a decrease in the influence of tradition. In short, architecture and literature are characterized as manifestations of specific stages in history. The rise of literature is regarded as the outcome of historical necessity; architecture cannot adapt to the next phase in the history of the human intellect.

The idea that the Renaissance represents the first stage in a process pointing towards decadence in architecture is a characteristically Romantic preconception. After the Middle Ages architecture was no longer an art of universal validity, it became relegated to the status of one of the arts. Unity was replaced by division.[21] The disintegration of art corresponds to the disintegration of faith, "Gutenberg was the precursor of Luther." Diversity is viewed as inferior to homogeneity. The two are contrasted as chaos and order: "there is a chaos of languages [...]. Mankind has a second tower of Babel."[22]

Notre-Dame de Paris can be read as a novel about the relations between image and writing, architecture and literature. Buildings have inscriptions and names, and decline is associated with end of the unity of the verbal and the nonverbal. The preface to the eighth edition (1832) also makes a link between gothic architecture and national identity, urging people to conserve the monuments of their past.[23] Yet it would be misleading to read *Notre-Dame de Paris* as a didactic work about the superiority of medieval art. The multiple allusions suggest a wide range of aesthetic qualities. This emphasis is especially clear in the scene marking the climax (book VIII, chapter 6). La Esmeralda is taken into the cathedral. "She resembled a virgin painted by Masaccio rather than one painted by Raphael: she was weak, thin, and skinny."[24] Three choirs are singing three different songs: a psalm, an offertorium, and the mass of the dead. The scene both summarizes and transcends the human condition and raises the multiplicity to a level of abstraction.

"It is horrible and beautiful." This statement quoted earlier suggests the self-contradictory character of aesthetic qualities that can be regarded as the most important principle underlying the cross-system quotations in Hugo's novel. Quasimodo is deaf, yet he makes music by manipulating the bells of the cathedral.

Beauty and ugliness, art and life are shown to be interrelated. Phoebus is handsome and superficial, Quasimodo is ugly and morally sophisticated. Mutually contradictory values are ascribed to both human beings and homemade objects. "Stone and crystal," the title of book IX, chapter 4 refers to two vases placed in la Esmeralda's window by Quasimodo: one of them is ordinary but functional, whereas the other is beautiful but cracked.[25]

Notre-Dame de Paris – unevenly organized as it is – may help us understand that one of the distinctive features of Romanticism is the undermining of the Platonic ideal of unchanging, "objective," transcultural, ahistorical values. The comparison of the two vases – just as Hoffmann's interpretation of Gluck and Mozart, Nerval's view of Watteau or Frenhofer's concept of a masterpiece – may remind us of the diversity and mutability of aesthetic values. These values are not "out there" waiting to be recognized. They come from inside those who do not merely perceive, but rather create them. The conclusion is inescapable that the effect of the frequent "appearance" of nonverbal art in Romantic fiction is that the reader understands that values in art are not to be found but created through the process of interpretation.

Notes

[1] "Dans une phrase comme '*Paris* est une grande ville', le nom *Paris* est *employé*, de manière transitive […]; dans 'Paris a deux syllabes', ce nom est *mentionné* (cité)."

[2] "bonnes têtes flamandes après tout, figures dignes et sévères, de la famille de celles que Rembrandt fait saillir si fortes et si graves sur le fond noir de sa ronde de nuit."

[3] "Par bonheur il trouva la loge de la maréchale remplie de femmes, et fut relégué près de la porte, et tout à fait caché par les chapeaux. Cette position lui sauva un ridicule; les accents divins du désespoir de Caroline dans le *Matrimonio segreto* le firent fondre en larmes."

[4] "Er schlägt dem Bräutigam den stählernen Galanteriedegen aus der Hand und bahnt sich durch das gemeine Gesindel, das er, wie der tapfere Roland die Armee des Tyrannen Cymork, durcheinanderwirft, daß alles gar possierlich übereinanderpurzelt, den Weg ins Freie."

[5] "Ces yeux brillants produisaient une certaine illusion qui rappelait la réalité, la vie."

[6] "je doute que le Ciel ait jamais produit une telle femme."

[7] "Je n'étais pas moi-même fort satisfait de mon explication."

[8] "Après la mort de son mari, le premier soin de Mme de Peyrehorade fut de la faire fondre en cloche […]. Depuis que cette cloche sonne à Ille, les vignes ont gelé deux fois."

[9] "La traversée du lac avait été imaginé peut-être pour rappeler le *Voyage à Cythère* de Watteau."

[10] "je la trouvais différente d'elle-même."

[11] "Et nous voudrions tant avoir écrit ces pages de *Sylvie*. […] ces pays de rêves où se promena Gérard."

[12] "les illusions tombent l'une après l'autre, comme les écorces d'un fruit, et le fruit c'est l'expérience."

[13] "vous cherchez un drame, voilà tout, et le dénouement vous échappe."

[14] "Il ne verra pas la femme en toi, il verra la beauté: tu es parfaite!"

[15] "Il ne pourra voir la femme en toi. Tu es si parfaite!"

[16] "egy darab vászonnak a színekkel való betarkítása ész, értelem és gondolat nélkül."

[17] "Je veux que le grand diable Neptunus m'enfourche si je ne vous rends pas la plus heureuse créature du monde."

[18] "Parmi tant de merveilleuse gravures, il y a en particulier une eau-forte qui représente, à ce qu'on suppose, le docteur Faust, et qu'il est impossible de contempler sans éblouissement. C'est une sombre cellule; au milieu est une table chargée d'objets hideux: têtes de mort, sphères, alambics, compas, parchemins hiéroglyphiques. Le docteur est devant cette table, vêtu de sa grosse houppelande et coiffé jusqu'aux sourcils de son bonnet fourré. On ne le voit qu'à mi-corps. Il est à demi levé de son immense fauteuil; ses poings crispés s'appuient sur la table, et il considère, avec curiosité et terreur, un grand cercle lumineux, formé de lettres magiques, qui brille sur le mur du fond comme le spectre solitaire dans la chambre noire. Ce soleil cabbalistique semble trembler à l'oeil et remplit la blafarde cellule de son

rayonnement mystérieux. C'est horrible et c'est beau."

[19] "Le livre tuera l'édifice."

[20] "Ceci tuera cela."

[21] "La sculpture devient statuaire, l'imagerie devient peinture, le canon devient musique."

[22] "il y a confusion des langues. [...] C'est la seconde tour de Babel du genre humain."

[23] "en attendant les monuments nouveaux, conservons les monuments anciens. Inspirons, s'il est posiible, à la nation l'amour de l'architecture nationale. C'est là, l'auteur déclare, un des buts principaux de ce livre."

[24] "Elle ressemblait à ce qu'elle avait été comme une Vierge de Masaccio ressemble à une Vierge de Raphaël: plus faible, plus mince, plus maigre."

[25] "L'un était un vase de cristal fort beau et fort brillant mais fêlé. Il avait lassé l'eau dont on l'avait rempli, et les fleurs qu'il contenait étaient fanées. L'autre était un pot de grès, grossier et commun, mais qui avait conservé toute son eau, et dont les fleurs étaient restées fraîches et vermeilles."

References

Balzac, Honoré de 1964. *L'OEuvre.* Publiée dans un ordre nouveau sous la direction d'Albert Béguin et de Jean A. Ducpurneau. Tome 12. Paris: Le club français du livre.

Balzac, Honoré de 1979. *La Comédie humaine X.* Paris: Gallimard.

Derrida, Jacques 1990. *Mémoires d'aveugle: L'autoportrait et autres ruines.* Paris: Réunion des musées nationaux.

Genette, Gérard 1999. *Figures IV.* Paris: Seuil.

Goodman, Nelson 1978. *Ways of Worldmaking.* Indianapolis – Cambridge: Hackett.

James, Henry Jr. 1878. *French Poets and Novelists.* London: Macmillan and Co.

James, Henry 1956. *Autobiography.* New York: Criterion Books.

James, Henry 1957. *Literary Reviews and Essays.* New Haven, Conn.: College and University Press.

James, Henry 1963. *Selected Literary Criticism.* London: Heinemann.

Levey, Michael 1992. *Rococo to Revolution: Major Trends in Eighteenth-Century Painting.* London: Thames and Hudson. (1st ed. 1966)

Márkosfalvi Barabás, Miklós (1944). *Önéletrajz.* Kolozsvár: Erdélyi Szépmíves Céh.

Nehring, Wolfgang 1981. "E. T: A. Hoffmanns Erzählwerk: Ein Modell und seine Variationen." in Steven Paul Scher (ed.): *Zu E. T. A. Hoffmann.* Stuttgart: Ernst Klett.

Pater, Walter 1986. *The Renaissance: Studies in Art and Poetry.* Oxford – New York: Oxford University Press.

Proust, Marcel 1965. *Contre Sainte-Beuve.* Paris: Gallimard.

Rosen, Charles 1998. *Romantic Poets, Critics, and Other Madmen.* Cambridge, MA – London, England: Harvard University Press.

Scher, Steven Paul 1968. *Verbal Music in German Literature.* New Haven: Yale University Press.

Vidal, Mary 1992. *Watteau's Painted Conversations: Art, Literature, and Talk in Seventeenth- and Eighteenth-Century France.* New Haven and London: Yale University Press.

Wordsworth, William 1988. *Selected Prose.* Ed., with an Introduction and Notes by John O. Hayden. Harmondsworth, Middlesex: Penguin Books.

Framing Texts as the Representations
of National Character
(From Enlightenment Universalism to Romantic Nationalism)

"Tradition ist nichts, was Einer lernen kann, ist nicht ein Faden, den Einer aufnehmen kann, wenn es ihm gefällt; so wenig, wie es möglich ist, sich die eigenen Ahnen auszusuchen. Wer eine Tradition nicht hat und sie haben möchte, der ist wie ein unglücklich Verliebter." (Ludwig Wittgenstein)[1]

"Der Sinn aller Tradition ist Konzentration des Seelischen. Das Wesen allen 'Fortschritts' ist Zertreuung, Macht und damit Verlassen des eigenen Zentrums." (Wilhelm Furtwängler)[2]

"Das Überlieferte, das uns anspricht – der Text, das Werk, die Spur – stellt selbst eine Frage und stellt damit unser Meinen ins Offene." (Hans-Georg Gadamer)[3]

"[…] Mahler said that tradition is laziness, and I agree with him." (Pierre Boulez)[4]

1. Imagined Communities

As Benedict Anderson argues, a community can be called imagined if its members have a sense of belonging together even though they have no direct, personal knowledge of each other.[5] This characterization applies to religious communities, the citizens of states, social classes, and nations. All of these are of a historical nature. Except in states in which ruling dynasties play a role, in most imagined communities canonized texts and "great narratives" guarantee continuity. For Christians the Bible and for Moslems the Koran is the sacred book, whereas for socialists the works of Marx and his disciples may constitute the core of the cultural canon. Most nations were defined in texts. The self-image of the Hungarians was at least partly created by Ferenc Kölcsey (1790–1838), the author of *Hymn* (1823), the text that became the national anthem after it was set to music by Ferenc Erkel in 1844. Four other works by Kölcsey, *Zrínyi's Song* (1830) and *Zrínyi's Second Song* (1838), two visionary poems predicting the death of the nation, and two longer essays, both published in 1826, *Mohács*, a meditation on the battle fought in 1526 that led to the partition of Hungary, and *National Traditions*, a work that is usually regarded as an early statement about the significance of folklore, have exerted a decisive influence on the interpretation of Hungarian identity. Since this last can be considered the most important contribution to the shaping of the Hungarian nation I shall focus on this text.

Nation and class emerged after the dissolution of communities attached to religions and ruling dynasties. Homogeneous Christianity was so closely linked to the Latin language that the decline of monolingualism coincided with that of the unity of written culture. The authority of ruling dynasties suffered a serious blow with the executions of Charles I and Louis XVI. The idea that "workers have no fatherland of their own" was formulated as an antidote to nationalism and seemed to replace it at some stage. For the time being this prediction seems to have proven wrong. The distinction between ruling and oppressed classes can no longer hold in view of the growing stratification of societies. The prophecy implicit in the universalism of social utopia that nations would disappear in the near future has lost its credibility.

The cult of national character must be interpreted in the context of changing values. Although it would be misleading to sustain a monolithic vision of the Enlightenment, it is possible to suggest that some of its representatives saw a link between the perfectibility of man and the gradual move towards the unity of the human race. Paradoxically, the imperialism of the French revolution and the Napoleonic wars could be regarded as a logical consequence of the cosmopolitan dream about a universal society. Such technological inventions as Jean-Rodolphe Perronet's bridges or Mongolfier's baloons could suggest both the impracticableness and the growing dimensions of war.

For Count István Széchenyi, the founder of the Hungarian Academy, the goal was to imagine and create a nation. The attitude represented by the poet Kölcsey and his successor János Arany (1917–1882) was more ambiguous. For them tradition was partly to be established and partly to be discovered. Kölcsey was brought up on empiricist philosophy, and Arany lived in an age dominated by Positivism. Both saw a link between tradition and oral culture.

What may be of lasting value in Kölcsey's approach is the observation that culture is not only a product of individual talent but also of a collective memory that is not a matter of personal choice. The validity of this argument seems to have been confirmed even by deconstruction criticism: "Those who do not study history are condemned to repeat it, though studying is also a form of repetition."[6]

The starting hypothesis in Kölcsey's essay is that poetry represents the highest form of culture, and the highest form of poetry is "deeply rooted in national traditions" and "stands close to the nation."[7] In his view the perfect realization of this idea can be found in Homer. This assumption is based on two preconceptions: a) the definition of a national character has to be found in early history, b) orality is superior to writing. The first of these hypotheses has never ceased to affect Hungarian culture, although some historians suggest that it is not possible to speak of nations before the Enlightenment and the rise of the bourgeoisie. The second served as the basis for the institutionalization of folklore in the nineteenth century and seems to have a revival, especially among those who speak of a second(ary) or second-degree orality.

It is one of the inherent qualities of history that perceptions that appear dated in the short term may prove to be significant in the long run. An obvious example is the reading of Ossian offered in Kölcsey's essay. The premise that "the disappearance of tradition makes it impossible for us to develop an authentic interpretation of the characteristics of the past,"[8] leads to the conclusion that "in a late phase of culture the ancient is given the features of the present age."[9] Other elements in the Hungarian Romantic's line of argument – the organicist view of national character, the emphasis on the capacity of the mother tongue to create reality or on cultural relativism – may be questioned, but the idea of the interdependence of past and present, of memory as a sine qua non of culture seems as valid as ever in the self-perception of nations.

The oppositions between exterior and interior, surface and depth, short-term and long-term processes suggest that the past is always rewritten by the ever-changing present and raise the thorny question how influence or success is related to value.

A disciple of both the Enlightenment and Romanticism, Kölcsey was aware of what lay outside the domain of national traditions. He saw Christianity and science as supranational fields. Literature he thought to be their antidote. The idea of this duality of human culture continued to be influential in the twentieth century. In a book written in defence of small states, published in neutral Switzerland during World War II, Jan Huizinga described the humanist of Christianity and science as cosmopolitan: "Die Teilung in Nationen mußte ihm als ein die wahre Kultur störendes Hindernis vorkommen."[10]

Today a similar gap exists between the international terminology of science and the language of the historians of national literatures. Generic concepts and periods differ according to linguistic areas and literary texts are still read as manifestations of national spirit.

2. National Character

In contrast to a view widely held, this concept was not born with Herder or the reaction against the wars fought by the French revolutionary army. The origins of counter-images can be traced back to earlier times. In Britain, for instance, a great number of articles were published with the aim of discrediting the Italian opera in the early 18th century. One could also refer to the self-contradictions of the Enlightenment, more specifically to some works of the author of *Essai sur l'origine des langues* and *Considérations sur le gouvernement de Pologne* (1772). The first among Jean-Jacques Rousseau's texts on national character dates from 1752. The comparison of organic and inorganic, familiar and alien, autonomous and imitative – closely reminiscent of Kölcsey's oppositions – is followed by the following observation: "Si j'étais chef de quelqu'un des peuples de la Nigritie, je déclare que je ferais élever sur la frontière du pays une potence où je ferais pendre sans rémission le premier Européen qui oserait y pénétrer, et le premier citoyen qui tenterait d'en sortir."[11]

Another relevant passage occurs in *Du contrat social*, published a decade later. Peter the Great is dismissed for imitating foreign models instead of letting national culture develop: "Pierre avait le génie imitatif; il n'avait pas le vrai génie, celui qui crée et fait tout de rien. [...] Il a d'abord voulu de faire des Allemands, des Anglais, quand il fallait commencer par faire des Russes; il a empêché ses sujets de jamais devenir ce qu'ils pourraient être, en les persuadant qu'ils étaient ce qu'ils ne sont pas."[12]

Rousseau's and Kölcsey's meditations on cultural universalism versus relativism have to be examined against the background of a wide-spread debate. No significant thinker was prone to an extremist position. Universalists were not necessarily conservative; utopias were often based on the monolithic idea of one "Weltgeschichte." Relativism, on the other hand, frequently implied the preservation of existing values.

Rousseau's relativism may have been inspired by his reading of Montaigne and Montesquieu. It is also possible that the Swiss thinker formulated his ideas in reaction against the essay *Of National Characters*, published in 1748, in which David Hume considered "the Negroes to be naturally inferior to the Whites," on the ground that they did not display "any symptom of ingenuity."[13] In other words, they could not develop a culture of their own.

Although in most cases national character was created in texts, it would be a mistake to ignore other factors. The evidence offered by the history of visual arts is summarized by a recent work in the following manner: "The gowing number of accessible international collections and the availability of prints from all over Europe allowed eighteenth-century artists of even the most mediocre fortunes to build up a cosmopolitan visual imagination. This, combined with the decline of the tradition of regional workshop training, established a social environment which, in general terms, did not favour the natural production of idiosyncratic regional styles of production. Increasingly, therefore, national and regional artistic character had actively to be invented or re-established in the wake of vigorous political campaigns to assert national identity. Being the artist of a certain locality or nation increasingly became a matter of choice rather than accident of birth."[14] In his *Treatise on Ancient Painting* (1740) George Turnbull argued that "the general and national Character of a People may be conjectured from the State of the Arts amongst them: and reciprocally."[15] From Jacques-Louis David's early *The Oath of the Horatii* (1784–5, Musée du Louvre) to Caspar David Friedrich's painting known as *The Stages of Life* or *The Three Ages of Man* (1834–5, Museum der Bildenden Künste, Leipzig) many works of art can be seen as the visual illustrations of the parallel between the cycle of the life of an individual and that of a nation. The belief that culture developed cyclically from a state of youthfulness towards maturity, old age, and death was supported by the cult of ruins.

Kölcsey was well-versed in the philosophy of the French Enlightenment, so the opening words of his essay have to be read in the context of the ideas on cultural universalism and realitivism formulated by such authors as Montesquieu, Voltaire, Buffon, Rousseau, Diderot, Condillac,

Helvétius, and Condorcet: "Nations have the same phases in their life as individuals. Their childhood is followed first by the promises of youth and later by the strength of maturity, which, in turn, is replaced by the decline of old age."[16] This old topos, inherited from Classical Antiquity, gained special significance in the late eighteenth and early nineteenth century. Széchenyi used it inconsistently, which today may appear more acceptable than Kölcsey's blunt statement, although it has to be admitted that many national literary histories seem to comply with an explicit teleology similar to the one underlying Kölcsey's work.

In marked contrast to Kölcsey and many others, Széchenyi often toyed with the idea that national character has to be created in writing. Innumerable fragments from his works were given a proverbial status by later generations and the closing sentence of *Credit* (1830), his most influential book – "Many think: Hungary has been; I like to believe she will be"[17] – served as a slogan in what is still called the Age of Reform, the period between Waterloo and the revolutions of 1848.

As a diary entry dated 7 April 1819 indicates, the source of Széchenyi's ideas on national character was *A Classical Tour Through Italy in 1802* by John Chetwoode Eustace, published in four volumes in London, in 1815. The quotation from this work starts with the following words: "National character, though it may be influenced both by the will and the climate, is not the effect of either. Government and education are the grand and efficient causes in the formation of character both public and private."[18] A month later Széchenyi made the following remark: "Eine Nation entstehet ebenso wie ein Kind geboren wird – gehet durch die Jahre der Adolescens, der Jugend, der Mannheit, und des Alters – und stirbt endlich ab – der einzige Unterschied nach dem Tode einer Nation und eines Menschen ist nur, dass der Leichnahm eines Menschen von Würmern gefressen wird, und zu sein gänzlich aufhört, indessen der verlebte Körper einer Nation – lange Jahre noch fortvegetirt –. Ob eine Nation gross werden oder unbedeutend bleiben soll, hengt von dem Zufall eben so sehr ab, als von der Erziehung die es in seinen Kinder Jahren bekommen hat."[19]

Since Széchenyi's diaries were not published until much later, it is not likely that Kölcsey had access to them. Széchenyi, however, could rely on the poet's essay when later he blamed Hungarians for the preservation of the outmoded and for superficial imitation: "We have no national habits; our existence and knowledge depend on imitation. Unlike other nations, we stick to the old and are superficial in imitating others."[20]

Are the characteristics of the Hungarian nation to be preserved or to be created? The main reason for Széchenyi's great influence on both conservatives and liberals is his inconsistency in answering that question. "Hungary is an old fortress that needs restoration." One page after this statement quite a different tone is set by the following remark: "The Hungarian is but a child. He has not achieved anything yet but the psychic and physical energy hidden in his young soul may enable him to do great things."[21] When defining the character the Hungarian nation should acquire in the future, he resorts to the figure of speech known as oxymoron: "Our country needs an old head attached to young shoulders."[22] The paradoxical nature of the combination of tradition and innovation suggests not only a compulsion to fuse contradictory experience into a unity but also the possible disappearance of national character. His declaration made in the Upper House, on 2 October 1844, refers to the second alternative: "It may be possible that those who will replace us will be more honest and intelligent, but I take it for certain that they will not be Hungarians."[23]

Throughout his life Széchenyi viewed national character as the product of literature. Here is a passage of a work entitled *Dust and Mud*, written on 13 June 1858: "If in youth an individual or nation had nothing similar to what mortals could never express but Schiller, Alfieri, Moore, Berzsenyi, Vörösmarty, and others suggested, that nation would sink to the level of a machine and may achieve material but no spiritual prosperity."[24]

A similar contrast of organic and inorganic, coupled with the idea of the different ages of nations, can be found in the works of numerous French authors. Several texts by Taine, *L'avenir de la science* (written in 1848) and *De l'origine du langage* (written between 1848 and 1858) by Renan, or Gobineau's notorious *Essai sur l'inégalité des races humaines* (written between 1853 and 1855) could be mentioned in this context.[25]

The last of these works may illustrate the damage theories about the diversity of human communities have done to human culture. Yet it cannot be denied that the preconception concerning the ages of nations sometimes went together with tolerance toward alterity – as the examples of Spengler, Toynbee, Berdyaev, Valéry, and Wittgenstein indicate. The traces of the same conception can also be found in the debates over the explanation of the end of the Habsburg Monarchy or in the revival that makes Spengler an early critic of Eurocentrism.[26]

In view of the international survival of the organicist interpretation of history, it cannot be called anachronistic that the questions raised by Kölcsey and Széchenyi continued to tempt Hungarian writers until the present day. Here I have no space for a summary of these later developments.[27] In the rest of this essay my intention is to focus on an issue that preoccupied virtually all the interpreters of Kölcsey's text: to what extent should texts be evaluated on the basis of their contribution to the shaping of national character.

3. The Driving Forces of Development: Originality, Language, and the Future

"In the age of public education the brilliance of individual greatness is more sporadic and less spectacular."[28] This statement may echo *Émile* and *Über naive und sentimentalische Dichtung*. It also reveals the ambiguity of Kölcsey's approach to progress: on the one hand, it seems an organic process, on the other, it leads from the natural to the artificial.

The duality of imagination and learning was a cliché throughout the nineteenth century. The double meaning of "original" implied that the specificity of a culture has to be discovered in early history. The fundamental question for Kölcsey was whether the early legacy of the Hungarian people was sufficient for the survival of their culture. He clearly saw that distance was a source of alienation. At the same time, the Greek example convinced him that the greatness of a culture consisted in its capacity to recognize itself in the other. No culture could do without foreign influence, yet imitation was a sign of the weakness of native traditions.

The language reform supported by Kölcsey represented a compromise between the legacy of the Enlightenment and the Romantic approach to language: it asserted the claims of the vernacular, yet it aimed at creating a standard "polished" idiom, purged of all signs of local dialect.

One of the reasons why Kölcsey's essay *National Traditions* could serve as a starting-point for so many and so different interpretations is that its message is rather ambivalent. Culture is both influence and self-reliance. On the one hand, it seems to suggest that the significance of a culture depends on its ability to make an impact on others; on the other hand, it draws a distinction between two relations between self and other: imitation and appropriation. Not all foreign occupations are viewed in the same way: the Arab settlers of Spain are said to have created a culture of their own, whereas the Ottoman Turks are harshly criticized for destroying the civilization of the peoples they conquered. A similar duality is ascribed to the oppressed: appropriation is contrasted with servile imitation.

The ideal of Greek Antiquity is upheld to exclude one extreme, that of unlimited cultural relativism. The other extreme would be the utopia of one mankind and one history. In recent years a similar critique of these two attitudes was formulated by Paul Ricoeur, who condemned both the racist interpretation of history and the belief in the unity of Weltgeschichte, the globalizing force of the American way of life that leaves no room for a dialogue with the histories of the different parts of the world.[29]

One of the possible readings of Kölcsey's essay was given by Mihály Babits (1883–1941), an outstanding poet and the author of two seminal discursive works, the long essay *Hungarian Literature* (1913) and its counterpart *A History of European Literature* (published in Hungarian in 1934–35 and in German translation in 1949). If Kölcsey's essay is viewed from the perspective outlined in these two works, its message is that the development of a culture depends not only on its unity but also on the multiplicity of the tasks it can handle, so that the main goal a nation has to reach is dialogue with other cultures. To preserve one's identity is linked to tolerance towards others. Kölcsey's emphasis on "influence" implies that a familiarity with the other is a precondition of culture. "I am another" also means "the other is myself." Culture is mediation and so depends on our ability to keep a distance from our own community and assimilate the alien. The duality of self and other need not cause schizophrenia, although it may not exclude opposition or conflict.

If read from the perspective of Romanticism, *National Traditions* marks a shift from the preconception that a) traditional rural culture was a barbarity to be forgotten, and b) the primary task for the national community was to absorb the culture of the other parts of Europe. After the universalist teleology of some Enlightenment thinkers committed to the task of dragging Hungarians out of a barbarous rustic dark age and towards a bright cosmopolitan future had been rejected, artists and writers created an ideology based on the notion that Hungary represented a unique cultural entity that had grown out of a distinctive landscape. In the 1840s, in the works of Petőfi and others, the untrammelled plainland, the "puszta" became an icon of national identity. Such long epic poems as *The Flight of Zalán* (1825) by Vörösmarty or *The Death of Buda* (1863) by János Arany expressed a deep, consecrating sense of belonging to one's own land and folk. It was at least partly due to Kölcsey's influence that in the nineteenth century some Hungarian writers regarded literature as a moral force to preserve the decorum of a national community threatened by cosmopolitan positivists.

Undeniably, it is also possible to make a more destructive interpretation of Kölcsey's essay. "What is national character? Bad habits." This categorical condemnation by Imre Madách (1823–1864), the author of *The Tragedy of Man*,[30] – a 4117-line-long dramatic poem on the history of mankind that contains no more than a single reference to Hungarian history – foreshadows Nietzsche's association of decline with parochialism and the ossification of national character: "Wenn nämlich ein Volk vorwärts geht und wächst, so sprengt es jedesmal den Gürtel, der ihm bis dahin sein *nationales* Ansehen gab; bleibt es stehen, verkümmert es, so schließt sich ein neuer Gürtel um seine Seele; die immer härter werdende Kruste baut gleichsam ein Gefängnis herum, dessen Mauern immer wachsen. Hat ein Volk also sehr viel Festes, so ist dies ein Beweis, daß es versteinern will und ganz und gar *Monument* werden möchte: wie es von einem bestimmten Zeitpunkte an das Ägyptertum war."[31] If the identity of a nation becomes easily recognizable, the next stage is the loss of that identity. "Ein historisches Phänomen, rein und vollständig erkannt und in ein Erkenntnisphenomän aufgelöst, ist für den, der es erkannt hat, tot."[32]

Although Kölcsey's essay contains no such explicit prediction, it does not exclude the disappearance of nations in a more distant future. In 1939, more than a century after the publication of *National Traditions*, a collection of essays appeared with the title *What Is Hungarian?* Edited by the historian Gyula Szekfű, this book was meant to suggest that the concept of national character had lost its validity by the twentieth century. As in so many other cases, the counter-identity of Germans supplied the background. What counted as a brave dismissal of racist theories at the time of the threat of Nazi Germany may be interpreted in a somewhat different way in 2000. It seems rather paradoxical that a historian made the following sweeping generalization: "People are everywhere, in every period, season, and climate the same; the same laws of life make them weep, laugh, relax, join groups, and kill each other."[33] While such a statement resembles the clichés of rationalistic universalism propounded by rather ahistorical representatives of the Enlightenment, the claims made by the poet Babits and the composer Kodály, suggesting that Hungarians take no interest in metaphysics and "labyrinthine" complexity in art, appear of rather doubtful value. More relevant might be the point made by the Protestant bishop László Ravasz that "there is no objetctive feature that could be considered to be a canonical measuring rod, an unambiguously Hungarian characteristic in literature or in the arts."[34]

Such a negative definition is compatible with the view that a national community can be defined only in linguistic terms. The idea that being Hungarian means using the conceptual map constituted by the Hungarian language is by no means absent from Kölcsey's essay. "Hungarians can achieve originality by the use of their language,"[35] the poet writes, lamenting that in the age of the rise of poetry composed in the vernacular, Janus Pannonius (1434–1472) "used a Roman lute when singing fine, yet foreign songs."[36] The opposition between the written language of the Latin Antiquity and Middle Ages on the one hand and the constantly changing, spoken vernacular tradition handed down by word of mouth on the other is related to the debate mentioned earlier: "the defenders of writing were inclined to universalism, whereas the adherents of orality preferred relativism."[37]

Put another way, it is possible to read *National Traditions* with the eyes of Dezső Kosztolányi (1885–1936), the most important exponent of a language-based cultural relativism in twentieth-century Hungarian literature. Understandably, this poet relied on Széchenyi's numerous works rather than on Kölcsey's essay. The idea that human consciousness is inseparable from language, implicit in Kölcsey's line of argument, was more consistently expressed by Széchenyi, who was convinced that the disappearance of even the tiniest linguistic community was an irreparable loss to mankind. "I have received my language from God and I will return it to Him upon my death." This declaration, made in the Upper House on 30 November 1835,[38] is symptomatic of the attitude Kosztolányi attributed to Széchenyi in his *To Be or Not to Be* (1930). This long essay is a counterpart of *Hungarian Literature* by Babits. Babits urged his reader to look at his/her culture with the eyes of an outsider. Kosztolányi's point is that a native reader can never keep that distance from his/her own literature. In that sense the gap between the self and the other cannot be bridged.

The idea that speaking a mother tongue means having preconceptions is more explicitly stated by Széchenyi but can also be detected in Kölcsey's text. Hungarian literature is the legacy of the language, taking language in a rather broad sense as the historical memory, belief system, and way of life of an imagined community. Irrespective of the possible disappearance of nations as imagined communities in the future, this language-based conception may be the most obvious manifestation of the role of texts in shaping national identity.

Notes

[1] Ludwig Wittgenstein, *Vermischte Bemerkungen*. Chicago: The University of Chicago Press, 1984, 76.

[2] Wilhelm Furtwängler, *Aufzeichnungen 1924–1954*. Wiesbaden: F. A. Brockhaus, 1980, 264.

[3] Hans-Georg Gadamer, *Wahrheit und Methode: Grundzüge einer philosophischen Hermeneutik*. Tübingen: S. J. C: B: Mohr (Paul Siebeck), 1986, 379.

[4] Pierre Boulez, "History in the Present Tense," CD Review, December 1990, 23.

[5] See Benedict Anderson, *Imagined Communities*. London: Verso, 1983.

[6] J. Hillis Miller, *Reading Narrative*. Norman: University of Oklahoma Press, 1998, 3.

[7] Ferenc Kölcsey, "Nemzeti hagyományok," Budapest: Szépirodalmi Könyvkiadó, 1950. Vol. I, 505–506.

[8] Kölcsey, ibid., 513.

[9] Kölcsey, ibid., 514.

[10] J. Huizinga, *Im Bann der Geschichte: Betrachtungen und Gestaltungen*. Burg: Burg-Verlag, 1943, 162.

[11] Jean-Jacques Rousseau, *Discours sur les arts et les sciences – Discours sur l'origine de l'inégalité*. Paris: Garnier-Flammarion, 1971, 117.

[12] Jean-Jacques Rousseau, *Du contrat social*. Paris: Garnier-Flammarion, 1966, 82.

[13] David Hume, *Essays: Moral, Political and Literary*. London: Oxford University Press, 1971, 213.

[14] Matthew Caske, *Art in Europe 1700–1830: A History of the Visual Arts in an Era of Unprecedented Urban Economic Growth*. Oxford University Press, 1997, 110.

[15] Quoted by Matthew Craske in *Art in Europe* 1700–1830, 24.

[16] Kölcsey, ibid., 490.

[17] István Széchenyi, *Hitel*. Budapest: Magyar Történelmi Társulat, 1930, 492.

[18] Gróf Széchenyi István, *Naplói*. Vol. I. Budapest: Magyar Történelmi Társulat, 1825, 577.

[19] Gróf Széchenyi István, *Naplói,* Vol. I, 629.

[20] István Széchenyi, *Világ vagy is felvilágosító töredékek némi hiba 's előítélet eligazítására*. Pest: Füskúti Landerer, 1831, 72.

[21] Széchenyi, *Világ*, 101–102, 103.

[22] Széchenyi, *Világ*, XXIX.

[23] Gróf Széchenyi István, *Beszédei*. Budapest: Athenaeum, 1887, 358.

[24] Gróf Széchenyi István, *Döblingi Hagyatéka,* Vol. III. Budapest: Magyar Történelmi Társulat, 1925, 862–863.

[25] See Tzvetan Todorov, *Nous et les autres: La réflexion française sur le diversité humaine*. Paris, 1989, 154, 174.

[26] See, for instance, Mireille Marc-Lipiansky: "Crise ou déclin de l'Occident?" *L'Europe en formation* 306–307, automne – hiver 1997, 47–79.

[27] See my essay "A *Nemzeti hagyományok* korszerűsége," *Valóság* 1999/5, esp. 36–38.

[28] Kölcsey, ibid., 492.

[29] Paul Ricoeur, *Histoire et vérité*. Troisième édition augmentée de quelques textes. Paris: Seuil, 1964, 185.

[30] Madách Imre, *Összes Művei*. Budapest: Révai, 1942, Vol. II, 757.

[31] Friedrich Nietzsche, *Menschliches, Allzumenschliches: Ein Buch für freie Geister.* Wilhelm Goldmann, 1981, 412.

[32] Nietzsche, *Unzeitgemäße Betrachtungen.* Frankfurt am Main: Insel, 1981, 106.

[33] Gyula Szekfű (ed.), *Mi a magyar?* Budapest: Magyar Szemle, 1939, 489.

[34] Gyula Szekfű (ed.), *Mi a magyar?* 32.

[35] Kölcsey, ibid., 508.

[36] Kölcsey, ibid., 515.

[37] Katalin Neumer, *Gondolkodás, beszéd, írás.* Budapest: Kávé, 1998, 38.

[38] Széchenyi István, *Válogatott Művei.* Budapest: Szépirodalmi, 1991, Vol. I, 692.

Romanticism, Biedermeier, and Realism

How can the position of Romanticism be determined in the continuity of European art and literature? The most serious difficulty in discussing this topic is related to a fundamental self-contradiction of our discipline. On the one hand, historians wish to develop value-free definitions of literary movements; on the other hand, this ideal can hardly be respected when speaking about such concepts as Romanticism, Biedermeier, Realism, Symbolism, Naturalism, and Jugendstil. Biedermeier, Realism, and Naturalism imply a functional view of literature, whereas Romanticism and Symbolism are bound up with the ideal of aesthetic autonomy. That is why it is easier to define both Biedermeier and Realism in terms of institutions rather than in terms of stylistic features. A Biedermeier "Lebensbild" or a Realistic novel is inseparable from illustrated almanacs, serial publications, and journalism, whereas an ode by Keats or a sonnet by Mallarmé comes closer to representing an autonomous verbal structure. In any case, Paul de Man's warning is worth remembering: "The terminology of traditional literary history, as a succession of periods or literary movements, remains useful only if the terms are seen for what they are: rather crude metaphors for figural patterns rather than historical facts or events."[1]

The literature on Romanticism is so vast that it is virtually impossible to find a starting hypothesis that cannot be called a distortion. I am inclined to reject the nominalist approach represented by Arthur O. Lovejoy half a century ago, yet I find too much self-contradiction in Romanticism to accept René Wellek's defence of the homogeneity of the movement. The fallacy of a finite and simple definition has to be avoided.

It is probably true that most of the other movements of 19th-century art have to be characterized with reference to Romanticism, which may have been the last great period in the history of European culture to be influential in all the arts and in most parts of the Western world. Our position in history is still largely determined by the awareness that we are "nach der Romantik – der letzten Epoche eines noch alle Künste umgreifenden Epochenbewußtseins," – as Hans Robert Jauß convincingly argued.[2] The relevance of all the later movements is more restricted. It would be difficult to speak about Naturalism in verse, and it is not much easier to distinguish a Symbolist current in novel writing. Some of the 19th-century movements may be tied to certain genres and/or seem to have implications that are inseparable from evaluation. Biedermeier art is often regarded as "abgesunkene Romantik;" Realism and Naturalism have undergone a radical devaluation in the course of the 20th century; and analysts of kitsch frequently take examples from Biedermeier and Jugendstil art. György Lukács adopted normative restrictions in his essays on Realism, written in his middle phase, and his legacy has made it virtually impossible for scholars working in the former Soviet bloc to use this term in a post-Communist world.

All these examples indicate that historicist objectivity is an illusion. The Romanticism of 1898 was different from the Romanticism of 1998. The following hypotheses are highly biased in the sense that they are formulated from the perspective of the end of the 20th century.

While (Neo-)classicism is a stylistic concept that has to be examined in relation to the ideology of the Enlightenment, Romanticism denotes both style and world picture ("Weltanshauung"). Those who seek to find the place of Romanticism in a "longue durée" continuity might take the rejection of the Rococo as a point of departure, a paradigm shift that occurred some time between the middle and the end of the 18th century in the various European countries. To locate the next stage is not as easy. Because of the gradual transformation of the (Neo-)classical style around 1800, at the time when the cult of "ut pictura poesis" was replaced by that of "ut musica poesis," the codified ideas of static beauty had disintegrated and a dynamic interpretation of the sublime prevailed. This distinction can also be rephrased as a contrast between the ideals of "natura naturata" and "natura naturans," inorganic and organic form, allegory and symbol, didacticism and implicit meaning, functionalism and the autonomy of the aesthetic sphere. With the rise of Romanticism the artist ceased to be a servant, and s/he no longer was an educated and civilized craftsman. Technical skill and profession were devalued in favour of mission or calling, which became the distinctive features of a genius. Institutions inherited from earlier periods were rejected and schools were replaced by movements. The change in the relations between patron and artist went together with a break with the idea that artists were either masters or disciples.

With some caution one could associate the rise of Romanticism with a shift of emphasis from representation to expression. In the middle of the 19th century Amiel gave the following retrospective definition: "Un paysage quelconque est un état de l'âme, et qui lit dans tous deux est émerveillé de retrouver la similitude dans chaque détail."[3] Paul de Man's hypothesis that the Romantic image is based on "a tension (and not a mere analogy or imitation) between a consciousness and a natural object,"[4] is but a variation on the French Romantic's remark.

While this thesis may help us understand the long survival of the Romantic legacy, it is no satisfactory premise for the conclusion that "there is little in the poetry of our century that cannot be included within this broadly considered framework of the romantic tradition."[5] Although this conclusion was formulated by de Man in 1958, before the debates on Postmodernism had started, a conception that would include all the avant-garde movements as extensions of Romanticism is not sufficiently historical. Another pitfall is a categorization according to what some would call subject-matter. There are also other simplifications a historian needs to avoid. While it is true that the imitation of Classical Antiquity was not cultivated by the Romantics, it is a gross simplification to believe that they devalued Graeco-Roman in favour of medieval art. We are much closer to the truth if we associate Classicism with a timeless and Romanticism with a historical approach to aesthetic values.

The philosophy of history and language are crucial for the understanding of Romanticism, but consistency is more than a little difficult to trace in the attitude taken towards these two domains by the representatives of this movement. The Risorgimento, German and East-European nationalism, pan-Slavic ideology, and Napoleonic and Victorian imperialism are all related to the cultural relativism that found its most sophisticated spokesman in Wilhelm von Humboldt. The works of Kleist, Pushkin, Mickiewicz, Petőfi, and Wagner testify to the ambiguity of Romantic liberalism. They advocated some form of world-wide revolution, but they were also inclined to emphasize the superiority of their own nation to others. The painting entitled *Finis Poloniae* (1832, in the Berlin National-Galerie) by Dietrich Monten exemplifies a German sympathy for the Polish uprising of 1830–

31, whereas *Germania an ihre Kinder*, a poem composed by Heinrich von Kleist in 1808 as a response to Napoleon's occupation of Austria, retrospectively may be read as the expression of a rather aggressive nationalism. Other works could also be cited as representing an unresolved conflict between equality and liberty.

Posterity means continuous development. The same words can be understood in different ways in different places and periods. There can be no final word on the link between Romanticism and the concept of national identity ("Volksseele" or "Volksgeist"). Let me quote Hans Sachs from the final scene of *Die Meistersinger von Nürnberg*, first performed in 1868:

> "zerfällt erst deutsches Volk und Reich,
> in falscher welscher Majestät
> kein Fürst bald mehr sein Volk versteht,
> und welschen Dunst mit welschem Tand
> sie pflanzen uns in deutsches Land;
> was deutsch und echt, wüßt keiner mehr,
> lebt's nicht in deutscher Meister Ehr."

This prophecy is comparable to the visions expressed in Kölcsey's poems *Zrínyi's Song* (1830) and *Zrínyi's Second Song* (1838), or in Vörösmarty's *Appeal* (1836). The predictions of the decay of a nation under foreign rule are susceptible of different readings. During the 1956 revolution Vörösmarty's poem acquired a special significance, and there is every reason to believe that Wagner's words may have had a similar effect on some citizens of the German Democratic Republic. The same words of Sachs, the reference to foreign mists and vanities proved to be vulnerable to manipulation in the Third Reich, although those who did not ignore the wider context could find a critique of chauvinism in the warning that German art remain true to its best traditions in evil times:

> "im Drang der schlimmen Jahr
> blieb sie doch deutsch und wahr."

A similar ambiguity can be felt in Petőfi's *Life or Death*, written on 30 September 1848, in which Serbs, Croats, Germans, Slovaks, and Romanians are called "disgusting hungry ravens." The 19th-century reader may have felt agreement where we sigh or feel uncomfortable.

Since one of the most important elements of the legacy of Romanticism is the idea that interpretation is a historical experience, no work can ever be completely understood either by the artists' contemporaries or by posterity. The literary movements of the 19th century have to be approached in terms of an interdisciplinary "Wirkungsgeschichte," rather than in terms of a purely literary "Entstehungsgeschichte." The history of each of the above-mentioned artistic movements is a history of redefinitions. The public of the mid-19th century was more attentive to what was described or painted than the readers and viewers of the late 20th century seem to be. That is one of the reasons why a Biedermeier portrait or a Victorian novel might have seemed more Realistic for a 19th- than for a 20th-century public.

Apart from the value-laden character of period concepts, there is another major difficulty for those who wish to describe the relations between the different artistic movements of the 19th century, the convention based on the idea that these movements represent a linear progress. As the author of a book on Biedermeier painting remarked, "around 1900, art history was being rewritten so as to present the development of nineteenth-century art as a logical sequence leading through Realism to Impressionism. History painting, formerly considered the highest achievement of the century, came to be dismissed as an aberration."[6] It is not at all self-evident that works composed at the same time can be labeled avant- or arrière-garde. A similar conclusion was drawn by Carl Dahlhaus from a comparison of the works of three musicians of the mid-19th century: "Niemand vermag zu sagen, ob Meyerbeers 'juste milieu' (wie Schumann es nannte) innerlich 'früher' oder 'später' ist als Schumanns Romantik oder Silchers Biedermeier."[7] The 1996 exhibition of the paintings of Jean Baptiste Camille Corot (1796–1875) in the Grand Palais proved that there may be important artists whose careers cannot be described in terms of a teleological process leading from Classicism through Romanticism and Realism to Naturalism and Impressionism. The uncertainty is especially striking in the use of the term Realism. Currently in the Musée d'Orsay paintings as different as *St. Sébastien, martyre* by Théodore Ribot (1823–1891), a work showing the influence of Ribera and exhibited in the Salon of 1865, the portrait of *Mme Tessier* (1872) by Adolphe Monticelli (1824–1886), an artist who could be called either a late Romantic or a forerunner of Van Gogh, and *Mrs. Heugh at the Age of 93* (1872) by the Pre-Raphaelite Sir John Everett Millais (1829–1896) are presented as examples of Realism. The confusion is no less obvious in literary history. Literary historians of one country characterize as Romantic works that literary historians of another country characterize as Realistic. This suggests that these two movements cannot be analyzed separately. It could be argued that Realism was an extension of some aspects of Romantic art, while other aspects were developed by the Symbolists.

"The ugly is dynamic where the beautiful is static." This statement made by the authors of one of the few synthetic books on the arts of the 19th century can be taken as a useful summary of those features that distinguish the aesthetics of Romanticism and Biedermeier.[8] One of the reasons why it is difficult to speak of a Biedermeier style is its eclecticism that is both a continuation of earlier movements and their transcendence. What we have after the fall of Napoleon has been called "the taming of Romanticism." The cult of originality was replaced by an emphasis on consensus and an inclination to dispense with the assumption that the artistic was in conflict with the pragmatic and that the artist's mission was to reject the rules, practices, and institutions which had been transmitted to him/her. The appropriation of devices borrowed from various periods of the past went together with a return to imitation. Immermann's novel *Die Epigonen* (1835) is about the "Lebensgefühl" of the late comers ("die Spätlinge") who lack originality. In his well-known analysis of *Auf eine Lampe* (1846), Emil Staiger wrote about Mörike's "epigonische Situation" and gave as evidence the variation upon the following line of the second part of Goethe's *Faust*:

"Die Schöne bleibt sich selber selig."[9]

The close of *Auf eine Lampe* – "Was aber schön ist, selig scheint es in ihm selbst" – is only one of the many examples illustrating the post-Romantic artist's heavy reliance on direct or indirect quotation.

The Empire style, Biedermeier culture, and Victorianism may be local variants of a transformation leading towards Realism. The similarities between earlier and later works, however, are so striking that it is tempting to stress continuity, rather than speak about a reaction against Romanticism. Petőfi's ars poetica, for instance, his self-characterization as "the wild flower of unrestrained nature" (in the poem *A természet vadvirága*, composed in December 1844) is reminiscent of Wordsworth's description of the anti-rhetorical natural poet who is attracted to humble and rustic life and manners.

It is no less difficult to find stylistic criteria which would make the interpretation of Biedermeier and Realism as radically different movements more than possible. The decorative element in Biedermeier culture is clearly destructive of the objective rendering of the sitter or of landscape, which was the main goal of the Realists. In the novels of Balzac or the paintings of Courbet a high price was set on "la recherche du détail pertinent." Keen observation of character became an important criterion for critics. In contrast to the stylization of landscape and character in the narrative fiction of Mörike and Stifter or in the paintings of Waldmüller and Barabás, the Realist prose writer or painter took the "original" of his work as his point of reference. As *La Comédie humaine* proves, the Realist writer's ambition was to obliterate the distinction between art and science. This reinterpretation of the function of art was a far cry from idealization, a principle which Biedermeier artists inherited from Neoclassicism.

The rise of Realism is inseparable from the discovery of photography, which – together with the growing popularity of water-colours and sketches, "feuilletons" and literary portraits – involved another rearrangement of the aesthetic sphere: artistic value was ascribed to the transitory. This meant a further challenge to the adherents of the Platonic ideal of timeless beauty.

It would be easy to go one step further and assert that the two movements can also be associated with a cult and a rejection of allegory, respectively. No such claim can be made. Allegory and Realism seem to be incompatible but they should be regarded as different modes of interpreting. Since the same text or painting can be seen as allegorical or a Realistic narrative, "Lebensbild," or description, we have to be content with the more modest hypothesis that Realism may be at least partly responsible for the shift from the cult of "Ideallandschaft," implying an anthropocentric view of nature still influential in Biedermeier art and literature, to the concept of "milieu," mentioned in the 1842 preface to *La Comédie humaine*. One of the far-reaching consequences of this change was the canonization of urban and industrial landscape, not only in such novels as *Mary Barton* and *Hard Times* but also in Baudelaire's cycle *Tableaux Parisiens* and his "petits poèmes en prose" published under the title *Le Spleen de Paris*. Petőfi's poem *On the Railway* (1847) foreshadows not only Whitman's *To a Locomotive in Winter* (1876) but the rise of industrial art and the avantgarde cult of the machine that was to replace the principle of organic form preached by the Romantics.

It is a telling evidence of the complexity of historical paradigm shifts that the two artistic movements in question also have important similarities. First of all, it is undeniable that the middle-class character of Biedermeier culture helped the rise of Realism. After the Vienna Congress the egotistical sublime of the solitary genius was questioned in the name of bourgeois rationality and common sense. Visionary prophecy was often replaced by an emphasis on the ordinary or the occasional. Under the influence of the Dutch landscape and genre paintings of the 17th century, open-air painting emerged and such poetic "Lebensbilder" were composed as Lenau's *Auf eine holländische Landschaft.* The refusal to ennoble the trivial led to a new conception of art: the importance of "subject" became minimized and aesthetic value was no longer defined with reference to a transcendental principle of beauty. The anti-bourgeois attitude of Romantic bohemians was replaced by an emphasis on middle-class values. While the Romantics drew inspiration from the later works of Beethoven, in Biedermeier culture a return to Mozart became the slogan. Needless to say, the works of both composers were interpreted in the 19th century in a way radically different from the way they are read today. While Beethoven was regarded as a genius at war with society, Mozart was considered to be an artist who seemed to live according to the norms of his age.

Romanticism, Biedermeier, and Realism can also be defined in terms of the changing relations between the artist and the market. In most parts of Central Europe the first auctions were held and the first circulating libraries opened in the decades following Waterloo. This was the period in which mass culture began to emerge in the most civilized countries. From the later perspective of the Symbolists a Biedermeier poet or a Realist prose writer made concessions to the general public. To such later writers as Henry James and Virginia Woolf it seemed that Dickens wasted his talents pandering to public taste and sacrificed his artistic conscience for money.

The strong sense of community underlying Biedermeier culture made it easier for the Realists to bring a reaction against the Romantics' emphasis on individual creativity. Such novelists as Balzac, Dickens, Gogol, or Trollope refused to ascribe to the novel any special status that would separate it from the life of the author or the reader. As Bourdieu pointed out: "Le réalisme se définit fondamentalement, avec Courbet, par la volonté de dépeindre 'le vulgaire et le moderne'. Champfleury revendique pour l'artiste le droit de représenter avec vérité le monde contemporain."[10]

The Romantics often seemed to maintain that the primary means of expression was dissonance. An important distinguishing feature of Biedermeier culture is an attempt to restore the credibility of resolution. One of the results of the desire to bridge the gap between high art and popular culture was that Biedermeier literature, painting, and music became closely tied to institutions. The dangers inherent in courting the support of the general public proved to be detrimental in the long run: the art of the "juste milieu" as represented by Paul Delaroche and Horace Vernet clearly indicates how the combination of Romantic and Realistic features turned into academic art.

The gap between commissioned and noncommissioned art had become considerably wide in the course of the century. The Biedermeier portraitist Barabás painted water-colours for himself that were free in handling and thus closer to Romanticism (*Lago Maggiore* 1834, *Sunset in Venice* 1834, *Italian Landscape* 1834, *Villa di Mecenate a Tivoli* 1834, *The Eruption of the Vesuvius* 1835, *The Blue Cave* 1835, *Shipwreck* 1835, *Sunset in Calabria* 1836, *Boat in a Storm with the Vesuvius in the Background* 1837, *Le Mont-Blanc* 1843), and Munkácsy, who won the gold medal at the 1870 Salon and became internationally famous with such works as *Milton and His Daughters* (1877–78) and *Christ Before Pilate* (1881), continued the Barbizon tradition with such landscapes as *Dusty Road* (1874) or *Park in Colpach* (1886). The origins of the attack made by Henry James on Dickens as a novelist who can produce only "figures" but no "characters," and on Trollope as a writer "for children," who is "a good observer," but "practically nothing else," in his reviews of *Our Mutual Friend* (1865) and *The Belton Estate* (1866),[11] or the later clash between "Ringstraße" art and "Wiener Sezession" can be traced back to the Biedermeier inclination to accept rather than transform the taste of the common reader or viewer. When some novelists and critics tried to restore the reputation of Balzac or Dickens in the 20th century, those aspects of their writing were stressed which seemed to contradict the ideals of Realism. In this spirit Kafka planned his novel *Amerika* as a "Dickens-Nachahmung,"[12] *La Comédie humaine* was reread as a Romantic work by Jean-Pierre Richard,[13] and Fontane's *L'Adultera* and *Der Stechlin* were revalued by Herman Meyer as novels developing the Romantic art of quoting to pave the way for the 20th-century techniques of intertextuality.[14] If such novels as *Le rouge et le noir* or *Anna Karenina*, *Mertvyye Dushi* or *A rajongók*, *Middlemarch* or *Effi Briest* may have been read in the 19th century as edifying tales, presenting "exempla" of behaviour patterns, today these works are interpreted from the perspective of 20th-century developments, just as Biedermeier narratives like *Die Judenbuche* or *Der Nachsommer*, Grillparzer's "bürgerliche Schauspiele," the "Volksstücke" of Nestroy and Szigligeti, such "Lebensbilder" in verse as Lenau's *Der Räuber im Bakony*, *Die drei Zigeuner*, the same poet's short narratives *Mischka an der Theiß* and *Mischka an der Marosch*, or Petőfi's descriptive poems *The Plains, The Puszta, In Winter,* and *Kis-Kunság* are viewed as representing a transition between Romanticism and Realism.

The cult of the vagabond who is a fugitive from injustice rather than from justice and preserves an unwritten code of honour, has special significance in the current of Romanticism which was to merge into Realism. At the same time, it is a manifestation of the interrelations between the various forms of art. In 1834, during his stay in Italy, Barabás painted an outlaw and made two portraits of "bandits" – one of these is a watercolour now in the Hungarian National Gallery, the other a drawing.[15] The interest the young Hungarian artist seems to have taken in the victims of an unjust political and social system may have been inspired by his readings. Karl von Moor, in Schiller's *Die Räuber* (1781), a play that was given a political significance in the French revolution of 1789, the title hero of *Rob Roy* (1817), a powerful and dangerous but also just and generous Highland outlaw, or Robin Hood in *Ivanhoe* (1819) were among those characters in literary works that served as models for several artists. *Bandit on the Watch* (1825) by the Swiss artist Léopold Robert (later acquired by the Wallace Collection) is a characteristic pictorial manifestation of the Romantic artist's sympathy for those who had been rounded up by the police. In Italy penniless "lazzaroni" – a word also used by Barabás in the catalogue of his works – frequently came into conflict with the troops of the Papal States and Bourbon kingdom. Their defiance of law and authority symbolized opposition to the political system introduced by the Holy Alliance. In 1822 Robert gave the following characterization of these outcasts: "Ever since I arrived here I have been struck by these Italian figures, by their manners and their picturesque and savage clothes. I hoped to render them with all possible truth, and above all with that simplicity and nobility which are marks in this people and which they inherit from their ancestors."[16]

The fascination which freedom-loving outlaws exerted on the Romantics is inseparable from the portrayal of gypsies. Petőfi's early "Lebensbild" *The Life of Wanderers*, composed in April 1844, was inspired by *A Gypsy Family Travelling in Transylvania*, painted by Barabás in 1843, the year of the composition of Mérimée's *Carmen*. Of course, both Barabás and Petőfi were familiar with Lenau's 1838 poem *Die drei Zigeuner*. The image of the gypsy – "ce peuple qui sait lui-même ni d'où il vient ni où il va, [...] qui n'a d'aucune foi et aucune loi, aucune croyance définie et aucune règle de conduite," as Liszt wrote in 1859[17] – became associated not only with the idea of unrestricted freedom but also with improvisation. In 1822 Liszt heard the gypsy band of János Bihari (1764–1827). This experience served as a starting point for the composer's experimentation with "rubato" playing.

To what extent are the "Hungarian rhapsodies" representative of the Romantic cult of freedom and to what extent can they be interpreted as a kind of abstraction of Hungarian national identity? It is hardly possible to find a satisfactory answer to this old question. A similar ambiguity can be detected in the descriptive poems of Petőfi. As is well-known, in July 1848 this poet hoped to be elected to the Hungarian parliament. The thrill of revolution that caught him made him compose a text in prose (*A kiskunokhoz*) and the poem *Kis-Kunság*. In both the image of the "puszta" becomes the symbol of a wide horizon. At the same time the "open" and internal landscape refers to the Hungarian national character. The structural development of the poem is incontestably Romantic. The first stanzas emphasize the temporal alienation of the lyric self from his vision and thus designate the ontological priority of consciousness over what is perceived. The speaker is not part of the landscape in a literal sense; surrounded by an urban environment, he is taken to the puszta by his imagination. It is no mere conjunction of psychic state and sense perception. A very close association is established between the internalized consciousness that contains the object of the description and a language that corresponds to the Wordsworthian ideal of the absence of rhetoric. Nevertheless, the conventionality of the writing becomes apparent if the poem is put in a wider context. Once again, Petőfi followed the example of Barabás, who in 1838 painted his *Puszta Landscape* (now in the Janus Pannonius Museum, Pécs) and two watercolours. One of these has a title with spatial, temporal, and even musical connotations (*Alföldi róna, esti hangulat*). Since all these works present a landscape that is in contradiction with the Romantic ideal of the sublime, they can be viewed as combining Romantic elements with the Biedermeier emphasis on the ordinary.

In a sense Biedermeier culture represented a return to the legacy of the Enlightenment: the communicative function of art was emphasized. Novels were viewed as instruments of moral education, and their readers were expected to develop strong positive or negative emotional attitudes towards the characters of narrative fiction. In so far as works of visual or verbal art were expected to support rather than undermine social norms, there was an overlap between Central-European Biedermeier culture and Victorianism. Similarities between the Biedermeier and Victorian value systems have inspired some scholars to apply the English term to mid-

19th-century culture in Central Europe or to argue in favour of an English Biedermeier.[18]

As Trollope insisted, "the novelist, if he have a conscience, must preach his sermons with the same purpose as the clergyman."[19] This ideal is inseparable from the assumption that language is subordinated to some extra-linguistic, nontextual purpose. In a Realist novel "the language should be so pellucid that the meaning should be rendered without an effort of the reader."[20] The public was expected to forget the arbitrariness and artificiality of the semiotic system. Narrative prose was meant to fulfill an obligation; it could be "needful" only by serving a social purpose. Utilitarianism involved a rejection of Kantian aesthetics: reception was not regarded as an act of disinterested contemplation.

As is widely known, the taste of the new middle class played a major role in the development of Realism. The function of many novels written in the middle of the 19th-century was to reinforce the ethical norms of the bourgeoisie which later were described as "the Victorian frame of mind."[21] The author of a sociological study of the art of the first half of the 19th century spoke of the world of "Gerichtstafelbeisitzer" in the less developed countries of Central Europe,[22] a term used in such literary works as Petőfi's fragmentary verse satire *The Lateral Judge* (1847) or Jókai's novel *The Good Old Lateral Judges* (1856). This value system was responsible for the happy endings of most narratives written in the middle of the nineteenth century, "a distribution at the last of prizes, pensions, husbands, wives, babies, millions, appended paragraphs, and cheerful remarks," as Henry James wrote in *The Art of Fiction* (1884), an essay heralding the end of Realism.[23]

By the 1880s the softening of the dichotomy between high and popular culture became outmoded. Biedermeier art was devalued and Realism disintegrated into Naturalism and Symbolism. On the one hand there were serious attempts to get rid of the rhetoric hidden in a Realist novel; on the other, metalinguistic devices were used to make language as important in narrative fiction as in lyric poems written in verse.

The continuity between Realist and Naturalist writing is so obvious that sometimes it seems impossible to distinguish them. Both are based on the idea that unmediated experience exists. At the end of the 20th century some would regard this as a misleading epistemological assumption. Realist novels are readable only in so far as they question their own "ars poetica." Such is the observation made by J. Hillis Miller: "What the good reader confronts in the end is not the moral law brought into the open at last in a clear example, but the unreadability of the text."[24]

The end of Realism was bound up with the reappearance of the belief that reality changed along with the observers, an idea formulated earlier by the Romantics. Shifts in narrative point of view were most systematically used and theorized by Henry James, but his experimentation was anticipated by Flaubert, whose oxymoron "bien écrire le médiocre"[25] clearly reveals that the French writer was aware of the contradictions of Realism. While in Realist novels the "contrat de lecture" asked for fast writing and reading and gave relatively little importance to the signifier, Flaubert's "culte du style" was in obvious contradiction with the ideal of the transparency of the narrator's language, "das positivistische Vertrauen in die kausale Transparenz seiner Welt."[26]

Flaubert had reservations about both Romanticism and Realism, "car c'est en haine du réalisme que j'ai entrepris ce roman," as he wrote about *Madame Bovary*. "Mais je m'en déteste pas moins la faute idéalité," he added.[27] The outcome of the disintegration of Realism was a dichotomy: Naturalism developed in the spirit of egalitarianism, whereas Symbolism was often coupled with a nostalgia for traditional hierarchies. At the end of the 19th century there was a strong revival of Romanticism: George drew inspiration from the poetry of Hölderlin, Maeterlinck stressed the continuity between Romanticism and Symbolism in his essay on Novalis, published in the volume *Le tréson des humbles* (1896), and Yeats returned to the legacy of Blake. Although the movement led by Mallarmé was largely restricted to the lyric, its influence contributed to the rise of the psychological novel, a type of narrative prose that superseded Realism. "L'ère du soupçon" had set in, and the communicative function of art had lost its validity in consequence of unreliable narrators and ambiguous characters. Since the 20th century was dominated by the modes of presenting consciousness, our perspective is largely determined by them. This is one of the main difficulties in any attempt to define the relations between Romanticism and Realism, the two artistic currents that played a major role in the 19th century.

Notes

[1] Paul de Man, *The Rhetoric of Romanticism*. New York: Columbia University Press, 1984, 254.
[2] Hans Robert Jauß, *Studien zum Epochenwandel der ästhetischen Moderne*. 2. Auflage. Frankfurt am Main: Suhrkamp, 1988, 7, 82.

[3] Henri-Frédéric Amiel, *Fragments d'un journal intime*. 31 octobre 1852. Genève: Georg et Co., 1911. Tome I., 62.

[4] Paul de Man, *Romanticism and Contemporary Criticism: The Gauss Seminar and Other Papers*. Baltimore and London: The Johns Hopkins University Press, 1993, 130.

[5] Ibid., 131.

[6] Geraldine Norman, *Biedermeier Painting 1815–1949: Reality Observed in Genre, Portrait and Landscape*. London: Thames and Hudson, 1987, 8.

[7] Carl Dahlhaus, *Klassische und romantische Musikästhetik*. Laaber: Laaber-Verlag, 1988, 169.

[8] Charles Rosen and Henri Zerner, *Romanticism and Realism: The Mythology of Nineteenth Century Art*. London: Faber, 1984, 19.

[9] Martin Heidegger: *Denkerfahrungen 1910–1976*. Frankfurt am Main: Klostermann, 1983, 44.

[10] Pierre Bourdieu, *Les règles de l'art: Genèse et structure du champ littéraire*. Paris: Seuil, 1992, 368.

[11] Henry James, *Selected Literary Criticism*. London: Heinemann, 1963, 8, 14.

[12] Franz Kafka, *Tagebücher 1910–1923*. Frankfurt am Main: Fischer, 1983, 391.

[13] Jean-Pierre Richard, *Études sur le romantisme*. Paris: Seuil, 1970, 7–139.

[14] Herman Meyer, *Das Zitat in der Erzählkunst*. Stuttgart: J. B. Metzler, 1961.

[15] *Márkosfalvi Barabás Miklós Önéletrajza*. Kolozsvár: Erdélyi Szépmíves Céh, 1944, 235, 302.

[16] Hugh Honour, *Romanticism* (1979). Harmondsworth, Middlesex: Penguin Books, 1991, 241–242.

[17] F. Liszt, *Des Bohémiens et de leur musique en Hongrie*. Nouvelle édition. Leipzig: Breitkopf und Haertel, 1881, 12.

[18] Gábor Halász, "Magyar viktoriánusok" (1942), in *Válogatott írásai*. Budapest: Magvető, 1977, 304–346; Virgil Nemoianu, *The Taming of Romanticism: European Literature and the Age of Biedermeier*. Cambridge, MA: Harvard University Press, 1984.

[19] Anthony Trollope, *An Autobiography*. Leipzig: Tauchnitz, 1883, 206.

[20] Ibid., 218.

[21] Walter E. Houghton, *The Victorian Frame of Mind 1830–1870*. New Haven: Yale University Press, 1957.

[22] Károly Lyka, *Magyar művészet 1800–1850: A táblabíró-világ művészete*. Budapest: Singer és Wolfner, (1922).

[23] Henry James, *Selected Literary Criticism*, 1963, 52–53.

[24] J. Hillis Miller, *The Ethics of Reading: Kant, de Man, Eliot, Trollope, James, and Benjamin*. New York: Columbia University Press, 1987, 33.

[25] Gustave Flaubert, *Correspondance II (1850–1854)*. Paris: Charpentier, 1894, 315.

[26] Hans Robert Jauß, *Ästhetische Erfahrung und literarische Hermeneutik* (1982). Frankfurt am Main: Suhrkamp, 1991, 158.

[27] Gustave Flaubert, *Correspondance III (1854–1869)*. Paris: Charpentier, 1892, 68.

The Tragedy of Man: a Reading

The Romantics *took* a passionate interest in history, yet they were often tempted to raise themselves to a suprahistorical vantage point. Inspired by Milton's *Paradise Lost* and Goethe's *Faust,* the *chef d'ocuvre* of Imre Madách (1823–1864) is a monumental work revealing such a double perspective, a meditation on the values of history and an attempt to look at something of which the 19th century was proud, a critique of the excesses of the historical sense.

History is presented by the Hungarian poet as Adam's dream, a succession of great moments in the struggle of mankind. The hero is accompanied by Eve and Lucifer, and the three main characters stand for three forces which seem to be in ceaseless conflict. Adam's belief in evolution towards a goal is annulled by Lucifer's concept of eternal recurrence, whereas both the hero's design and the philosophical parodist's interpretation are questioned by the unhistorical creative instinct represented by Eve. The scenes of becoming are counterpointed by the idea that the world reaches its finality at each and every moment, and the historical sense of the 19th century is at variance with the unhistorical visions of a lost paradise and of a future marked by slow degeneration. Catastrophes are repeated at regular intervals, and the final outcome points to Madách's distrust of teleology.

Written in the winter of 1859–60, *Az ember tragédiája* ("The Tragedy of Man") is a late Romantic lyrical drama which suggests a loss of illusions characteristic of a post-revolutionary age.

After the repression of the Hungarian revolution by the army of the Russian tzar in 1849, some Hungarian intellectuals reached the conclusion that all forms of superficial patriotism were not only cheap but also harmful. Laying the blame (and not without reason) upon certain Liberal governments (the British, for example), they became convinced that the Western world failed to understand the revolution led by Kossuth, because foreigners had an inauthentic image of Hungary based upon the impression that the provinciality of Hungarian conditions made upon travellers. Few, perhaps none, of these intellectuals went as far as Madách, who considered patriotism almost irreconcilable with artistic creation.

"Patriotism can be the subject of poetry only with us, who are struggling for our very existence; no great poet has ever resorted to it," he wrote once, and this must have been a recurrent thought with him, because there is another slightly different statement in the same notebooks: "Patriotism could be a poetic principle only with Hungarians, for the reason that other nations have no idea of the struggle involving existence and non-existence." On a third occasion he even gave a more specific explanation of what he regarded as the main reason why Hungarian poets insisted on patriotism: "Other nations do not know of conditions like those in the political life of Hungary. We are in a constant struggle for our life, in one cage with the beast which is ready to devour us at any moment. If they are fighting, their goal is no more than a change from good to better."

Although the dating of some texts by Madách is uncertain, it is beyond any doubt that the observations just quoted were made by him in the 1850's. He learned a bitter lesson about the political isolation of his people after Lord Palmerston, the Prime Minister of the most Liberal of countries, asked the Austrian Emperor to crush the Hungarian revolution as quickly as possible. Because of his frail health, Madách could not fight as a soldier in 1848-49, but his brother died of an illness caught in the war and his sister, brother-in-law, and their child were killed by Romanians supporting the Austrian monarch against the revolutionary army. What is more, after the defeat of the revolution, the poet was imprisoned for having given shelter to Kossuth's secretary.

The memory of the revolution continued to cast a long shadow over the rest of his life. In the pre-revolutionary decade, under the influence of the vigorous theatrical life which produced a great number of plays inspired by Romantic nationalism, he composed historical tragedies about medieval Hungary – *Nápolyi Endre* ("Andrew of Naples"), *Mária királynő* ("Queen Mary"), and *Csák végnapjai* ("The Last Days of Csák"), whereas in the post-revolutionary period his chief aim became to give some global interpretation of the history of mankind, having come to the conclusion that the lack of understanding the Hungarians met with may have been due at least partly to their reluctance to think in international terms. "What is national character? – Bad habits," he observed, after having realized that the idea of national character, a concept at the basis of most historical tragedies written by the Hungarian Romantics of the first half of the 19th century, was invalidated by Positivist science.

In one respect Madách's somewhat far-fetched conclusion seems to have been justified; his most important work has been translated into more languages than any other piece of Hungarian literature. Despite, furthermore, the fact that it is very difficult to translate a lyrical drama with a diction full of commonplace-like maxims and gradually unfolding symbols, *The Tragedy of Man* has attracted the attention of writers as different as Maxim Gorky and James Joyce.

The great variety of interpretations this work has enjoyed may indicate that its influence has been the result not only of its general subject matter but also of the ambitions of the text. Some of these derive from the way the Biblical material is treated by the poet. The first speech of the Lord in the opening scene suggests a Deist conception of God. The created universe is compared to a machine just completed. The wheels go round, and the Creator may rest, for ages may pass before one spoke will need repair. Yet this static interpretation of the universe is immediately challenged by Lucifer, the spirit of Negation. The Lord could not have created anything without his support, he argues, and so he must have his share. This claim appears to be justified, because the Lord gives Lucifer two trees in the garden of Eden, having doomed them first.

Lucifer is further characterized in the next scene, which portrays the story of the Fall. His view of existence echoes that of Schopenhauer: time has no direction, it is no more than eternal recurrence. Individuals may be different, but the roles played by them are the same. Man must have knowledge, because it enables him to choose; thus it brings maturity.

Some interpreters of *The Tragedy* claim that Adam and Lucifer are the heroes of the play, and their dialogues reflect a dilemma with which Madách had to struggle in the post-revolutionary decade; Adam's values are those of a Romantic Liberal, whereas Lucifer's mistrust of generalizations, value-judgments, normative statements, and teleology may remind one of Positivist reasoning. Scene 3 – in which Adam is presented as living outside of Eden in a godless universe and Lucifer's interpretation of time is further elaborated by his arguments that the present has no duration and thus no existence and that the universe is constantly created and destroyed by forces which work in silence and secrecy – undoubtedly supports such an interpretation.

After three scenes of introduction, the main body of the text offers us samples from human history. Adam is anxious to know the fate of his race, and Lucifer gives him a chance to have a vision of the future through a long dream consisting of eleven episodes.

The first of these is one of the best parts of the work, as far as the sheer quality of the writing is concerned. An unfinished pyramid, symbolizing human ambition, is seen in the background. Its creator, the Pharaoh, is a Romantic Titan, a man who has become a god unto himself. Apparently he has more power than God, but he is tormented by solitude. Eve, the wife of a dying slave, teaches him to hear his people's anguish. The Pharaoh renounces his power and liberates the people.

At this point comes the ironic twist so characteristic of the writing of Madách. The crowd has an everlasting longing for a master, Lucifer argues, and it will certainly look for a new tyrant before long. What we see does not contradict Lucifer's argument. Adam cannot help admitting that he has wasted too much time in an aimless attempt to transform man. Although Eve suggests that they could find happiness in private life, Adam finds her horizon very limited and asks Lucifer to lead him to new adventures.

The Egyptian scene enacts a vision of interpreted enterprise. Adam is presented as an example of the egotistic sublime, whereas Lucifer is a commentator who is able to philosophize and can unveil the ontological preconceptions underlying what others say. For him truth is never given; its mode of existence is not eternity. In his interpretation, being is understandable only as projected upon the horizon of temporality. What he seems to suggest by the vision of the pyramid, covered by dust and sand, is that being must be interpreted by way of time. How then does time show itself? What is the truth-character of time? Such are the questions asked by him, and his focus is on something very different from the common sense of time which we have, "use," spend, read from the clock and which we perceive as presence, as an infinite and linear sequence of "nows". Lucifer views life from the perspective of being-toward-death. That is why some interpreters draw a parallel between Madách's conception of being and Existentialism.

The author of *The Tragedy* was a well-read man, and he drew upon various sources when writing his masterpiece. Himself a Roman Catholic,

112

his close friends were Protestants, and his approach to *Genesis* was influenced by Milton and the Satanic readers of *Paradise Lost*. The symbol of the unfinished pyramid echoes *Childe Harold's Pilgrimage,* and the picture of Greek Democracy in the next scene may have been inspired by Shakespeare's presentation of the crowd in *Julius Caesar* as well as by Toqueville's ideas on American society. Adam's reincarnation, Miltiades, the brave soldier, is sentenced to death by the people whose city he has just saved from the enemy. The focus is on his disillusionment; what he calls the majestic people proves to be a mob selling its vote. Questions asked previously are answered here, thus creating a sense of continuity, yet the first two parts of Adam's dream are also contrasted: the lyric monologues and symbolism of the previous scene are replaced by dialogues full of theatrical intensity.

If the example of Athens has shown that the general mood of the people can be manipulated by democracy and man does not need freedom, the next scene presents Adam with an antidote. All values are contested, including the life of the individual. Nihilism prevails in Rome until the city is menaced by a pestilence. Unable to continue to live in an atmosphere of total disillusionment, Adam craves for some guiding principle. Remembering those few who have been crucified for their belief in universal brotherhood and in the liberation of the individual, he listens to Peter the Apostle, who speaks of the arrival of a new faith.

Soon, however, he must learn a bitter lesson. History seems to justify Lucifer's skepticism: the poor want no brotherhood once they have become rich and the same Christianity which appears as a healthy reaction against the relativism prevailing in Rome will turn into a new form of tyranny in medieval Byzantium.

At this point one could assume that the message of the play is based on the underlying idea that all principles lead to disaster once they have been put into practice, but the following scenes show this to be a gross simplification.

The presentation of sensuality in Rome may be one of the less successful sections of *The Tragedy*. Taken as a whole, the sixth scene resembles *A kegyenc* ("The Favourite," 1861), the only play by Count László Teleki (1811–1861), an outstanding Liberal statesman, without having any of the more profound intellectual implications of the earlier play. Chance stands for the loss of teleology in both worlds, but in *The Favourite* the presentation of gambling is subordinated to a devastating vision of the total absence of meaningful human relations. In the opening scene Valentinianus Caesar, the hero of Teleki's Romantic parable, drinks to the health of a monkey, thus suggesting the deterioration of understanding and the impossibility of human communication in a society without communal values. As compared to this portrayal of the Roman Empire, the interpretation of decadence in Madách's work seems to be more conventional.

Something similar could be said about the second half of the next part, the love scene between Tancred, just returning from a Crusade, and Isaura, a nun from a convent. Still, the first half of Scene VII is crucial to the understanding of the ideological aspect of the meaning of the work as a whole. Christianity has triumphed but only at a heavy cost: words are contradicted by deeds. Appearance is in conflict with reality; the soul has departed and only the carcass of the ideal survives. The rights of the individual are denied; those who depart from the officially sanctioned and institutionalized interpretations are persecuted.

Once fully institutionalized, the movement becomes self-destructive. Heretics are executed in Constantinople. The conflict between the advocates of "homoousion" and of "homoiousion" is presented as a ridiculous hair-splitting debate. Like John Stuart Mill, one of the most influential Western thinkers in Hungary in the post-revolutionary years, Madách seems to have shared Hegel's condemnation of Byzantine society. One could argue that in *The Tragedy* this unfavorable judgment is made by Lucifer and that he falsifies evidence in order to convince Adam that all ideas deteriorate once they have triumphed, but this possibility is ruled out by the fact that Adam is forced to endorse Lucifer's conclusion by his own experience. Mill was an agnostic; in this sense his total condemnation of Byzantine Christianity was quite understandable. In the case of Madách, however, a similar value-judgment begs some kind of explanation. In his essay *Madách tragédiája* ("*The Tragedy of Man* by Madách"), first published in 1955, the Marxist philosopher György Lukács argued that the question whether Jesus was man or God had lost its relevance for the author of *The Tragedy,* and so the message of the work could not be reconciled with Christianity.

Such an interpretation, however, must be discarded as irrelevant. Lukács seems to have overlooked a crucial passage in the final scene of the play. Having reached the conclusion that history is meaningless, Adam intends to commit suicide, but he is stopped by Eve, who tells him that she feels she will become a mother. Lucifer warns her that the child was conceived in sin and will bring only misery to the Earth, but she responds that God has the power to create somebody who can bring redemption from both sin and misery.

In other words, it would be an exaggeration to maintain that some kind of Positivist lack of faith is asserted in *The Tragedy*. In Constantinople Adam learns to question the legitimacy of any power which claims to render justice in the name of any ideology. In vain Lucifer tries to convince him that the abuse of power should be seen from a comic rather than a tragic perspective, Adam feels desperate that ideals have died for him.

Exhausted, he tries to seek relief by taking rest in an age marked by indifference, but he cannot find happiness in passivity. Re-incarnate as Kepler, he looks for new interpretations of the world. While for others existence is governed by a stable hierarchy, he identifies rank with curiosity and an inclination to question the legitimacy of existing laws and to see a contradiction between *de facto* and *de jure* authority. Ideas may change, but their total absence results in boredom, a form of existence that knows neither aims nor struggles. That is why Kepler yearns for excitement in life.

And now follows one of the most brilliant as well as paradoxical scenes, a dream within a dream, a kind of *mise-en-abyme,* a variation upon the themes of earlier parts. Like Miltiades, Danton subordinates his individual interests to a common cause, but the movement becomes institutionalized and condemns him as a traitor. Passion becomes a destructive force, and those who have power are alienated from the people. In his solitude Danton makes a desperate attempt to understand his opponents, the aristocrats, but communication between people with different beliefs seems impossible. The revolution is transformed into inquisition. Even the guillotine has ears.

The Paris scene is similar to a mirror in so far as it brings together all the basic motifs of *The Tragedy*. Eve has two incarnations: as a marquise she is sublime and idealized, as a woman from the mob she is vulgar and grotesque. Ironically, in retrospect, after its fall, the old aristocracy seems to have a superiority over the class that has been oppressed for such a long time, but this conclusion proves to be superficial if we compare the Paris scene and the one that follows it. Danton seems to be a kind of arch-liberal, who hates the ruling class but tolerates all individuals. The crowd cannot understand his attitude; and so he, too, is sentenced to death by the Sovereign People he has served. One would expect a sense of disillusion on the part of the hero, but when awakened by Lucifer, Kepler calls his dream magnificent. Violence as such, it seems, is not rejected in *The Tragedy*, because in the tenth scene Kepler strongly condemns rules which protect long established power relations and reaffirms his belief that the false virtues of habit make man forget to walk upon his feet and to exercise his mind.

Yet the next scene, a huge and well constructed *danse macabre*, gives another twist to the argument. Adam has grown older and no longer plays an active part in the action. A London Fair symbolizes free competition, the democracy of a capitalist society, characterized by unlimited private property, free enterprise, and the freedom of the stronger to do down the weaker by following market rules. The anachronistic class barriers of feudalism have crumbled, superstitions are left behind, and people are led by the assumption that wealth brings happiness. Hope of gain is regarded as the most important incentive to productivity and many of those who rebelled against capitalism in their youth would endorse possessive individualism in their later life. Every citizen is governed by what he considers to be his vital interest, and thus society seems to be a mere collection of self-interested individuals who are in perpetual conflict with each other because they are infinite consumers whose only desire is their own private benefit.

There is little doubt that the London scene was inspired by the ideas of Bentham, whose works were widely read in Hungary at the time Madách studied in Pest. *Hitel* ("Credit," 1830), the second and most influential book by Count István Széchenyi (1791–1860), a work that had exerted a profound influence on all the intellectuals of Madách's generation, contained both a summary and an implicit but also radical critique of Benthamism. Following the lead of Széchenyi, Madách relied upon the Romantic interpretation of capitalism when presenting workers who reject mechanical civilization and students who detest the prosaic urban life. In the London scene Adam's disappointment is unquestionable: the French Revolution has led to a utilitarianism which kills not only religious faith, but also belief and creative imagination. What is more, it makes people cruel. If the only thing that matters is personal greed, individuals seek power over each other and their main wish is to exploit others.

Since anarchy has brought a dog-fight for a bone instead of liberty, the only antidote to this chaotic yet ruthless world Adam can think of is some kind of centralized community controlled by science and guided by the intellect. Yet when his ideal is realized in the form of a phalanstery, it proves to be even more destructive than the world of competition. Utilitarianism is pushed one stage further, material welfare being the only guiding principle. Individuality is repressed by division of labour. Life is ruled by excessively centralized plans, egalitarianism implies standardization,

116

history is reduced to a heap of preconceptions, and the legitimacy of art is denied together with the rights of the individual. All that is left is "solid mediocrity"; the age no longer requires genius. The symbolic figures of Plato, Luther, and Michelangelo are reduced to the size of average men.

Like some other Hungarian intellectuals of his time, Madách was familiar with the works of such Socialist theoreticians as Saint-Simon and Fourier. Inspired by his readings, he created a negative Utopia, a vision of a totalitarian state in which the network of such traditional communities as nation and family is replaced by the ideal of official truth. The state presented in the twelfth scene of *The Tragedy* seems to act from benevolent motives, but if one looks behind the rhetoric, the sole purpose of the methods of the aged man who embodies authority is to prevent people from using whatever may have been left of their freedom. Madách's phalanstery is behaviouristic; it does not care what people may think.

The conclusion reached by Adam at the end of this scene is that although free market and central planning seem to represent opposite poles, they behave alike; both deny self-developmental freedom. Although the leader of the phalanstery preaches equality, what he forces upon people is uniformity. Madách's Liberalism was similar to the conception of freedom formulated by John Stuart Mill; he regarded liberty as the equal, effective freedom for all to develop their capacities.

Having found no society in which the individual is judged by the extent to which he has realized his capabilities, Adam looks for freedom in space. By now an aged man, he is flying with Lucifer, having left the Earth behind. It is dusk, turning gradually to night. Having lost all sense of direction, Adam cannot get over the sensation that life is not worth living if one has no goal in view. He has learned to accept mortality, but cannot do without some meaningful occupation.

Asking Lucifer to show him the end of human history, he is taken back to Earth. Lucifer lives up to his principle, and deprives Adam of his last illusion. The last human beings are Eskimo-like creatures living in a region that once belonged to the tropical zone. Adam understands that traditional forms of energy have been used up and that scientists have failed to find appropriate substitutes. Life is doomed to a slow death.

The fourteenth scene, which prophesies an end to all life on earth, clearly indicates that Madách viewed himself as a latecomer who lived in an Alexandrine age characterized by self-irony, incapacity for action, parodistic deformity, and an awareness that its twilight mood would eventually turn into a grotesque deterioration of the human race. Adam has become a broken old man. Leaning on his stick, he is a symbol of spiritual decline. Science has been defeated and noble deeds and ambitions have disappeared. Creative efforts are obliterated by material needs, and man is reduced to the status of animals.

This gloomy perspective makes Adam cry out in despair; and his long dream comes to an end. We are taken back to the landscape of the third scene. Adam cannot forget his dream and decides to save mankind from future sufferings by committing suicide, but Eve tells him that she is expecting a baby. Thus, Adam's conclusion is refuted by Eve's suprahistorical unwisdom.

"Das Ewig-Weibliche/Zieht uns hinan" ("The eternal womanly draws us upward"). These words from the "Chorus mysticus," ending the second part of Goethe's *Faust* and sung at the conclusion of *Eine Faust-Symphonie* (1854), one of the major works by Madách's compatriot Ferenc Liszt, may have been in the Hungarian poet's mind when writing the last scene of his lyrical drama. Yet the closure of *The Tragedy of Man* also foreshadows Nietzsche's reflections on the disadvantages of history for life. Adam's obsession with history has led to the paralysis of personality, a loss of self-respect, and the belief in the old age of mankind.

The hero's last words reaffirm his despair over the slow passing away of his race, a nightmare vision he is unable to forget. The Lord tries to comfort him, but the point he makes does not seem to be very strong. When affirming the value of struggle, he relies on a principle which Adam himself tried to assert before it became invalidated by the vision of the end of life on the Earth. If this is so, it is possible to suggest that *The Tragedy of Man* disqualifies any theological interpretation of human existence. It is no wonder, then, that some critics have characterized the message of the play as non-Christian.

Still, in view of certain other passages in the final scene, such a conclusion may seem to be somewhat simplified. When Lucifer reminds Eve that her child has been conceived in sin, she affirms her belief in God's freedom to create a child to bring salvation. The allusion to the Messiah is made more important by the angelic choir calling eternal grace the most fundamental characteristic of the Lord.

Madách's interpretation of God may owe something to a distinction drawn by Kant, a philosopher whose works were fairly well known in the years following 1837, when Madách began to study at the University of

Pest. In his essay *Der einzig mögliche Beweisgrund zu einer Demonstration des Daseins Gottes* ("The sole possible argument for a demonstration of God's existence," 1763), Kant defined existence (*Dasein*) as absolute position, whereas in the *Kritik der reinen Vernunft* ("Critique of Pure Reason," 1781) he seemed to identify being (*Sein*) with "mere position." Although Madách was not a systematic thinker, what *The Tragedy of Man* suggests is that existence might be regarded as belonging to God's essence, whereas being as "mere position" is a characteristic of man. In any case, the end of the play seems to be in harmony with the conclusion Kant reached in his *Critique of Pure Reason:* the whole of our knowledge finally ends in unanalyzable concepts.

Besides the ability to struggle, two other values are mentioned by the Lord in his final speech. Poetry and music are called curative forces, reminding us that the conflict between the historical sense and the creative imagination is a leading motif in *The Tragedy of Man*. Historicizing is presented as the activity of the old age of mankind, a malady against which art is the only medicine. In an age of Positivistic science Madách affirmed man's right to forget and tried to lead the eye away from culture, interpreted as becoming, to art, regarded as representing the eternal and stable.

One of the reasons for the disagreements among critics about the message of the Hungarian poet's lyrical drama may be that several alternative conclusions are left unreconciled in the final scene. This open ending may also have something to do with the success of the work. At any rate, it is in keeping with the structure of the text. The fifteen scenes constituting the surface structure are subordinated to a thematic deep structure, the dialogue of Adam and Lucifer being a projection of an inner debate between the teleology of Romantic Liberalism and the cyclical view of existence held by some Positivists. To present this dialogue, Madách resorted to the device of the double (*Doppelgänger*) used by many Romantics. The relation between Adam and Lucifer is somewhat similar to that of Deianeira and Jolé, or Forgách and Palizsnay, in *Férfi és nő* ("Man and Woman") and *Queen Mary*, plays which Madách wrote in the early 1840's.

A comparison of *The Tragedy of Man* with the poet's earlier works may reveal his double intention when composing his most important work: while keeping the general framework of a Romantic genre, he also wished to move beyond some of its limitations. Heracles in *Man and Woman*, Palizsnay in Queen Mary, Csák in *The Last Days of Csák*, or Lucifer in the Biblical poem *A nő teremtése* ("The Creation of Woman," c. 1855), are all

Romantic rebels guided by emotion, whereas the Lucifer of *The Tragedy* is a highly intellectual descendant of Romantic rebels; his Satanism is more akin to that of Baudelaire and Lautréamont than to that of earlier poets. He has a cyclic conception of life, yet his irony is mixed with pathos. The lyrical character of the drama is manifest in his somewhat uneasy, reluctant laughter at the end of most of the historical scenes which prove him right. He foresees Adam's failures, but registers them with a wry smile. He finds no satisfaction in his knowledge that Adam's teleological claims are mistaken, because he seems to be aware that the commentator is as much part of an interpreted design as the hero.

Although one could say that an intellectual monologue projected into dialogue is the most essential part of *The Tragedy*, it would be misleading to underestimate the contribution of Eve and the Lord to the ambiguities of the play. It is true that in some passages Eve seems to have none of the complexities of the two protagonists. Ready to accept the truth of Lucifer or the Lord, she lives in an eternal present. In Constantinople she is no more than a nun who observes the rules of a convent, in Prague she is selfish and empty-headed, in Paris her lack of personality is emphasized by the fact that she appears in two roles: first as the sister of an average *marquis*, then as a ruthless woman of the people, and in the second to last she is reduced to a mere caricature of herself. On the other hand, there are crucial moments when she is able to exert a decisive influence on the outcome of the events. In Paradise she has a deeper understanding of the intricacies of the relation of man to God, in London her faith resists mortality, and in the final scene she is the one who can foresee the advent of the Messiah.

No less riddled with contradictions is the character of the Lord. A Jesuit author Jakob Overmans has accused Madách of irreligious views. This is obviously an exaggeration, but, as already suggested, it is undeniable that certain passages of *The Tragedy* cannot be reconciled with Christianity without some difficulty. On the basis of his first words, János Arany, the great poet and first critic of Madách, called the Lord "complacent like a craftsman," and indeed in the first scene the Creator seems to be not only passive, but even alienated from his Creation.

Furthermore, the opening lines of the Choir of Angels may strike us with their ambiguity:

> our share is but the shade he casts on us.
> We glorify him for that endless grace
> that granted us this share in his effulgence.

This metaphoric ambiguity is further strengthened by another contradiction when the text swerves from *Genesis*: the Lord gives two trees to Lucifer but forbids anyone to touch the fruit of immortality: "he who eats thereof shall die." The Arian Milton and his Satanic interpreters may have inspired Madách to stress this ambiguity, especially in Scene II, when Eve summarizes man's relation to God in the following way:

> Why should he punish us? If he has set
> the path we are to follow, surely then
> he made us such that sinful impulses
> will not mislead. Or has he placed us over
> a dizzying abyss, doomed to be damned?
> Or if sin, too be part of his design,
> as is a storm among bright, sunlit days,
> then who dares call that storm the guiltier
> than is this blaze that warms us into life?

Has Adam any chance to resist his fall? Lucifer says no, and the Lord does not care to contradict him. Adam cannot reconcile himself to his fate, and Lucifer's joy is mixed with sadness. Both of them defy the Lord. Surrounded by Calvinist friends, living in an age when the fate of Hungary was determined by external forces and the intellectual climate by Positivism, Madách dramatized a polemic consciousness. The line of argument underlying the dialogue between Adam and Lucifer follows a sequence of four statements:

1. my existence must have a purpose;
2. I cannot see this purpose;
3. it must have been set by somebody/something mightier than me;
4. to learn that purpose I have to find this mightier force.

Madách's conception of history is somewhat akin to that of Ranke, who started his career as a disciple of Hegel and moved toward Positivism. This German historian, widely read in Hungary in the middle of the nineteenth century, compared the history of ideas to a sequence of theses and antitheses. He also claimed that the spirit of denial was an inalienable attribute of God. In *The Tragedy of Man* Lucifer's role is that of ironic denial, without which new historical reality cannot be apprehended. In the historical scenes Lucifer not only becomes the *Doppelgänger* of Adam, but also grows into a humanized instrument of a God who is absent from history. Such an overlapping in the heroes is a further proof for the lyrical character of the play. For Adam it is easier to follow Lucifer's arguments than the Lord's advice, because Lucifer stays with him through all the adventures and cannot help guiding him in his search for an answer to his questions, while God punishes him for a deed the significance of which he is permitted to see only after having committed it. The two protagonists are brought together precisely because not only Adam, but occasionally even Lucifer is tormented by the aloofness of the Lord. There is some evidence suggesting that Madách may have been preoccupied with the alienation of God from man long before he started working on *The Tragedy of Man*. Let it suffice to quote two lines from his earlier lyric *In Winter:*

> Where God rules over death and winter
> Holy monotony sets in for ever.

Most interpreters have laid emphasis on the discrepancy between the ten historical scenes and the rest of the play. Explicitly or implicitly they missed a homogeneous organizing principle in *The Tragedy* as a whole. This must be considered the result of a rather superficial analysis confined to the level of action. On a deeper level the episodic plot is subordinated to a structural sequence following a strict inner logic that can be detected from the opening Choir of the Angels to the final words of the Lord. The thematic structure of the work is based on a sequence of disjunctions which is in sharp contrast to the ideal of a homogeneous paradise, the memory of which accompanies Adam and Eve throughout history. The disjunctions result in the falling apart of previous unities and the irreconcilable contradiction between the parts.

Right after the beginning of the drama, the disunion of God and the universe, relatively independent from the moment it has been completed, is already taking place, followed by the separation of God and man in Paradise. In Scene III Adam is forced to leave his original surroundings, and becomes a wanderer in exile. When writing these opening scenes, Madách could rely on his earlier lyrics: in *Isten keze, ember keze* ("God's Hand, Man's Hand") Nature without Man, in *Hazaérkezéskor* ("Homecoming") and in *Gyermekeimhez* ("To My Children") childhood symbolized the harmony of an undivided world as well as the unity of the inside and the outside, whereas in *Önvád* ("Self-reproach") the wanderer in exile stood for man's alienation from his surroundings.

In the historical scenes of *The Tragedy of Man* culture is shown to be unable to reach a synthesis. Scenes IV and V (Egypt and Athens) present the conflict between the masses and the individual from both sides. In Scene VI (Rome) the unity of existential freedom and material welfare disintegrates, while in Constantinople Adam abandons his previous ideal, losing his trust in religion. In the Kepler scenes man and culture, *de facto* power and *de jure* authority, become estranged; Scenes IX (Paris), XI (London), and XII (Phalanstery) show stages in the disintegration of end and means. In the vision of a capitalism based on free competition and in the satirical utopia of a perfectly planned and utilitarian society the continuity of the past with the present is lost; this anti-historicism, together with the disappearance of individual rights may indicate a Romantic rejection of the ideas of Auguste Comte. In the Phalanstery scene analysis and synthesis, biological and moral, international and national, and public and private values are in conflict, and the former effaces the latter. In some respects Madách almost foreshadows Nietzsche's objections to Positivism, not only by his cult of the individual, which both he and Nietzsche inherit from Romanticism, but also by his claim that activity is inseparable from contemplation. In fact, the negative utopia of Scene XII is more akin to the picture of the utilitarian society presented in *Martin Chuzzlewit, Hard Times,* the works of Tocqueville and Matthew Arnold, or the interpretation of American society given in the 329th aphorism of *Die fröhliche Wissenschaft* than to Fourier's idea of a *phalanstère*. It is about an era which sees its salvation in public opinion and associates knowledge not with the liberation but with the suppression of the individual. Synthesis is more distant than ever and this message is confirmed by Scenes XIII and XIV, in which nature and society, quantity and quality, surface and depth, and material needs and spiritual values are brought into opposition, and in each case the latter is obliterated by the former.

In short, the structure of *The Tragedy* may be compared to a regressive sequence. The last stages in this sequence indicate that Madách foresaw the threat of technocracy in a period when he could have no first-hand experience of its influence in his own country, and when some Positivist thinkers, living in the most highly developed capitalist societies, were unaware of such a danger. The Hungarian poet attacks mediocrity and uniformity and considers artistic creativity a possible antidote. Like certain other Romantics, he regards music as the highest form of artistic creation, and in the best parts of his play he attempts to imitate the organic unity of musical form. An example of a gradually developed symbol can be drawn from Lucifer's speech on mortality in Scene IV:

do you not feel
the languid breeze that fans your face and then flies on?
It leaves a filmy gossamer of dust,
no more than just a layer in a year,
but many cubits in a century.
Two thousand years will raze your pyramids,
your name interred beneath the drifting sands;
inside your pleasure gardens jackals howl
and servile beggars squat upon the wastes.
And all of this is consummated not
by heaven-rending storms or roaring quakes,
but by the playful breeze caressing you.

In passages like this a symbol is created in which abstract idea and concrete language, signified and signifier, form an indissoluble unity, with
threads connecting the unfolding symbol so organically to preceding and
subsequent passages that the boundaries of the symbolic unit are hardly
discernible. This is especially worthy of consideration in view of the
great aphoristic skill Madách shows in the notebooks. The originality
of the style of *The Tragedy* is partly due to a tension between aphoristic
statements and gradually unfolding symbols. The structural function of
these latter may remind one of the role of Wagner's "infinite melodies." Besides their encyclopaedic bent, this may be another similarity
between the art of Madách and that of Wagner, another late Romantic
struggling with Positivism.

This similarity, however, may exist only on a very abstract level, for the
interpretation of existence given in the Wagnerian musical dramas is radically different from that suggested by *The Tragedy*. Madách does not seem
to believe in any of Wagner's alternative values; ecstasy (*Tristan*), a greed
for power (*Der Ring des Nibelungen*), or redemption (*Der fliegende
Holländer, Tannhäuser, Lohengrin, Parsifal*). There is evidence to suggest
that the Hungarian poet may have struggled with the idea of a universe
empty of values. In some of his short poems – in *Őszi ének* ("Autumn
Song") and in *Sárga lomb* ("Yellow Leaves") – autumn symbolized a
gradual loss of values, and the speaker of *Ifjan haljak meg* ("Let Me Die
Young") is a sailor who throws all his possessions into the sea, until he
himself gets immersed. Yet when composing his *chef d'oeuvre*, Madách
did not go as far as suggesting nihilism. The contradictions of the final

scene indicate that while raising the most troubling issues of his age, the Hungarian poet gave no definitive solution to any of them.

It should not be forgotten that this is the only work of Madách which has an open ending. Of the two other plays dating from his best creative period, *A civilizátor* ("The Civilizer," 1859), a burlesque comedy ridiculing the doctrine that the state is the highest goal of mankind and that man has no higher duty than to serve the state, has a melodramatic happy ending, while *Mózes* ("Moses," 1861), a Biblical drama of considerable pathos, affirms teleology through suffering. Although both are interesting works, it is quite possible that the greater success of *The Tragedy of Man* is inseparable from its inconclusiveness, the tensions it creates between different and sometimes even antagonistic conceptions of human existence.

The Christian, Romantic, Positivistic, and Existentialist interpretations of *The Tragedy of Man* seem to be almost equally valid. The final message of the Hungarian poet's lyrical drama seems to be that to have unqualified faith in any system of ideas is self-destructive, because none of them can be followed without misgivings. Since no belief offers an asylum to man into which tyranny cannot force its way, through a premature devotion to any ideology we may consume the moral capital we have inherited from our forefathers. Unless we are content with existing on the level of animals or automata, we must strive to be independent of the ruling opinions of the time and should not fear to enter into the most hostile relationship with the existing order because fate will never take from us the responsibility and even obligation of thinking for ourselves.

Toward a Historical Definition of Realism

Past scholarship "has contributed astonishingly little to clarifying the essence of Realism." This statement was an accurate description of the state of affairs some forty years ago, when made in a review of one of the most important books on Realism written in German since World War II.[1] What is more, my perception is that the argument still holds good because there has been no breakthrough in the definition of the term in the last decades. As evidence, I could refer to various dictionaries of literary terms published recently, which summarize earlier theories rather than conceptions more recently developed,[2] indicating that Realism may not be one of the concepts in the forefront of contemporary scholarship. In any case, the task of formulating rules that define Realism in a historical sense is not like the task of defining a term with an established usage.

My first intention is to examine some of the criteria which have been used in definitions of Realism. Although I tend to regard most of these as questionable, I do not aim at an indiscriminate dismissal of the term. My assumption is that a reappraisal of the existing criteria may lead us away from sweeping generalizations and help us formulate less rigid and more convincing conclusions about the narrative structures than may be specific to nineteenth-century Realism. Without attempting any comprehensive or even systematic survey, I wish to comment on some of the processes that go into the worldmaking of such novels as Balzac's *La Vieille Fille*, Trollope's *He Knew He Was Right,* and Fontane's *Effi Briest.* My choice is purely arbitrary, except that I would like to transcend national boundaries. Originally I planned to include two other novels, one by Dostoevsky and one by the Hungarian writer Kemény, but the technical difficulties of quoting from Russian and Hungarian texts have deterred me from trying to be more comprehensive. In any case, my choice may be justified on the ground that the three novels date from different subperiods and are widely considered to be representative of Realism. We may therefore ask the question as to whether the strategies commonly associated with Realism are characteristic of these three works of narrative fiction.

To see if the facts square with the theory, it is convenient to start with René Wellek's highly influential definition of Realism because it is meant to be historical, which gives it an enormous advantage over prescriptive approaches. For him Realism is "a system of norms dominating a specific time, […] which we can set apart from the norms of the periods that precede and follow it."[3] Although the identification and characterization of these norms would amount to a highly appropriate definition of Realism, the way René Wellek proceeds to specify the historical position of this literary trend strikes me as somewhat problematic. Arguing that it emerged with "the end of Romanticism,"[4] he makes the following observation: "It rejects the fantastic, the fairy-tale-like, the allegorical and the symbolic, the highly stylized, the purely abstract and decorative. It means that we want no myth, no *Maerchen*, no world of dreams."[5]

It would be foolish to deny the partial truth of this statement. What I wish to suggest is that it depends at least partly on the reader whether a mythic structure is recognizable or not in a given text. *La Vieille Fille* has been interpreted as a new version of the tale of "La Belle au bois dormant,"[6] and I tend to accept this as one of its possible readings, in the same way as I would be inclined to give legitimacy to the interpretation of *The Turn of the Screw* as a new version of Genesis. What is at issue here is intertextuality, and it would be difficult to deny that the reading of a novel by Balzac may be influenced by the fact that the author and the reader share a common tradition. Some statements made by Realist writers to the effect that they planned to make their public forget it was reading books instead of having an experience of "life" should not blind us to their habit of reminding the reader of other texts. At several stages of the story Balzac's narrator presented scenes as variations upon scenes in earlier works of literature, or at least referred to a passage in Voltaire's *Œdipe*, Beaumarchais's *Le Mariage de Figaro*, or Shakespeare's *Richard III* as giving the clue to the understanding of his own novel.[7] It would be tempting to detect ironic reversal as the guiding principle behind the strategies of overt or covert intertextuality in Realist fiction, but even this might prove to be a simplification. The point of the many allusions to *Othello* in *He Knew He*

Was Right – from the first hint that the wife, Mrs. Trevelyan, is from an alien world to the central episode set in Venice – is exactly how relevant the old pattern is in a seemingly new world.

At this point, it is probably worth emphasizing that evidence based upon the analysis of a novel by Trollope may be decisive, because unlike Stendhal or Dickens or even Balzac he cannot be described as a novelist marking a transition from Romanticism to Realism. His world would suggest that Realism should be viewed as post-Romantic rather than anti-Romantic, because the values of Romanticism are not so much invalidated as taken for granted in a Realist novel. Needless to say, not only Wellek's definition may be called too rigid on this ground, but also a more recent description of the conventions of Realism such as the one outlined by Philippe Hamon. His claim that "le héros réaliste voyagera sans doute fort peu loin de son milieu," because Realists reject the Romantic value of "un ailleurs"[8] is in sharp contrast with the prominent role of the exotic in *He Knew He Was Right*, and in this context one could also refer to another major work of Trollope's maturity, *The Way We Live Now*, as well as to many other examples of European Realism. One may even wonder whether Realist fiction is not bound up with the portrayal of tensions between value systems belonging to different parts of the world. From the early works of James to Realist fiction written in Russia or in Central Europe, numerous novels could be cited in this context.

Without pursuing this line of argument any further, my intention is simply to suggest that the relation between Romantic and Realistic worldmaking may be more than a matter of simple contrast. In many cases Romantic values are not invalidated but rather admitted as an existing frame of reference in Realist fiction. To take another example from *He Knew He Was Right*, when her sister tries to urge Nora Rowley to become the wife of Mr. Glascock, a rich man with great moral integrity, Nora's answer is that she has to think of her own feelings, thus reminding the reader that Romanticism has liberated emotions from the control of reason. Passion may turn out to be a destructive force – as in the case of the jealous Trevelyan – or it may prove to be a supreme moral value – as with Nora Rowley and Hugh Stanbury – but in either case it has an autonomy never questioned by the narrator. In consequence, the barrier breaks down between Romanticism and Realism, especially if it serves as a proof of a radical break between pre-capitalistic social formations and capitalism, or of the claim that "capitalism has effectively dissolved all the older forms of collective relations, leaving their cultural expressions and their myths as incomprehensible to us as so many dead languages or undecipherable codices."⁹

A more helpful definition of nineteenth-century Realism can be suggested by Foucault's thesis that there are "deux grandes discontinuités dans l'épistémè de la culture occidentale: celle qui inaugure l'âge classique (vers le milieu du XIXᵉ siècle) et celle qui, au début du XIXᵉ, marque le seuil de notre modernité."¹⁰ The transitions from general grammar to philology, from natural history to biology, and from the analysis of wealth to political economy, as well as the emergence of literature and history, "la constitution de tant de sciences positives," and "le repli de la philosophie sur son propre devenir"¹¹ could be taken as preconditions of Realist writing, and Foucault's idea of an earlier discontinuity may also caution us against overemphasizing the connection between Positivist philosophy and Realist fiction.

A nominalist distrust of general abstractions, a phenomenalist denial of any distinction between phenomenon and essence, surface and depth, a rejection of value judgments of normative statements, and even a belief in the universal validity of the empiric methods of natural science may well have exerted an influence upon the ideals of the leading novelists of the second and last thirds of the nineteenth century, but it is hard to say how deeply that influence affected their artistic practice. In some cases their attitude revealed elements of anti-Positivism, partly because they had to justify the relative independence of literature, a status which had hardly existed before the Romantics. It would be too easy to refer to *Hard Times* or point out the fairy-tale structure in several other novels by Dickens, but it is probably worth recalling that there is hardly any novel written by a nineteenth-century Russian author in which transcendence does not play a major role, while Victorian novels almost never fail to correspond to the rules of a Christian ethic, and many works of Realist fiction contain a hidden metaphysics. In other words, they seem to confirm Foucault's claim that Kantian criticism, Romantic metaphysics, and Positivism may be viewed as integral parts of the same intellectual context,¹² so that the emergence of Realism can be taken as a proof that from the early nineteenth century "l'homme est apparu comme doublet empirico-transcendantal."¹³

There is, however, one basic hypothesis underlying Foucault's conception of history which must be rejected if we aim at a workable tentative definition of Realism. The conclusion that "dans une culture et à un moment donné, il n'y a jamais qu'une *épistémè*, qui définit les conditions de possibilité de tout savoir"[14] is almost as far-fetched as some of the conclusions drawn by Lukács or Jameson. The underlying assumption of Realist fiction that the world as a whole is describable and reality is accessible to verbal formulation certainly echoes the Classicist view of language, "la grande utopie d'un langage parfaitement transparent où les choses elles-mêmes seraient nommées sans brouillage."[15] What is more, the realists' claim that language could be reality's direct and unmediated expression was based on the conception that signs had a binary structure, an idea which did not emerge until the advent of Classicism in the seventeenth century, before which "le système des signes dans le monde occidental avait été ternaire, puisqu'on y reconnaissait le signifiant, le signifié et la «conjoncture»."[16] If there was any element of anti-Romanticism in the goals of the Realists, it must be conceded that those who formulated them relied heavily on Classicist conceptions of language. Their program was based upon the stubborn belief that the phenomenality of words naturally corresponded to the essence of things. In other words, they seemed to ignore that "what *materiality* names can never be encountered as such because it is always mediated by language or other signs, as Hegel and Marx, each in his own way, recognized. [...] we are forbidden ever to have direct access to what the word *materiality* names or nicknames. We can know the material only through names or other signs." Since Realism was bound up with a cult of the proper name, the distance between nineteenth-century Realism and our own age can be explained in terms of our belief that "no name is 'proper.' All names, proper or common, are sobriquets, nicknames, figurative substitutes for proper names that can never be given and that cannot exist."[17]

It could, of course, be argued that whatever the intentions of some Realists may have been, most of them did not write in a style that could be called transparent. In *Effi Briest*, for instance, major events are anticipated on the level of surface structures. At the end of Chapter 3, Vetter Dagobert makes the remark that "Fräulein Cousine stehe zwar auf dem Punkte, sich zu verheiraten, es sei aber doch vielleicht gut, die 'Insel der Seligen' schon vorher kennengelernt zu haben,"[18] and this early indication is followed by a wide range of metaphorical statements and puns pointing towards the conclusion, or hinting at what is assumed to be inexpressible in the novel. It is thanks to the connotative character of his language that Fontane can combine brevity with depth. Less than a page is devoted to the duel between Crampas and Innstetten, the central scene of the whole novel, and the same terseness makes the reader constantly aware of Fontane's great stylistic achievement so that s/he may feel it necessary to stop at sentences which seem to have multiple meanings.

"Mythologie war immer mein Bestes." This remark, made by Effi to her daughter Annie near the end of the novel,[19] may remind us that metaphoric statements often serve as modes of expressing mental states. In Kessin Effi is fully convinced that she lives in a haunted house, and she often has hallucinations, dreams, and nightmares. Far from being absent from the novel, the fantastic has a psychological motivation. Once again, it seems desirable to replace the strong thesis formulated by some theoreticians by a weaker one: in Realism it is not necessary that the fantastic and the metaphorical be rejected; what seems to be essential is a 'dévalorisation' de l'intrigue,"[20] which may involve an ironic distance towards the characters. What we have is low rather than high mimesis, the events take place in a "*bon* siècle (par opposition au *grand* siècle)," as Balzac maintained,[21] but even this feature should be called post- rather than anti-Romantic, for "la peinture des moeurs intimes," the emphasis upon "le génie de la province"[22] may owe much to the Romantic cults of "couleur locale" and of cultural relativism.

The foregoing thus appears to suggest that there may be two reasons why it is difficult to produce a satisfactory definition of nineteenth-century Realism: on the one hand, artistic practice may contradict intentions, especially when seen in retrospect; on the other hand, some features which seem to represent anti-Romanticism on a first impression may prove to be in harmony with Romantic poetics on a deeper level. The battle Petőfi fought against artificiality in poetic diction in the 1840s started as a self-conscious reaction against Vörösmarty's highly metaphorical style, but in the long run it turned out to be another stage of Hungarian Romanticism, somewhat reminiscent of the cult of simplicity propagated by some German and English Romantics. Coleridge almost immediately saw the contradiction between Wordsworth's ideals and his practice, and a similar discrepancy characterized the activity of Balzac. His aspirations toward scientific accuracy were based on the false assumption that the line between artistic and scientific judgment coincided with the line between subjective and objective and on the equally untenable notion of the real as that which resisted symbolization. Yet whatever Balzac's program may have been, his narrator almost never ceased to make the narratee aware of the artificiality of the world presented, reminding the reader that "a work of literature constructs its own 'reality' while simultaneously describing it."[23] *La Vieille*

Fille is certainly not one of the novels with conspicuously Romantic elements, but even this work is full of passages emphasizing fictionality: Suzanne, one of the main characters, is compared to women painted by Titian and Rubens, Agnes is contrasted to a character in Molière, and at one point the reader is reminded that he must turn to *Les Chouans*, another part of *La Comédie*, if he wants to have a proper understanding of a certain passage in *La Vieille Fille*.[24]

A similar discrepancy can be observed in the scenes or tableaux which are often regarded as macrostructural units specific to Realist fiction. While it may be true that Champfleury spoke for most Realists when he insisted on "la qualité suprême de l'horreur de la composition,"[25] the structure of a long scene in a novel by Kemény or by Tolstoy shows an arrangement as strict as a ritual: the beginning and the end are presented from a distant point of view, while the central part of the episode seems to be close to both the narrator and the narratee, so that the contrast between background and foreground is supplemented by an opposition between fast and slow rhythm.

"Realism bears the great handicap that in order to ascertain how real it is one ought to know the real."[26] Simple as this statement may seem to be at first sight, it may be taken as a sound formulation of the most fundamental reason why it is more difficult to define Realism than almost any other literary trend. The term itself seems to suggest an irreconcilable contradiction. Offering an alternative to conventionality, it demands the transparence of the signifier, an ideal that cannot be realized without a heavy dependence upon a socio-cultural code full of stereotypes, creating maximum readability, which is hardly possible without an emphasis upon intertextuality, one of the chief sources of conventionality. If Realist novels are predictable, they are so because of a coherence produced by causal motivation. In other words, the credibility which may be a *sine qua non* of Realism is a form of redundance inseparable from phatic procedures whose conventionality is at variance with the claim that Realist style is free of artificiality.

At this point we must remind ourselves of the fact that once our aim is a historical definition of Realism, we cannot ignore the historical nature of reading. What may have passed for "empirical" narrative in the nineteenth century might turn out to be tradition-bound, even heavily conventional, at the close of the twentieth century. Just as a historical survey of photography will reveal how that allegedly objective form of art has always been

132

vulnerable to the influence of changing habits of visual interpretation, the synecdochic arrangement of descriptions and the metonymic structure of plot – two distinguishing features of Realist fiction – will appear to be highly stylized if seen in retrospect. Even the outside knowledge of science that a writer may bring to bear on his novel is exposed to historical changes – as the cases of Balzac and Kemény testify, whose physiological learning, manifest in their ideas of human character, has been invalidated by later developments.

In view of this, the claim, which Wellek surprisingly shares with Lukács, that Realism is "the objective representation of contemporary social reality,"[27] can be taken as a definition of ideals rather than of artistic practice. The only specific interpretation of objectivity I can think of is based on the alleged absence of a narrator, an ideal that was most consistently formulated by the author of *The Awkward Age* but had been a guiding principle underlying Realism from the first half of the nineteenth century. The climax of *La Vieille Fille* is written in a dramatic form, and many scenes in other novels have a central passage indicating the hypothesis that pure dialogue may have the highest mimetic value. Yet even this tendency is vulnerable to the self-contradictions of Realist objectives. The aim of a writer who tries hard to remove his narrator from the scene may be to give maximum information, but to be able to achieve this the story-teller must assume authority, and this he cannot do without making his presence felt. That is why the practices of Trollope and James are less different than their ideals, and the omniscience of the narrator does not seem to be a useful term when applied to actual novels.

"Wilke schmunzelte. 'Is doch ein Daus, unser Fräulein,' so etwa gingen seine Gedanken."[28] These words seem to illustrate a strategy characteristic of most works of Realist fiction. As if he did not care to know everything, the story-teller may have both more and less information about the events than the characters. Accordingly, new information may be given either directly or indirectly, and both narrated consciousness and interior monologue are possible. Both naming what is familiar and explaining the unknown may play a significant role in Realist fiction, and explaining can hardly exist without evaluation, so that instead of associating Realist fiction with the value-free ideal of Positivism it seems more advisable to assume that collective norms are at play in the world presented in such works. It is at least partly the historical nature of these norms that makes prescriptive interpretations of Realism hardly acceptable.

Among these the conception developed by Lukács may have been the most sophisticated and most widely influential. It lies beyond my scope to deal with the circumstances under which he wrote most of his essays on the subject in the Soviet Union in the 1930s, conditions which cannot be ignored if one wants to avoid errors of judgment. For our purposes it is enough to say that normativity is almost never absent from them; it impairs his ability to follow a historical argument, even when what he seems to aim at is a comparison between nineteenth-century Realism and later trends: "Aber der Dichter muss eine feste und lebendige Weltanschauung haben, er muss die Welt in ihrer bewegten Widerspruchlichkeit sehen. ... Dieser verkehrte Weg kann zu keinem Ergebnis führen. ... Und diese Krise muss sich im Laufe der Zeit noch verschärfen."[29] The categorical imperatives setting the tone reflect a kind of normativity which goes hand in hand with a reluctance to examine the terms used and with an almost wilful disregard of the historical nature of artistic conventions: "Die Porträts von Cézanne sind ebenso blosse Stilleben, verglichen mit der menschlich-seelischen Totalität der Porträts von Tizian oder Rembrandt, wie die Menschen Goncourts oder Zolas im Vergleich zu Balzac oder Tolstoi."[30]

My quotations are from the essay on description and narration, but I could also refer to other texts. In "Grenzen des Realismus,"[31] for instance, Lukács maintains that a Realist concentrates on the essential qualities of reality and he remains faithful to them; his works are literary reflections of the objective reality of human life. Accordingly, Hoffmann is a Realist, while Karl Kraus is not. From this line of argument it is clear that Lukács seems to have ignored that history is constituted by interpretation; rather, he has assumed the objective status of a stable point of reference. Still, his conception is not only insufficiently historical, but is also self-contradictory: his long essay on Tolstoy clearly indicates that his immanent, essentialist definition of Realism is at variance with his idea of *Weltliteratur*, based on the concept of influence:

So eigenartig diese Wirkung Tolstois in Europa auch gewesen sein mag, es handelt sich hier doch nicht um eine vereinzelte Erscheinung. Die Periode, da Tolstoi in der Weltliteratur wirksam wird, ist zugleich jene Periode, in der plötzlich und mit beispielloser Geschwindigkeit die russische Literatur und die der skandinavischen Länder eine führende Rolle in der europäischen Literatur erringen. Bis dahin wurde im 19. Jahrhunder der grosse Strom der Weltliteratur von den führenden westlichen Ländern, von England, Frankreich und

Deutschland beherrscht. Schriftsteller anderen Nationen tauchen nur vereinzelt und episodisch am Horizont der Weltliteratur auf.[32]

What is more, the concept of *Weltliteratur* is bound up with that of *Weltgeschichte*, because

> Nur solche Illusionen des Schriftstellers, die in der gesellschaftlichen Bwegeung notwendig begründet sich, deren dichterischer Ausdruck der Schriftsteller ist, die als Illusionen, oft tragische Illusionen, von einer welthistorischen Notwendigkeit sind, werden für eine solche objektive Gestaltung der Gesellschaft kein unüberwindliches Hindernis sein.[33]

In sum, the basic criterion of Realism derives from social history: "Die subjektive Aufrichtigkeit der Schriftstellers kann nur dann zu einem grossen Realismus führen, wenn sie der schriftstellerische Ausdruck einer bedeutenden gesellschaftlichen Bewegung ist."[34]

For Lukács Realism is an ideal, his terminology is based not on historical considerations but rather on a dichotomy of acceptance and rejection. A contrast is made between the "Grundlage der richtigen Empfindungen und des richtigen Denkens" on the one hand, and "falscher Objektivismus" and "falscher Subjektivismus" on the other,[35] and the conception of "man" underlying this opposition is not only abstract but even anti-historical. One may go even as far as suspecting that his prescriptive view of Realism may have something to do with the positivist assumption that "fiction is fabricated and fact found."[36] At first glance the terms "Erzählen" and "Beschreiben" seem to have been given a historical dimension, since they are characterized as representing "Mitleben" and "Beobachten," "notwendige Verhaltensweisen der Schriftsteller zweiter Perioden des Kapitalismus,"[37] but the ground of the distinction is again questionable. The stand Lukács takes seems to correspond to the conservative position as described by the young Jakobson: he regards any departure from the system of representation to which he has become accustomed as a deformation of reality.[38]

The key words in the definition offered by Lukács – "eine richtige und tiefe Widerspiegelung der objektiven Wirklichkeit"[39] – can be misleading, because they may be read without an awareness that both the concept of reality and the ways of creating have changed in the course of the centuries. Lukács fails to recognize that "What we often mistake for the actual world is one particular description of it. And what we mistake for possible worlds are just equally true descriptions in other terms. We have come to think of the actual as one among many possible worlds. We need to repaint that picture. All possible worlds lie within the actual one."[40]

No historical definition is possible before it has been admitted that the real is always a system of institutionalized values. What seemed to nineteenth-century readers to be natural in a novel by Trollope may strike a late-twentieth-century reader as strangely artificial for various reasons, e.g. the growing temporal distance, which cannot be ignored, because the real is not reconstructed but constructed from the text. As credibility is indispensable for Realism, I am almost tempted to think of a Realist way of reading, or at least to view Realism as both style and performance, a mode of reception with certain rules. It is precisely because I regard the hypothesis that there is no fixed, permanent reality shared by author and reader across the last two centuries as a precondition of the understanding of Realism that I cannot accept the definition given by Lukács nor take the structuralist viewpoint and associate Realism with "une *détonalisation* du message,"[41] an absence of narrative modality, a concept which seems to do as little justice to history as Barthes's earlier term of "le degré zéro de l'écriture." Despite its somewhat rhetorical formulation, Jameson's caution against these conceptions "that neither the reader's reception of a particular narrative, nor the actantical representation of human figures and agents, can be taken to be constants of narratives' analysis but must themselves ruthlessly be historicized"[42] seems to be highly pertinent.

No critic of the ideas of Lukács on Realism can do justice to his theory without mentioning the concept of "type," which even Wellek accepted as a term that could resolve the tension between description and prescription.[43] Yet here again Jameson's remarks are very much to the point. In his view Lukács' theory of typification is objectionable on two counts:

> on the one hand, it fails to identify the typifying of characters as an essentially allegorical phenomenon, and thus does not furnish any adequate account of the process whereby a narrative becomes endowed with allegorical meanings or levels. On the other, it implies an essentially one-to-one relationship between individual characters and their social or historical reference, so that the possibility of something like a system of charters remains unexplored.[44]

What has been called type by Marxist theoreticians from almost the very beginning of that tradition may turn out to be a manifestation of a more general rule observable in Realist fiction, an assumption underlying low mimesis that life is neither good nor bad. "Was ich vom Leben halte? Viel und wenig. Mitunter ist es recht viel und mitunter ist es recht wenig." This answer, given by Pastor Niemeyer to a question asked by Effi near the end of the novel,[45] may be typical of the conclusions of works which can be read as pieces of Realism. The outcome in most of them is a change of perspective, which may be regarded as a guiding principle in Realist fiction. "Er mass seitdem mit anderem Masse, sah alles anders an."[46] These words about Innstetten apply to Effi as well, and to so many other characters in nineteenth-century fiction that I am tempted to associate Realism with the frequency of a spiral conception of time. In any case, from *The Way We Live Now* to *A rajongók* (The Fanatics) by Kemény, many novels seem to suggest an eternal recurrence, a return to a balanced status quo, thus leading us to the assumption that "le réalisme, en général, tend à proclamer le nivellement, l'égalité et la neutralisation éthique du train quotidien."[47]

In Hungarian literature there are two writers, Kemény and Jókai, who were almost exact contemporaries, yet their works represent an epitome of what a Realist can and cannot do. Jókai's novels are full of "flat," i.e., black and white characters, while for Kemény the credibility of such a dichotomy is suspect, and thus his characterization is based on neutral (neither ... nor) or complex (both ... and) structures. What must be emphasized, though, is that the difference is not between Romanticism and Realism – it could be argued that of the two writers Kemény had the more profound understanding of the Romantic legacy – but rather between romance and novel. In Realism the protagonist can have none of the distinguishing features of an exceptional human being – it is worth recalling that *Vanity Fair* was subtitled "a novel without a hero" because there is no privileged focus. It could even be suggested that Realism was the product of a historical process pointing the way from the teleology of the *Bildungsroman* to a neutralization of character. During that process, the "personnage de la 'bande'"[48] emerged as a representative of social codes, narrowing the gap between principal and major characters. From Balzac to Trollope most nineteenth-century novelists made their narrators quote public opinion, sometimes in the form of proverbs or stories illustrating communal values.

It is by no means easy to say at what stage the decline of the status of the major characters and the growing importance of the role played by anonymous communities may have led to the dissolution of the conventions of

Realism. If later events can transform earlier happenings, this would apply also to the nineteenth-century novel. In any case, from the perspective of the late twentieth century, several of the earlier definitions of Realism may appear to be outdated. It is possible to read *Henry Esmond* in the light of the eighteenth century, but it is no more absurd to read *Bleak House* in the light of *The Trial*. Twentieth-century developments may have taught us that continuity based on a causal arrangement of events is less pervasive a determining force in Realist narratives than it may seem to be. In some cases crucial links in the action may be missing. We do not know much about the honeymoon of Effi and Innstetten or about what actually happened between Effi and Crampas, and we are never told what Crampas wished to say before his death. All these gaps, due to the use of a limited point of view and of a narrator who is far from being omniscient, may lead to differences in interpretation and are sources of indeterminacy hardly less obvious than the story-teller's silence about the exact nature of the illness of Milly Theale or about the events of a certain hour of Mathias's journey on the island in *Le Voyeur*. In view of such forms of absence, the claim that "le discours réaliste a horreur du vide informatif"[49] will prove to be exaggerated. The hypothesis that some novelists may have abandoned the use of a central focus because they intended to present a more credible vision of reality seems to be more convincing. In the same way that Manet, Degas, Seurat, and Toulouse-Lautrec painted human figures moving in different directions and occasionally even beyond the frame of the picture, Trollope cut some of his characters in half to make the impression that the reality he was portraying went beyond the limits of his narrative. An interesting example of this kind of indeterminacy is characteristic of the treatment of Priscilla Stanbury, a highly intelligent, self-effacing, independent woman who attracts the attention of the narrator of *He Knew He Was Right*, but later fades from view.

If indeterminacy plays a far from negligible role in nineteenth-century fiction, it seems questionable whether Realism can be associated with the use of a referential speech act. To prove or refute the accuracy of the hypothesis underlying Ian Watt's conception of Realism that Defoe, Richardson, and Fielding were the first writers to give full proper names to their characters,[50] cannot be my concern here – not only Allworthy, but even Lovelace is a name that would hardly qualify as such – but I would risk the hypothesis that both the metonymic arrangement of the plot and the synecdochic structure of descriptions may have set limits to the use of full proper names in Realist fiction. Novelists intent on the portrayal of communal values certainly could not help creating names which it would be hardly possible to regard as proper names in the strict sense. In *He Knew He Was Right* the private detective hired by Trevelyan is given the name Bozzle, "an amalgam of blue-bottle and the noise the fly makes,"[51] and his name is repeated so many times and in such a specific context[52] that the reader learns to accept it as a sign of an impersonal destructive force that can smear anybody or anything it touches.

It might be urged that the foregoing argument unduly simplifies or at least fails to do justice to the complexity of the theses formulated by Watt in his book. In any case, it is certainly necessary to ask how our literary movement is related to generic considerations; in other words, to what extent the emergence of Realism was bound up with the rise of the novel.

Although some German and Central or East-European theoreticians have made desperate attempts to define Realism in lyric verse, the case against their thesis is quite formidable: if Realism is to be interpreted as a trend in nineteenth-century literature, it must be associated with a detailed presentation of a socio-historical milieu, and this is hardly possible beyond the scope of a generic combination whose basic components are narrative and descriptive. The semi-narrative and semi-discursive genre of the portrait as developed by journalists and as raised to a high artistic level by Hazlitt, Macaulay, Sainte-Beuve, and Kemény among others, exerted a considerable influence on novelists who devoted whole chapters to individual characters.

Description, which Lukács viewed as "ein schriftstellerischer Ersatz für die verlorengegangene epische Bedeutsamkeit,"[53] is in fact indispensable for Realism; most nineteenth-century novelists show a keen topographical interest and look upon reality as a kind of inventory which can be decomposed into discrete items. The great emphasis put on detail is certainly an inalienable quality of the writing of Balzac, Dickens, or Trollope, and is a source of complexity because of its double character, so aptly analyzed by Barthes:[54] on the one hand, the minute details of realistic descriptions seem to be insignificant, even superfluous from the point of view of narrative structures; on the other, they create the impression that the real has a solidity which is resistant to meaning, and thus it will never cease to be a mystery that defies interpretation.

Yet, despite the fact that descriptions may create an impression of plenitude, the most important source of the complexity of Realist worldmaking must be sought on a deeper level. The urge James constantly felt to dramatize and the way of structuring for which Bakhtin gave the somewhat unfortunate, because misleadingly metaphorical, name "polyphonic," may be two aspects of this more fundamental characteristic: the novelist's desire to depart from a monologic form of discourse, his aspiration to cover a wide range of different idioms, and his attempt to present a clash between different value systems, conflicting truths, and multiple actual worlds. Once again, we must regard Realism as a stage in a longer historical process. Dialogue taken in an axiological sense is certainly less obvious in *Oliver Twist* than in *Bleak House, Barchester Towers* is monologic if compared to *The Way We Live Now,* and it is for similar reasons that we consider the late novels of Dostoievsky more complex than the works of Turgenev. It cannot be doubted, however, that this line of development eventually led towards ideals hardly compatible with Realism, since the disorientation of the reader undermined the principle of credibility and deconstructed the chronotopes characteristic of nineteenth-century fiction.

Besides the breakdown of communal belief systems, changes in the modes of publishing and in reading habits were also responsible for the dissolution of Realist conventions. The more close-knit structure of the novels of Flaubert, Fontane, and James owes much to the fact that they were not written for serial publication. Neither Balzac nor Dickens could resist the temptation to create suspense at the end of the installments, and few could deny that constant delays may create an impression of longwindedness or of melodrama when the text is read in book form by late twentieth-century readers accustomed to more economic ways of structuring.

Apart from this surface segmentation, many nineteenth-century novels follow the pattern set by the principal parts of *La Comédie humaine*: they start in the durative mood, and "le cercle de la vie quotidienne n'est rompu que par l'intervention d'un élément étranger."[55] The first chapters would present a kind of *Lebensbild* – scenes from provincial life, bringing into relief certain pervasive features of the life of a more or less closed community – which later on may be interrupted by some unexpected occurrence – the arrival of a visitor from the outside, for instance, questioning the relevance of the local value system, bringing about all sorts of complications, until the balance is redressed. From *La Vieille Fille* to *The Europeans* many novels seem to follow this pattern. Seemingly arbitrary montage, which the story-teller does not care to justify, hardly ever occurs in these works; different localities are linked together by embedding (a scene outside a building, involving a great many characters, is followed by a scene of intimacy inside the building, or vice versa), by a forward movement (the narrator follows the steps of a traveller), or by the successive presentation of simultaneous events (two characters say good-bye to one another, and the narrator follows one of them and later returns to the other).

This linear arrangement is often thrown into relief by a structuring principle based upon the distinction between foreground and background, mentioned above. The rhythm of narrating events in the background is fast, whereas the events of the foreground are related either in a durative mood or at a slow pace. In many cases, the central part of the action does not cover more than a relatively short period – two or three years – but it contains specific indications of when and where. "Eine kurze Spanne Zeit [...] Und doch, was war alles seitdem geschehen!" These words from Effi's indirect interior monologue[56] are symptomatic: the underlying idea is that significant events are clearly distinguishable from the usual state of things, which appears to be almost timeless, since it shows people playing games with rules that are taken for granted by the members of the community and thus obliterate chance for the participants.

A further emphasis was given to dimensionality by the introduction of historical figures. In most novels they belong to the background. Whether the gap is considerable between the period in which the narrated events take place and the story-teller's own period (as in Kemény's *Özvegy és leánya* [The Widow and her Daughter]), or less wide (as in *La Vieille Fille, Vanity Fair, War and Peace*, or *Effi Briest*), not to mention cases in which the two overlap (as in *He Knew He Was Right*, started in 1867 and written about events taking place in the same year), the guiding intention is always to create the impression that private life, even patriarchal intimacy, is closely related to history.

Because of its relative lack of complexity, *La Vieille Fille* can be regarded as a text showing the most general rules in the use of chronotopes which are observable in Realist fiction. The first words refer to historical time and are followed by a longer passage in the durative mood. Next, time is arrested by a minute description, which is later replaced by another portrayal of habitual actions, and then gradually transformed into a characterization. It is only after such a careful preparation that individual scenes are presented, separated from each other by shorter durative passages and/or by the narrator's comments bringing the action to a virtual standstill. The closure is anticipated by a return to the durative, and the end of the novel is cast in the present of the narrator and the narratee.

The final sentences are in fact a manifestation of what Jakobson called the phatic function of language. This seems to be an almost indispensable ingredient of Realism. While relating the story, the narrator also carries on a dialogue with the narratee. Prime among his functions is that of a generalizing observer, but he also orders the sequence of events and orients the narratee in time and space. If his main intention is to convey information, he might speak in the first person and address the narratee in the second, but from time to time he will resort to the first person plural, whenever he wants to create a sense of community. Both the allusions to historical figures and to intertextuality may indicate what kind of narratee the story-teller has in mind: he draws upon a tradition he shares with his audience. These factors also serve credibility, together with topical, anecdotal allusions, and proverbs indicating common sense, which forms the basis of all the value judgments made by the narrator with the intention that they be accepted.

If I can draw any conclusion from these tentative remarks, I must put great emphasis on the communication between a narrator and narratee. Instead of associating it with anti-Romanticism, the rejection of the fantastic, the transparence of the signifier, the dominance of the referential speech act, a reluctance to present the consciousness of the characters, the absence of narratorial interference, or the omniscience of the story-teller, I would like to highlight chronotopes and the phatic use of language as terms crucial for a hypothetical definition of Realism. In my interpretation the most important distinguishing features of this literary trend, important in nineteenth-century fiction, are the distinctions between background and foreground, durative and singulative, open and closed space, and a language game played by the narrator and the narratee. This game is based on the tacit acceptance of certain communal beliefs which guarantee the credibility of the story-telling and the reliability of the narrator's value judgments, two conditions without which no Realism is possible.

Notes

[1] Henry H. H. Remak, "Richard Brinkmann, Wirklichkeit und Illusion. Studien über Gehalt und Grenzen des Begriffs Realismus für die erzählende Dichtung des neunzehnten Jahrhunderts," *Germanic Review* 34:2 (April 1959), 155.

[2] See, for instance, *Metzler Literatur Lexikon* (Stuttgart: Metzler 1984), 353–54.

[3] René Wellek, "The Concept of Realism in Literary Scholarship," in *Concepts of Criticism* (New Haven and London: Yale University Press 19G3), 225.

[4] Wellek, 240.

[5] Wellek, 241.

[6] Nicole Mozet, Introduction to Balzac, *La Comédie humaine*. Paris: Gallimard, 1976, IV, 806.

[7] Balzac, 818, 842, 930.

[8] Philippe Hamon, "Un discours contraint," in *Littérature et réalité*, by Roland Barthes, Leo Bersani, Philippe Hamon, Michael Riffaterre, Ian Watt. Paris: Seuil, 1982, 137.

[9] Fredric Jameson, *The Political Unconscious: Narrative as a Socially Symbolic Act*. Ithaca, N.Y: Cornell University Press, 1981, 69.

[10] Michel Foucault, *Les mots et les choses. Une archéologie des sciences humaines*. Paris: Gallimard, 1966, 13.

[11] Foucault, 233.

[12] Foucault, 258.

[13] Foucault, 332.

[14] Foucault, 179.

[15] Foucault, 133.

[16] Foucault, 57.

[17] J. Hillis Miller, "Presidential Address 1986: The Triumph of Theory, the Resistance to Reading, and the Question of the Material Base," *PMLA* 102:3 (April 1987), 289.

[18] Theodor Fontane, *Effi Briest*, in *Sämtliche Werke*, IV. München: Carl Hanser, 1963, 23.

[19] Fontane, 273.

[20] Philippe Hamon, *Texte et ideologie. Valeurs, hierarchies et évaluations dans l'oeuvre littéraire*. Paris: Presses Universitaires de France, 1984, 89.

[21] Balzac 817.

[22] Balzac, 865, 851.

[23] Benjamin Harshaw [Hrushovski], "Fictionality and Fields of Reference: Remarks on a Theoretical Framework," *Poetics Today* 5:2 (1984), 232.

[24] Balzac, 822, 859, 852.

[25] Hamon, *Texte et idéologie*, 71.

[26] Henry H. H. Remak, "Peasant Sentimentalism or Peasant Realism? George Sand's *La Petite Fadette* and Gottfried Keller's *Romeo und Julia auf dem Dorfe*," *Beiträge Zur Romanischen Philologie* 17:1 (1978), 129.

[27] Wellek, 242.

[28] Fontane, 14.

[29] Georg Lukács, *Probleme des Realismus*. Berlin: Aufbau, 1955, 132–33.

[30] Lukács, *Probleme des Realismus*, 129.

[31] Lukács, "Grenzen des Realismus?" *Deutsche Zeitung* 17 Feb. 1939.

[32] Lukács, *Der russische Realismus in der Weltliteratur*. Berlin: Aufbau, 1952, 156–57.

[33] Lukács, *Der russische Realismus*, 165.

[34] Lukács, *Der russische Realismus*, 164.

[35] Lukács, *Probleme des Realismus*, 133–34.

[36] Nelson Goodman, *Ways of Worldmaking*. Indianapolis and Cambridge: Hackett, 1978, 91.

[37] Lukács, *Probleme des Realismus*, 111.

[38] Roman Jakobson, "On Contemporary Realism," in *Readings in Russian Poetics*, comp. Ladislav Matejka (Ann Arbor: Department of Slavic Languages and Literatures 1971), 23.

[39] Lukács, *Probleme des Realismus*, 115.

[40] Nelson Goodman, *Fact, Fiction, and Forecast*, 4th ed. Cambridge, Mass., and London: Harvard University Press, 1983, 57.

[41] Hamon, "Un discours contraint," 150–51.

[42] Jameson, 152.

[43] Wellek, 253.

[44] Jameson, 162.

[45] Fontane, 281.

[46] Fontane, 285.

[47] Hamon, *Texte et idéologie*, 187.

[48] Hamon, *Texte et idéologie*, 79.

[49] Hamon, "Un discours contraint," 161.

[50] Ian Watt, *The Rise of the Novel: Studies in Defoe, Richardson and Fielding*. London: Chatto and Windus, 1957.

[51] John Sutherland, "Introduction to Anthony Trollope," *He Knew He Was Right*. Oxford and New York: Oxford University Press, 1985, xvii.

[52] Trollope, 363–65.

[53] Lukács, *Probleme des Realismus*, 118.

[54] Roland Barthes, "L'effet du réel," in *Littérature et réalité*, by Barthes *et al.* (see n. 8 above), 81–82, 87.

[55] Mozet, 796.

[56] Fontane, 191.

Henry James and the
Hermeneutic Tradition
(The Figure in the Carpet)

In volume III of his *Temps et récit* Paul Ricoeur insists on the necessity of refuting the illusion that literary works are self-structured. "Pour ruiner cette suggestion," he argues, "il peut être de bonne stratégie de se tourner vers quelques textes exemplaires qui théorisent leur propre lecture."[1] My intention is to focus on *The Figure in the Carpet*, a work that anticipated the hermeneutics of the twentieth century.

A decade after the composition of this tale, in the preface to volume XV of the New York Edition of his works, James remarked that the "collective mistrust of anything like close or analytic appreciation" in the English-speaking world served as the main incentive to write *The Figure in the Carpet*.[2] Characteristically, the pioneers among the interpreters of this text came from outside the English-speaking world. From Ezra Pound's long essay (*Little Review*, August 1918) to Edmund Wilson's "The Ambiguity of Henry James" (first published in 1938, enlarged in 1948) and *Maule's Curse* (1938), a book on 19th-century American literature by Yvor Winters, several influential works by American authors failed to mention this tale, and a similar neglect characterized British criticism. Virginia Woolf, an avid reader and great admirer of James, never referred to it in her essays or diaries and in *The Great Tradition* (1946), F. R. Leavis merely cited the author's own comments on the story as illustrating his loneliness of spirit, instead of attempting an interpretation of the tale itself. Tzvetan Todorov was one of the first to take a more serious interest in *The Figure in the Carpet*. He included it in his general discussion of the stories dealing with writers and artists by James in his collection of essays published under the somewhat misleadingly ambitious title *Poétique de la prose* (1971). Although he gave no detailed analysis of any particular text – his ambition

145

was to describe the most general feature of the short stories of James, what he called "la quête d'une cause absolue et absente"[3] – his work had the merit of emphasizing the metafictional interest present in a fairly large number of works. By contrast, Wolfgang Iser limited his interest to *The Figure in the Carpet*. He gave it a special status in the opening chapter of *Der Akt des Lesens*, calling it a work that anticipated the "Theorie ästhetischer Wirkung," "die im Rückblick wie die Prognose für eine Wissenschaft wirkt."[4] His interpretation may be regarded as the most important to date insofar as it makes the point that the hidden meaning the narrator desperately intends to discover turns out to be insubstantial. It is not of morphological nature but is an effect of text: "Sinn ist dann nicht mehr erklärbar, sondern nur als Wirkung erfahrbar."[5] Yet this treatment has one shortcoming: ignoring Todorov's essay about the self-reflective works of Henry James, Iser describes the strategy underlying *The Figure in the Carpet* as a "sicherlich nicht bewußte Antizipation des kommenden Interpretationsbetrieb."[6]

Joseph Hillis Miller had the advantage of being familiar with both Todorov's and Iser's work in translation. His analysis, first published in 1980,[7] provoked a debate with Shlomith Rimmon-Kenan.[8] One of the conclusions to be drawn from this debate is that narratology, with its emphasis on structure and ambiguity, cannot help the interpreter of *The Figure in the Carpet*. As Miller says in the reworked version of his essay: "Self-referentiality does not subvert the assumptions and procedures of realistic fiction, since self-reference is still reference. As such it is assimilable within the assumptions of mimetic representations. [...] The notion of undecidable meaning must be distinguished [...] from a definition of ambiguity in literature as plurisignificance or richness of meaning."[9]

The last analysis I want to mention is by Roy Chambers. The most important contribution of this critic is the emphasis on internal repetition. The narrator's failure to learn the secret of Hugh Vereker's fiction from the author is echoed by Gwendolen's reluctance to tell others about her late husband's discovery of the figure in the carpet: "What the narrator encounters in Gwendolen [...] is what he earlier encountered in Vereker, not the availability of the secret but the resistance of a text."[10]

Before trying to add some observations of mine to those made by other critics, let me mention that I became interested in *The Figure in the Carpet* before my acquaintance with hermeneutics. In fact, this "nouvelle" has led me to the theory of interpretation. My first essay on James appeared in

1965, when I was an undergraduate in Budapest. Then I was not familiar with *The Figure in the Carpet*, but *The Real Thing* (1892), a tale that can be read as an attack on Naturalism, made me aware of James' complex approach to fictionality, while the long *nouvelle The Aspern Papers* (1888) made me aware of the inadequacy of two modes of interpretation: biographical criticism and the Positivist use of written documents. In 1984 I published a paper read at an international conference on *The Figure in the Carpet,* and for my 1995 book on interpretation I rewrote this essay in Hungarian.[11] This is my third attempt to discuss the short story that was first published in 1896 in the magazine *Cosmopolis.* While preparing the present paper, I deliberately avoided a rereading of my earlier essays.

One of the misconceptions the story refutes is the identification of the author and his work. The reader can never know what, if anything, the author wanted to say. The meaning of the text is not the "mens autoris"; it cannot be identified with the subjective intention of the author. What the interpreter must make his own is not the personality or the world view of the author. Hugh Vereker makes a set of statements that are inconsistent. They therefore cannot be attributed to a single self. In this respect the tale belongs to the large group of narrative works by the author which undermine the integrity and identity of human personality. The novelist's aim is to cast doubt on final vocabularies and on distinctions between accident and essence, appearance and reality, and surface and depth.

The idea that intentions are annihilated by the finished work (the "rounded form") also occurs in several other texts by James, including the notebooks in which he recorded the phases in the composition of his works. In the Preface to *Roderick Hudson* "the buried secrets, the intentions" are called "the dead reasons of things" that "are buried [...] in the texture of the work, [...] buried too deep to rise again."[12] This statement is in harmony with the hermeneutic assumption that understanding has a temporal aspect, "daß man *anders* versteht, *wenn man überhaupt versteht.* "[13] In the tale the narrator's metaphors – "a sort of buried treasure," "the tail of something," "a complex figure in a Persian carpet," "some safe preserve for sport," etc. – are joined by others used by Vereker, referring to playing a game or to "the very string that my pearls are strung on."

The "inner meaning" of the literary work is to be seen or heard. It is a pattern and "faint wandering notes of a hidden music." James often draws a comparison between texts and visual or musical compositions to remind the reader that in a work of art nothing is stated, everything is presented, and the text is comparable to a score that has to be performed; it lives in its interpretations and there is no such thing as *the* objectively correct interpretation of a work of art.

The language of painting, sculpture, architecture, and music grew into his vocabulary. In *The Lesson of the Master* (1888) "the great thing" to which the artist aspires is defined as the sense "of having drawn from his intellectual instrument the finest music that nature had hidden in it," and in a letter addressed to Joseph Conrad in 1906, the highest praise is expressed in the following manner: "I read you as I listen to rare music."[14] In *The Tree of Knowledge* (first published in 1900), a story about a sculptor, about how "tradition," "belief," "understanding," and "explanation" are interrelated, the focus is on the productive power of prejudice on all understanding. What this tale suggests is that although understanding is possible only through an individual learning process, in certain respects one can grasp what one "has always, always known." Understanding is portrayed as a circular process; everything that is said stands under anticipations and prejudgments. Other works by James could also be mentioned in this context. *The Sense of the Past*, an unfinished novel published in 1917, suggests that learning is a kind of remembrance, and the message of *The Sacred Fount* (1901) is that overcoming bias and attaining objectivity is a misconception.

When writing about the phenomenological movement, Gadamer drew a parallel between William James's critique of the concepts of psychology and phenomenology. He also recalled that he knew about the works of William James through Paul Natorp, who had been a friend of the American thinker.[15] It seems possible to argue that the rejection of the copy theory of knowledge was as crucial to William James's psychology as to Henry James's point-of-view technique, which implies the situatedness of subjects as a determinant of understanding. This might be the background to the presentation of the hermeneutic situation in *The Figure in the Carpet*. The text has no intrinsic nature; its identity is interpretation-relative; reading is like perception or performing a piece of music. Reconstruction is rejected and dialogue, meeting, encounter, interpretation grounded in conversation is affirmed. Agreement seems neither the condition of interpretation, nor the telos of understanding. To understand a work means to recontextualize it, and the interpreter's moves are "those of a chess-player," his/her activity is a "chase," an "adventure," it is motivated by an "expectant" "curiosity." There is a close resemblance between the vocabulary James used in his numerous essays on painting and literature. In this respect a comparison is possible with Proust, who also wrote about the other arts and shared James's interest in Ruskin. In 1913, shortly after the publication of *Du côté de chez Swann,* the French author used the Jamesian metaphor in an interview: "Je suis comme quelqu'un qui a une tapisserie trop grande pour les appartements actuels et qui a été obligé de la couper."[16]

Besides standing for a rhetorical concept, the word "figure" evokes the visual arts. "The subject of 'Roderick' figures to me vividly this employment of canvas," James wrote about his first full-length novel.[17] He used the term "figure" to denote not only the subject of a portrait but also the composition of a work of art. The "literary arrangement," "the constructional game" that makes the textual elements "hang together" and produces "that whole march of the fable"[18] is defined with reference to pictorial "developments," "the painter's subject consisting ever, obviously, of the related state, to each other, of certain figures and things."[19] "To exhibit these relations," the artist has to face a dilemma: "Really, universally, relations stop nowhere, and the exquisite problem of the artist is eternally but to draw, by a geometry of his own, the circle within which they shall happily *appear* to do so." Describing the artist as an "embroiderer of the canvas of life," James urged him to "work in terror, fairly, of the vast expanse of that surface, of the boundless number of its distinct perforations for the needle, and of the tendency inherent in his many-coloured flowers and figures to cover and consume as many as possible of the little holes."[20] Other texts by James could also be cited to disprove Iser's claim that *The Figure in the Carpet* represents an "unconscious" anticipation of certain interpretive strategies.

In this tale the use of the word "figure," meaning both "character" and "figure of speech," leads to the suggestion that meaning is either undecided or absent. Indeterminacy goes together with irony, the effect of several related oppositions. The periodical in which the critics review the books mentioned in the story is called "The Middle," referring to the most vulnerable part in the structure of the novels, and the title of the first novel by the 19-year-old Gwendolen Erme, "Deep Down," suggests a hidden meaning, although the work is characterized as superficial. What the narrator believes to be his "acute little study" of Vereker's art is dismissed by the novelist as "the usual twaddle." The novelist insists that while his fiction is "as deep as the ocean," the author of the article "doesn't see anything."

Vereker's writing is not "popular." Both the favourable and the derogatory criticism leveled against his works is unfounded: "Having missed my little point with a perfection exactly as admirable when they patted me on the back as when they kicked me in the shins." The interpreter's mistake is that his ambition is to "find" a "thing." He views the work as an object and asks for some help, instead of performing the task of reading. This miscalculation is responsible for the lack of understanding between author and critic:

"'You call it a little trick?'
'That's only my little modesty. It's really an exquisite scheme.' [...]
'Don't you think you ought – just a trifle – to assist a critic?'
'Assist him? What else have I done with every stroke of my pen? I've shouted my intention in his great black face!' [...]
'Is it a kind of esoteric message?'
His countenance fell at this – he put out his hand as if to bid me goodnight. 'Ah my dear fellow, it can't be described in cheap journalese!'"

The narrator-critic's request is for a clue. His idea is that a work of art resembles a puzzle. Once the mystery has been unveiled and the problem solved, the text is no longer resistant, it has been appropriated. Vereker dismisses such an approach as inadequate. For him understanding is not grasping something given but a creative, imaginative activity. "Seeing" means "seeing as." The narrator's mistake is to believe that the meaning of the novelist's work is some naked thing which is directly accessible, present-at-hand. The novelist, on the other hand, is convinced that his message has to be unveiled by an act of appropriation, grounded in a fore-sight or fore-conception and done under the guidance of an evaluative perspective, a point of view – a concept crucial for any reader who wants to understand Henry James. What "stands there" in the text is the assumption of the person who does the interpreting. The approach to interpretation suggested by *The Figure in the Carpet* resembles the definition of "Auslegung" in *Sein und Zeit*: "In der Auslegung wird das Verstehen nicht etwas anderes, sondern es selbst. [...] Die Auslegung ist nicht die Kenntnisnahme des Verstandenen, sondern die Ausarbeitung der im Verstehen entworfenen Möglichkeiten. [...] Wenn sich die besondere Konkretion der Auslegung im Sinne der exakten Textinterpretation gern auf das beruft, was 'dasteht', so ist das, was zunächst 'dasteht', nichts anderes als die selbstverständliche, undiskutierte Vormeinung des Auslegers, die notwendig in jedem Auslegungsansatz liegt als das, was mit Auslegung überhaupt schon 'gesetzt', das heißt in Vorhabe, Vorsicht, Vorgriff vorgegeben ist."[21]

Vereker insists on the organicity of his works and on the inadequacy of the interpreter's strategy and language.

"I scratched my head. 'Is it something in the style or something in the thought? An element of form or an element of feeling?' [...]

He hesitated. 'Well, you've got a heart in your body. Is that an element of form or an element of feeling? What I contend that nobody has ever mentioned in my work is the organ of life.'"

Since Vereker does not take his critic too seriously, it is not quite clear how he views the relations between the organic and the inorganic. In Romantic hermeneutics there was a strong temptation to regard speech as organic and writing as inorganic, and the works of Nietzsche, Heidegger, or Wittgenstein testify to the survival of this tradition. The narrator of *The Figure in the Carpet* gives an account that is written and retrospective, yet the text is full of elements resembling spoken discourse. Gwendolen's characterization is a good example of the play of shared language, the bearer of a tradition: "She had indeed no sense of humour and, with her pretty way of holding her head on one side, was one of those persons whom you want, as the phrase is, to shake, but who have learnt Hungarian by themselves. She conversed perhaps in Hungarian with Corvick, she had remarkably little English for his friend."

French words and phrases, a sentence from Virgil and other allusions create an impression of literary language. The tale is, after all, the narrative of a critic who recalls the past with his pen in hand and has a tendency to polish words to make their earlier meaning to come through. About Corvick it is stated that "he was prepared to out-Herod the metropolitan press." This modernized adaptation of "It out-Herods Herod," comes from what is usually called Act Three, Scene 2 of *Hamlet,* in which the hero gives instructions to the players by telling them how not to speak. The following explanation by Richard Aczel, the editor of a recent selection of the shorter works by Henry James, suggests that the phrase is used to indicate the distance between the narrator's understatements and George Corvick's vulgar style: "In the medieval mystery plays Herod was represented as a ranting and raving tyrant. Thus to 'out-Herod' suggests to 'shout louder than'."[22]

Although the narrator's discourse indicates his literary culture, he is unambiguously treated as a reader who fails to understand Vereker's art. "He evidently didn't think me intellectually equipped for the adventure." This admission is just one of the many elements indicating that *The Figure in the Carpet* is about insufficient understanding, despite the fact that the characters in the tale are seriously committed to reading: "for the few persons, at any rate, abnormal or not, with whom my anecdote is concerned, literature was a game of skill, and skill meant courage, and courage meant honour, and honour meant passion, meant life. The stake on the table was a special substance and our roulette the revolving mind, but we sat around the green board as intently as the grim gamblers at Monte Carlo."

At some point Corvick, the narrator's rival, is said to have "discovered" the "secret," solved the "problem": "there were to be no particulars till he should have submitted his conception to the supreme authority." In view of Vereker's earlier statement about the identity of text and message and the linguistic nature of the otherness the reader has to understand, this claim can be dismissed as unjustifiable. That Corvick believes that he has acquired "the final knowledge" and so appropriation is a finite process proves that he is even less qualified to understand Vereker's novels than the narrator, who records his confession of failure, candidly admitting that he is unable "to trace the figure in the carpet through every convolution, to reproduce it in every tint."

It belongs to the irony of the tale that all those who claim to have "seen the idol unveiled" pay a high price; both George Corvick and his wife Gwendolen die before they can inform others about their discovery. Gwendolen's second husband, Drayton Deane proves to be ignorant, and the narrator describes his own state as one of helplessness: "I was shut up in my obsession for ever – my gaolers had gone off with the key."

The two survivors are "victims of unappeased desire." There is no enlightenment. "The mouth of the cave" is never found, the reader is confronted with a hermeneutic circle. The image of the circle, used in the Preface to *Roderick Hudson*, a text that repeats several metaphors from the tale about the interpretation of Vereker's novels, has led James to the idea that understanding is a circular process and what is decisive is not to get out of the circle but to come into it in the appropriate ("right") way – one of the principles of hermeneutics.[23]

A close reading of *The Figure in the Carpet* may suggest several approaches. Besides illuminating an important aspect of the works of James, it can be taken as an attack on the Realist conception of "truth of description, truth of character, human truth as to men and women," as formulated by Trollope,[24] as well as on the Naturalist willingness to substitute science for art, expressed by Zola in *Le Roman expérimental* (1880). The notebooks of James prove his conscious decision to refute the idea that what has to be understood in a work of art can be identified as a fixed entity – a "lesson" or a "sermon," in Trollope's terminology.[25] The artist is not in the position to do the work of the interpreter. "There's a general idea *qui s'en dégage*: he doesn't tell what it is – it's for the reader to find out."[26] *The Figure in the Carpet* can be read as a therapeutic text that explores the hermeneutic situation and thus anticipates Heidegger's and Gadamer's theory of interpretation. The tale reminds us of the world-constituting power of language. Understanding is language-bound. What the readers of Vereker's novels fail to see is that every understanding is only "underway"; it never comes to a definitive end. Canonical interpretation is a self-contradictory concept. The idea of the discovery of truth is replaced by that of the happening of truth. It is suggested that tarrying or lingering (the equivalent of what Gadamer called "Verweilen"[27]) is the distinguishing mark of the experience of art. The meaning of the work of art is not a thing, it is not an object to be grasped, but an event, something new that comes into existence with the work of art itself. It is a conflict between emergence and hiddenness, what is created and what is left unsaid.

Notes

[1] Paul Ricoeur, *Temps et récit.* Tome III. Paris: Seuil, 1985, 239.

[2] Henry James, *The Art of the Novel: Critical Prefaces.* New York: Charles Scribner's Sons, 1961, 227.

[3] Tzvetan Todorov, *Poétique de la prose (choix), suivi de Nouvelles recherches sur le récit.* Paris: Seuil, 1980, 83.

[4] Wolfgang Iser, *Der Akt des Lesens: Theorie ästhetischer Wirkung.* München: Wilhelm Fink, 1976, 12.

[5] Ibid., 22.

[6] Ibid., 12.

[7] J. Hillis Miller, "*The Figure in the Carpet*," *Poetics Today* 1 (Spring 1980) 1: 107–18.

[8] Shlomith Rimmon-Kenan, "Deconstructive Reflections on Deconstruction," *Poetics Today 2* (Winter 1980–81), 185–88; J. Hillis Miller: "A Guest in the House: Reply to Shlomith Rimmon-Kenan's Reply," *Poetics Today* 2 (Winter 1980–81), 189–91.

[9] J. Hillis Miller, *Reading Narrative.* Norman, Oklahoma: University of Oklahoma Press, 1998, 96–7.

[10] Roy Chambers, *Story and Situation: Narrative Seduction and the Power of Fiction.* Minneapolis, MN: University of Minnesota Press, 1984, 165.

[11] Henry James, *London ostroma.* Budapest: Európa, 1965, 331–342; "Henry James: European or American?" in Tibor Frank, ed.: *The Origins and Originality of American Culture.* Budapest: Akadémiai, 1984, 239–45; *"Minta a szőnyegen": A műértelmezés esélyei.* Budapest: Balassi, 1995, 139–47.

[12] Henry James, *The Art of the Novel*, 11.

[13] Hans-Georg Gadamer, *Hermeneutik I: Wahrheit und Methode: Grundzüge einer philosophischen Hermeneutik.* Tübingen: J. C. B. Mohr (Paul Siebeck), 1986, 302.

[14] Henry James, *Selected Letters.* Cambridge, MA: Harvard University Press, 1987, 367.

[15] Hans-Georg Gadamer, "Reply to Thomas M. Alexander," in Lewis Edwin Hahn, *The Philosophy of Hans-Georg Gadamer.* Chicago and La Salle, IL: Open Court, 1997, 346.

[16] Marcel Proust, *Journées de lecture.* Paris: 10/18, 1993, 173.

[17] Henry James, *The Art of the Novel*, 4.

[18] Ibid., 14–17.

[19] Ibid., 4–5.

[20] Ibid., 5.

[21] Martin Heidegger, *Sein und Zeit.* Dreizehnte, unveränderte Auflage. Tübingen: Max Niemeyer, 1976, 148, 150.

[22] Henry James, *The Turn of the Screw and Other Stories.* Köln: Könemann, 1996, 355.

[23] "Das Entscheidende ist nicht, aus dem Zirkel heraus-, sondern in ihm nach der rechten Weise hineinzukommen," in Martin Heidegger: *Sein und Zeit,* 153.

[24] Anthony Trollope, *Autobiography.* Leipzig: Bernhard Tauchnitz, 1883, 213.

[25] Ibid., 206.

[26] *The Notebooks of Henry James.* New York, Oxford University Press, 1961, 220.

[27] Hans-Georg Gadamer, "Zwischen Phänomenologie und Dialektik – Versuch siner Sebstkritik," in *Gesammelte Werke 2 Hermeneutik II: Wahrheit und Methode: Ergänzungen, Register.* Tübingen: Mohr, 1986, 7.

Bilingualism and Literary Modernity

Multilingualism is closely related to the intertextual character of literature. On some level all texts are multilingual in the same way as all texts
can be read as translations. Textual voice is always composite and quota-
tional, so that every utterance is permeated with heteroglossia. At the same
time, on some other level few texts as unified wholes can be other than
language- and culture-bound. The difference may be one between deep
and surface structures, but it is safer to suggest that what we have here are
two different aspects of reading. When I am reading a text in English, a
different set of expectations will be brought into play from those involved
in my construction of a text in French.

What is sometimes called Modernism was associated more than many earlier movements with multilingual aspirations. Still, if we disregard concrete
and sound poetry, there were relatively few among the outstanding twentieth-
century writers who succeeded in composing major works in languages other
than their mother tongue. The poems composed in French by Rilke, T. S. Eliot,
and Ashbery are inferior to their verse in German and English, and the essays
of the young György Lukács published in Hungarian were dismissed as written in bad Hungarian, using "horrible German terminology," by the eminent
poet and critic Mihály Babits in a review published in 1910 (Babits 1978, p.
158). Most of the outstanding literary works of the last hundred years seem to
be monolingual. Despite the quotations in various languages and the incalcu-
lable textual play, Celan's verse is part of German poetry, whereas *The Cantos*
and *The Waste Land* belong to literature in English. Even *Finnegans Wake*
may be culture-bound and thus remind its reader of Joyce's dictum that "you
must write in your own tradition. Borrowed styles are no good. […] In the
particular is contained the universal" (Ellmann 1959, p. 520.).

My intention is to examine briefly the activity of three authors who published major works in an adopted language: Joseph Conrad, known as an English prose writer, Vladimir Nabokov, whose output can be divided into a Russian and an American phase, and Samuel Beckett, the only writer among the three who could be called bilingual in a strict sense.

Some Poles may resent Conrad's decision to write in English. While most critics would offer a biographical explanation for this language shift, there may have been other reasons why Conrad used the English language. As Ford Madox Ford, who co-authored several works with Conrad, pointed out, the Polish-born writer's second language was French. "Again and again during the writing of, say, 'Nostromo' he expressed passionate regret that it was then too late to hope to make a living by writing in French, and as late as 1916 he expressed to the writer an almost equally passionate envy of the writer who was in a position to write in French" (Ford 1989, p. 225). What Conrad aimed at was a kind of objectivity, even impersonality. An adopted language that was free of subjective or even sentimental associations seemed to be preferable for such an artist. Yet he had difficulties with English which were described by Ford in the following way: "Conrad's indictment of the English language was this, that no English word is a word; that all English words are instruments for exciting blurred emotions. [...] The consequence is that no English word has clean edges: a reader is always, for a fraction of a second, uncertain as to which meaning of the word the writer intends. Thus, all English prose is blurred. Conrad desired to write prose of extreme limpidity" (Ford 1989, p. 229).

Unlike Conrad who never wrote any fiction in his mother tongue, Nabokov published numerous books in Russian before he started writing in English. Most of his works are available in both languages. The status of these texts is somewhat uncertain. Let us take a single example, the book that was published in 1964 under the title *The Defense*. According to the title page, this work is a novel "translated by Michael Scammell in collaboration with the author." In the Foreword, written in Montreux at the end of 1963, Nabokov admits that *Zashchita Luzhina*, published in 1930, is full of highly functional, aggressive wordplay that is absent from the English text. The heavy-witted punning starts with the Russian title, a pun on "illusion." The chess defense invented by the hero, Grandmaster Luzhin, is an illusion. What the reader of the English text may learn at the end of the novel is known to the reader of the Russian text from the very beginning. The impact is radically different in the two cases. While *Zashchita*

Luzhina is a novel about the hopeless existence of people living in exile, *The Defense* is a playful novel that can be associated with Postmodernism.

Nabokov was perfectly aware that he occupied two radically different positions in two cultures. As mentioned earlier, when asked, three years after the publication of *The Defense*, if he had "any conspicuous or secret flaw as a writer" Nabokov gave the following answer: "The absence of a natural vocabulary. [...] Of the two instruments in my possession, one – my native tongue – I can no longer use, and this not only because I lack a Russian audience, but also because the excitement of verbal adventure in the Russian medium has faded away gradually after I turned to English in 1940. My English, this second instrument I have always had, is however a stiffish, artificial thing, which may be all right for describing a sunset or an insect, but which cannot conceal poverty of domestic diction when I need the shortest road between warehouse and shop. An old Rolls Royce is not always preferable to a plain jeep" (Nabokov 1967, p. 110).

Just as Conrad was helped by Ford, so Beckett had co-authors in the years when he started writing in French. One of these was Suzanne (Georgette Anna) Deschevaux-Dumesnil – the woman he married for legal reasons in 1961 – who could not speak English. One reason why I have such a hypothesis is that a story of hers, *F–*, which appeared as translated by Beckett in the periodical *transition* in January 1949, is remarkably similar to Beckett's own works. Although the Irish writer was familiar with Parisian argot, some of his contemporaries referred to the limits of his French. In Georges Belmont's view he had a strong Irish accent, and Josette Hayden went so far as to say his French was "deplorable" (Cronin 1999, p. 440). At their first meeting Anthony Cronin, who later became one of Beckett's biographers, was immediately able to place the writer's speech "as south Dublin Protestant, even to a slight lisp and a difficulty with 'r' sounds which was common in that class" (Cronin 1999, p. 479). As late as 1957, during the rehearsals of *Fin de partie,* the actor Jean Martin "wanted Beckett to realize that no matter how well he spoke the language, he was still a foreigner who writes in French" (Bair 1978, p. 483.). Peter Lennon, a young Dublin journalist who visited Beckett in the 1960s was taken aback "by the idiomatic Dublinese of his discourse" (Cronin 1999, p. 514), a sociolect which had been given literary status by Joyce and Flann O'Brien. Later on, when he read Beckett's works, he realized how deep the influence of this sociolect was on them.

In view of the richness of the Anglo-Irish style of a novel like *Watt*, it is not meaningless to ask why Beckett started writing poems in French before World War II. From the late 1920s he paid regular and long visits to Kassel, where his father's sister Cissie Sinclair lived with her family. Thanks to these trips he became fluent in German. What I would regard as his most important statement on language is in a letter written in German in 1937: "Es wird mir tatsächlich immer schwieriger, ja sinnloser, ein offizielles Englisch zu schreiben. Und immer mehr wie ein Schleier kommt mir meine Sprache vor, den man zerreissen muss, um an die dahinterliegenden Dinge (oder das dahinterliegende Nichts) zu kommen. Grammatik und Stil. Mir scheinen sie ebenso hinfällig geworden zu sein wie ein Biedermeier Badeanzug oder die Unerschütterlichkeit eines Gentlemans. Eine Larve. Hoffentlich kommt die Zeit, sie ist ja Gott sei Dank in gewissen Kreisen schon da, wo die Sprache da am besten gebraucht wird, wo sie am tüchtigsten missbraucht wird. Da wir sie so mit einem Male nicht ausschalten können, wollen wir weningstens nichts versäumen, was zu ihrem Verruf beitragen mag. Ein Loch nach dem andern in ihr zu bohren, bis das Dahinterkauernde, sei es etwas oder nichts, durchzusickern anfängt – ich kann mir für den heutigen Schriftsteller kein höheres Ziel vorstellen. [...] Mit einem solchen Programm hat meiner Absicht nach die allerletzte Arbeit von Joyce gar nichts zu tun. Dort scheint es sich vielmehr um eine Apotheose des Wortes zu handeln" (Beckett 1984, p. 52–53).

This letter sheds light on two of the possible motives behind Beckett's desire to write in French: his wish to escape from the oppressive influence of Joyce and his intention to eliminate language. *Murphy* was too close to the Joycean apotheosis of the word. His French vocabulary was far more limited; he was less aware of the connotations inherited from the past. He wrote in French, "parce qu'en français c'est plus facile d'écrire sans style" (Gessner 1957, p. 53.). Of course, there may have been another reason why he started writing in French. The Parisian avant-garde was much stronger than its British equivalent, so he might have had a better chance of success in French.

The shift must have been difficult for him. After the departure from English into French was begun before the war, a major work, *Watt*, was written in English. In comparison with this novel the earliest longer texts in French, the novel *Mercier et Camier* and the play *Eleutheria* were still very uneven. It was only after it became clear that *Murphy*, published in London in 1938, did not sell, and *Watt* was turned down by several publishers that Beckett stopped writing in English. He felt reassured when the story *Suite* (later rebaptised as *La Fin*) was accepted by *Les Temps modernes* in July 1946. What is more, before the end of the same year the same periodical, founded by Sartre, published the twelve poems composed before the war, between 1937 and 1939.

It is worth remembering that Beckett became aware of the fundamental difference between the historical legacy of French and English very early in his career. When "Anna Livia Plurabella" appeared in the *Nouvelle Revue Française* in 1931 in a translation for which he had been at least partly responsible, the young author "dashed off a note to the master to say that it was impossible to read the text without thinking of the futility of the translation process" (Cronin 1999, 155).

Like the Hungarian poet and prose writer Dezső Kosztolányi, whose first major essay on translation was written and published earlier and represented a more radically target-oriented approach than Walter Benjamin's somewhat overestimated *Die Aufgabe des Übersetzers*, (Kosztolányi 1990, pp. 561–566), Beckett was obsessed with the idea of untranslatability. That is why he was reluctant to translate the work of others. Most of his translations have to be regarded as occasional pieces. The Spanish poems in a collection selected by Octavio Paz published in 1949 are obvious examples. In the words of his biographer: "Many of his translations were hackwork, done mechanically and without a great deal of enthusiasm and many were unsigned. In these cases he could not afterwards say with certainty what he had done and what not" (Cronin 1999, p. 395). One of the exceptions is his translation of Robert Pinget's play *La Manivelle*. As the title (*The Old Tune*) suggests, this is a free adaptation. At the same time, it may remind us of Beckett's willingness to be associated with the "nouveau roman." In 1959 he even allowed himself to be photographed with the main representatives of this movement. This gesture was in marked contrast with his refusal to be associated with the so-called theatre of the absurd.

Like Nabokov, Beckett made self-translations in his later career. The status of these versions is different from translations made by others. His earliest attempt at self-translation was the French version of the story *Love and Lethe*, which had been in the collection *More Pricks Than Kicks*, published in London in 1934. This was followed by a French adaptation of *Murphy*, started by Alfred Péron and Beckett in 1938 and not completed until after the war, which the author called "my own translation and not a very good one" (Cronin 1999, p. 367). The absence of the rich English and Irish associations is so striking in these texts that they have to be called inferior to the originals. In 1948 three short poems by Beckett appeared both in French and in English in the first number of the new series of *transition*. This was the first indication that he expected his readers to reinterpret their ideas on bilingualism. Yet the gap continued to be wide between the different versions of his works. This may explain why his humour is hardly noticed in France, whereas in the English-speaking countries the innovative aspects of his narrative prose are usually underestimated.

Beckett's first biographer insisted that *Molloy* was co-authored by Marie Péron; in 1947–48 the author met daily the wife of Alfred Péron "to go over what he had written the night before" (Bair 1978, p. 368). Some years later, when Richard Seaver, a young American, offered him help to translate this novel into English, he warned his enthusiastic reader that this work could not and should not be translated; instead, they had to write "a new book in the new language" (Bair 1978, p. 439). In view of the fact that Beckett collaborated on the German translation of *En attendant Godot*, *Happy Days*, and *Play*, and followed the instructions of his American friends when eliminating unamerican rhythms, idiom, and atmosphere in *Malone Dies*, it might be somewhat misleading to call him a bilingual author. It is probably more appropriate to emphasize his target-oriented approach to interlingual intertextuality. This approach is also manifest in the translation of six maxims by Sébastien Chamfort made in 1975-6. The originals are in prose, the English versions are in verse. It seems likely that no generalization is possible about Beckett's self-translations. The English title *Waiting for Godot* could easily become proverbial and the text relied upon the tradition of music-hall cross-talk. By contrast, *Fin de partie* may be finer in French. This is the least sentimental of his dramatic works, and clearly shows the influence of Racine, an author whose notoriously limited vocabulary served as a model for Beckett's attempt to realize the aims he defined for himself in the letter written in German in 1937.

The longer works are so closely attached to specific linguistic and cultural traditions that it is probably better to speak of adaptation or recreation than translation. The short pieces may be the only exceptions, yet even in these texts the shift from one language to the other involved significant changes. My random examples are taken from the series called *Textes pour rien*, written in 1950 and translated in the late 1950s and early 60s. It suffices to quote the first two sentences from the sixth piece: "Entre ces apparitions que se passe-t-il? Et s'il se passait ceci, que mes gardiens se reposent et dorment, avant de m'entreprendre à nouveau, s'il se passait cela?" In marked contrast to the emphasis on finite and active verbs, the English has a conspicuously nominal, indirect and circumstantial character: "How are the intervals filled between these apparitions? Do my keepers snatch a little rest and sleep before setting about me afresh, how would that be?" Even greater is the difference between the two versions of the twelfth piece. What may strike the reader first is the rhythm of the monologue: "C'est une nuit d'hiver, là où je fus, serai, remémoré, imaginé, n'importe, croyant en moi, croyant que c'est moi, non, pas la peine, du moment qu'il y a les autres, où ça, au monde des autres, des longs parcours mortels, sous le ciel, avec une voix, non, pas la peine, et de quoi bouger, de temps en temps, non plus, du moment que les autres passent, les vrais, mais sur terre, sûrement sur terre, le temps d'une nouvelle mort, d'un nouveau réveil, en attendant qu'ici ça change, que quelque chose change, qui fasse naître plus avant, mourir plus avant, ou bien ressusciter, au fond de hors de ce murmure de mémoire et songe." This rhythm is different in the English text, and the abstract ("serais") is transformed into the concrete ("I'm going"), the general ("les vrais," "de quoi bouger") into the specific ("the true others," "the power to move"), and the temporal ("plus avant") into the spatial ("deeper"): "It's a winter night, where I was, where I'm going, remembered, imagined, no matter, believing in me, believing it's me, no, no need, so long as the others are there, where, in the world of the others, of the long mortal ways, under the sky, with a voice, no, no need, and the power to move, now and then, no need either, so long as the others move, the true others, but on earth, beyond all doubt on earth, for as long as it takes to die again, wake again, long enough for things to change here, for something to change, to make possible a deeper birth, a deeper death, or resurrection in and out of this murmur of memory and dream."

In 1956 the Third Program of the BBC commissioned Beckett to compose a radio drama. This meant a return to the English language. The last longer text written in French, *Comment c'est*, had given its author more trouble than any of the earlier novels. It hardly needs to be said that this second language shift may have been necessitated in part by the greater emphasis on autobiographical elements. *All That Fall* was followed by *Krapp's Last Tape*, another radio play entitled *Embers*, *Happy Days*, *Play*, a piece based on Beckett's painful relations with his wife and with Barbara Bray, who commissioned the radio plays, and *Company*, a prose work about the author's childhood. *Play* is of special interest from the perspective of bilingualism. The original English version reads like a parody of Noël Coward's cheap plays about love triangles. The husband, the wife, and the mistress live in a world in which one rings for the servants. The upper-middle-class British English sociolect is entirely absent from the French version, entitled *Comédie*.

In the 1960s Beckett's social life was conducted mainly in the Falstaff bar in the rue du Montparnasse, where his associates formed a preponderantly Irish group. By this time it became clear that bilingualism for Beckett reflected a double identity, a rejection of Irish provincialism and a nostalgia for Ireland. The return to Anglo-Irish discourse went hand in hand with a change in Beckett's working method: he often heard the voice of an actor or actress while writing. *Krapp* and *That Time* were written for Patrick Magee; *Not I* and *Footfalls* for Billie Whitelaw; *Embers* and *Eh, Joe* for Jack MacGowran. Some of the late works prove that in some cases intertextuality and translation may work at cross purposes. *Worstword Ho*, the author's last longer narrative, published in 1983, is, among other things, a parody of *Westward Ho!*, Charles Kingsley's patriotic historical tale about Elizabethans and Spaniards, a work that was published in 1855 and read by Beckett in childhood.

In the last decades of his career Beckett's bilingualism was pointing in three directions. The difference between *Happy Days* and *Oh les beaux jours*, *Sans* and *Lessness*, *Le Dépeupleur* and *The Lost Ones*, *Stirring Still* and *Soubresauts*, *Comment dire* and *What Is the Word* is so great that these texts could be taken as individual works rather than translations from one language into another. The French versions rely upon the cultural tradition of the French language, just as the English versions distort texts written in English by earlier authors. Beckett's dissatisfaction with translations of his works made by others can be seen in his handling of Elmar Tophoven's German version of *Fin de partie*, published in 1956. When Beckett was invited to direct this play in Berlin in 1967, he made substantial revisions. The Spitz dog, for instance, was replaced by a poodle in honour of Schopenhauer, one of Beckett's favourite philosophers, and the line "Der Spass ist zu Ende" was changed to "Der Fest ist jetzt zu Ende," which is a deliberate echo of Friedrich Schlegel's well-known rendering of the line from *The Tempest*: "Our revels now are ended" (Cronin 1999, p. 556).

The two other directions are related to Beckett's desire to eliminate language. In *Comment c'est* punctuation was replaced by gaps of white space, and syntax became elliptical, whereas in *Fin de partie* a tendency towards "acte sans paroles" became manifest. The culmination of this tendency was *Film*, a silent movie. If one compares the original script with the finished product, the discrepancy between the two is so great that this work can be regarded as a joint venture of the author and the great comedian Buster Keaton.

With *Film* the wheel has come full circle. Bilingualism may lead to silence. That is one of the possible conclusions one may draw from the career of Samuel Beckett.

References

Babits, Mihály 1978. *Esszék, tanulmányok.* Vol. I. Budapest: Szépirodalmi.

Bair, Deirdre 1978. *Samuel Beckett: A Biography.* London: Jonathan Cape.

Beckett, Samuel 1984. *Disjecta: Miscellaneous Writings and a Dramatic Fragment.* New York: Grove Press.

Cronin, Anthony 1999. *Samuel Beckett: The Last Modernist* (1997). New York: Da Capo Press.

Ellmann, Richard 1959. *James Joyce.* New York: Oxford University Press.

Ford, Madox Ford 1989. *Joseph Conrad: A Personal Remembrance* (1924). New York: The Ecco Press.

Gessner, Niklaus 1957. *Die Unzulänglichkeit der Sprache: Eine Untersuchung über Formzerfall und Beziehunglosigkeit bei Samuel Beckett.* Zürich: Juris.

Kosztolányi, Dezső 1990. "A holló" (1913), in *Nyelv és lélek.* Budapest: Szépirodalmi – Újvidék: Forum.

Nabokov, Vladimir 1967. "An Interview." *The Paris Review* 41 (Summer – Fall).

Conservatism, Modernity, and Populism in Hungarian Culture

> Sing we for love and idleness,
> Naught else is worth the having.
>
> Though I have been in many a land,
> There is naught else in living.
>
> And I would rather have my sweet,
> Though rose-leaves die of grieving,
>
> Than do high deeds in Hungary
> To pass all men's believing.
>
> (Ezra Pound: *An Immorality*, 1912)

To celebrate the fiftieth anniversary of the unification of the cities of Buda, Pest, and Óbuda, a concert was given by the Budapest Philharmonic Orchestra on November 19, 1923. The three works written for this occasion were a *Festive Ouverture* by Ernő Dohnányi, *Psalm 55* by Zoltán Kodály, and *Dance Suite* by Béla Bartók. The first composition could be called conservative in the sense that it was written in a tonal idiom. The aesthetics of the second anticipated the interpretation of the past developed by the Populists. The third opus was admired mainly by the supporters of the Modernist movement. The goal of this essay is to examine the interrelations among these three trends in Hungarian culture.

Between 1867 and 1914 Budapest was the fastest growing city in Europe. Its drawing power increased over this period – a drawing power that attracted not only people from elsewhere but also pulled intellectuals into urban groups and coteries. It had now become the outright point of concentration for Hungarian culture, overtaking the role of the provincial cities. Its technological face made for a sense of excitement and stimulus. Despite periodic threats of political, social, and ethnic conflicts, not only the upper but also the middle classes enjoyed freedom and security. With light taxation, hardly any inflation, cheap food and labour, and a plentiful supply of domestic servants, many middle class families led comfortable and sheltered lives. Intellectuals were being urbanized, feeling those emotions of stability and alienation that characterize city life. By 1910 the majority of the Hungarian bourgeoisie and working class lived in Budapest; understandably, therefore, after the end of World War I, it was in the capital city where both the bourgeois and the Communist revolution had started. In view of this, it might be surprising that the hero of the most imaginative works of fiction written in this period is a conservative aristocrat. Although he spends much of his time in Budapest, Eduárd Alvinczy, a highly respectable gentleman, ignores the twentieth century. There might be a slight touch of irony in the way the narrator treats him, but more important is the storyteller's almost unqualified admiration for this "impossibility," as a minor character calls him in *A vörös postakocsi* (The Red Stage-Coach, 1913) by Gyula Krúdy, one of the first Hungarian novels to break with the narrative conventions of the nineteenth century by questioning the idea that the self has an instrinsic nature.

In 1919, Krúdy published *Pesti Album*, a collection devoted to the life of the capital. One of the chapters ends with the following statement made by Alvinczy:

> "I am suffering from indigestion," he thought. "Salmon is no longer enjoyable."[1]

It is not quite impossible to read these words as the writer's response to the contemporary situation. In any case, they indicate a distance from political and social events and might be considered a warning against assuming that the socio-economic process of modernization ran parallel with artistic evolution. While the Naturalistic *tranche de vie Budapest* (1901) – by Tamás Kóbor, a Jewish novelist now almost forgotten – was enthusiastic about urbanization, the most innovative prose writer of the same period harboured strong reservations about the loss of intimacy in the modern city. Krúdy hardly ever ceases to identify himself with the ethos of Eduárd Alvinczy, an aristocrat whose ambition is to live according to the principles of Count István Széchenyi (1791–1860), the greatest representative of his class in the nineteenth century. In the act of paying tribute to the values of the man whose ambition was to transform his country from a stronghold of feudalism into a modern democracy, he voices his own nostalgic awareness of the distance that separates him from the beliefs of pre-industrial Hungary. The past is available to him not in its continuity into the present, not as a living tradition, but as the reconstructed object of his imagination. The fall of feudalism is thus counterpointed by another story: as the wordly and vital powers of the nobility decline, so its consciousness grows. Industrialization seems at odds with an understanding of world and self.

Linguistic isolation can be the only possible reason why the conflicts between the supporters of urbanization and some representatives of artistic modernity have been ignored by Western scholars. By way of example, I may quote the following remark from one of the best works on the intellectual trends in Central Europe in the early twentieth century: "the first vernacular poetry in Hungarian was produced among the sons of the Hungarian nobility at the leading Habsburg *Gymnasium*, the *Theresianum*."[2] This statement would suggest that poetry had not been written in Hungarian before Viennese influence made itself felt in the second half of the eighteenth century. The authors seem not to know that from the late thirteenth century there is an unbroken continuity in the history of Hungarian written verse. Accordingly, their idea of the Hungarian contribution to what represented "modernity" in the Dual Monarchy is based on insufficient evidence.

It might distort the picture if we view Hungarian culture from a Viennese perspective or assume that a scholar interested in the Habsburg Empire "can interpret the culture of these areas provided he is fluent in German," to quote an American publication that gives a one-sided treatment of Hungarian intellectual life in the early twentieth century by identifying it with the activity of a very small group of writers who were born in Budapest, but left Hungary at an early age, or at least wrote most, if not all, of their works in German.[3]

In some cases even a historian who is familiar with the language may seem to be unable to see the complexity of the interrelationships between urbanization and artistic innovation. My last example is taken from a recently published monograph aimed at analyzing the activity of György Lukács and his circle in the context of intellectual life in Budapest:

"Lukács and his friends were correct to see themselves radically out of touch with the cultural realities of Hungary, where the majority of the population still lived in conditions of rural backwardness, insulated from the benefits, as well as the discontents, of modernity. But they were almost equally estranged from the progressive artistic and intellectual circles of Budapest, which were too closely associated with a complacent liberalism and a superficial eclecticism to constitute a congenial intellectual world for them."[4]

166

No indication is given by the author as to the meaning of "progressive" in her book, but it is safe to assume that she may have the poet and journalist Endre Ady in mind, since the term was often applied to his activity at the time she wrote her monograph. Neither complacent liberalism nor superficial eclecticism characterized the social prophecy or the tragic vision expressed in his writings.

Before attempting to examine the complex relation of modernization to literary modernity, I cannot bypass a terminological issue. The term "modern" has been used in too many different ways. Some cultural historians, including the author of the monograph on Lukács and his circle quoted above, have drawn upon the distinction made by Stephen Spender between "modern" and "contemporary,"[5] although the English poet's book-length essay is mainly about British literature and does not claim to have theoretical value.

In any case, it is far from self-evident what Modernism denotes. I am inclined to agree with those who maintain that unlike "the terms Gothic, Renaissance, Baroque, Mannerist, Romantic or Neo-Classical, it designates no describable object in its own right at all," because it is a "portmanteau concept" whose referent is a wide variety of very diverse aesthetic practices.[6] What is more, it is doubtful whether it can be regarded as a term denoting exclusively artistic phenomena. Rather, it represents a broader cultural response to pressing issues which were the consequences of industrialization. According to one critic, four variables: "secularism, individualism, bureaucracy, and pluralism" have formed the core of modernity."[7]

The idea of the modern is closely tied to a teleological concept of history. As is well-known, it was developed in the course of the "querelle des anciens et des modernes," and was defined as the last stage in the succession of Classical antiquity, Middle Ages, and modern times. In contrast to the two other members of the triad, it implied the primacy of novelty and was based on the assumption that there were more and less advanced forms of consciousness. It became inseparable from a monolithic conception of world history and a canonical view of culture. Some followers of Hegel developed a normative interpretation of modernity. By the end of the nineteenth century, however, the concept became problematic, largely due to the influence of Nietzsche. Rival conceptions of modernity were formulated. Broadly speaking, such is the context in which the Hungarian culture of the early twentieth century has to be examined.

167

At the beginning of the twentieth century, four new trends emerged in Hungarian intellectual life. Each was characterized by a specific attitude towards urbanization. Only two of them, the movement centered around the journal *Nyugat* and the somewhat later avant-garde led by Lajos Kassák, could be called artistic in the strict sense of the word. The journal *Huszadik Század*, started in 1900, was the organ of sociologists and political scientists, whereas the primary interest of what was to become the Sunday Circle in 1915 was metaphysics. If modernity has any sense in Hungary in the early years of the twentieth century, it must be viewed as a complex of interrelationships among these four trends. Each claimed to represent modernity, but their definitions of the goals the country should achieve were different. In 1911 György Lukács won a competition with a two-volume monograph entitled *A modern dráma fejlődésének története* (The History of the Evolution of Modern Drama), in 1914 Dezső Kosztolányi published a collection of translations with the title *Modern Költők* (Modern Poets), and both authors published books in the series called *Modern Könyvtár* (Modern Library) edited by Jenő Gömöri, but their views on modernity were far from the same.

Although all these trends were opposed to some form of establishment, the representatives of each had a different notion of conservatism. The contributors to *Nyugat,* whose first issue came out in the last days of 1907, were creative writers. Born in the province, most of them drew inspiration from their early years spent in the country-side. Their poetry and fiction were dominated by a backward glance. To be of one's own time, as far as they were concerned, was a measure of failure rather than an achievement. Endre Ady made significant returns to his village, both in a physical and in a psychological sense, Mihály Babits evoked memories of his native Transdanubia in numerous poems and in his long novel *Halálfiai* (Sons of Death, 1927), and Dezső Kosztolányi's major works, from the verse cycle *A szegény kisgyermek panaszai* (The Complaints of the Poor Little Child, 1910) to the novels *Pacsirta* (Skylark, 1924) and *Aranysárkány* (Golden Kite/Dragon, 1925), were imaginative recreations of his childhood in Szabadka (today Subotica). In Budapest they were newcomers who never felt at home in the metropolis. This may have been one of the reasons why few of them tried to experiment with dramatic genres.

The Hungarian capital had a vigorous theatrical life, dominated by Ferenc Herczeg and Ferenc Molnár. Herczeg became a member of the House of Representatives in 1896, the year in which the country celebrated the thou-

sandth year of its creation, and supported the prominent conservative statesman Count István Tisza during his second term in the Hungarian parliament
between 1910 and 1918. Aesthetically, both Herczeg and Molnár were conservative, although they came from the same bourgeoisie that formed the
social background of most of the contributors of *Huszadik Század* and of
the members of the Sunday Circle, in sharp contrast to the majority of those
writers who made *Nyugat* the organ of artistic and intellectual modernity.

Oszkár Jászi, the founder and editor of *Huszadik Század,* had a better
knowledge of and a greater respect for the past of Hungary than György
Lukács, but to criticize that past was no self-torture for him, as it was for
Ady, Krúdy, Babits, or Kosztolányi, who were proud of their social origin
and insisted on their continuity with old, i.e. pre-capitalistic Hungary. The
authors of *Huszadik Század* were convinced that they were the true representatives of modernity, yet they often found the poetry, fiction, and essays
published in *Nyugat* obscure. The aesthetics of evocation and suggestion,
as represented by such poems as *A fekete zongora* (The Black Piano) by
Ady or *Fekete ország* (Black Country) by Babits, was a far cry from the
Positivistic ideals of the intellectuals of *Huszadik Század.* The interests
and values of the two groups were different: while the sociologists and the
political scientists believed that modernity meant a faith in the scientific
claims to total explanation, the creative writers discarded both scientism and functionalism. They were attracted to Symbolism, *Jugendstil*
(*Sezessionismus*), psycho-analysis, and other trends representing a reaction against Positivism. The philosophers of what was to be called the Sunday Circle occasionally published in *Huszadik Század* and in *Nyugat,* but
they spoke contemptuously of Positivism, and their understanding of the
new poetry and fiction was rather limited: Lukács, for instance, never came
to appreciate the novelty of Krúdy's fiction. With the publication of *A Tett,*
Kassák's first avantgarde periodical, founded in 1915, the gap became
even wider.

Undeniably, there were overlaps among the activites of the different
groups. Béla Balázs, a close friend of Lukács, was also a poet, and Emma
Ritoók, another member of the Sunday Circle, published several novels.
Occasionally their work appeared in *Nyugat,* but their creative writing was
far more conservative in the aesthetic sense than that of the major representatives of *Nyugat.* Some poets of *Nyugat,* including Ady, took a serious
interest in *Huszadik Század.* The first issue of *A Tett* was introduced by
Dezső Szabó, who at that time joined the first generation of *Nyugat,* and

169

Kosztolányi wrote a favourable review of Kassák's first published volume of poetry, *Éposz Wagner maszkjában* (Epic Poem in Wagner's Mask, 1915). Still, the overlaps were of secondary importance in comparison with the fundamental clashes among the four movements.

For a long time the bourgeois radicals of *Huszadik Század* sought to define the purity of scientific discourse in the spirit of Herbert Spencer. This effort made Oszkár Jászi and his associates seem pedestrian and old-fashioned in the eyes of the members of the Sunday Circle, who aspired to discover a new metaphysics. *Művészet és erkölcs* (Art and Morals, 1904), Jászi's early book which had won him a prize from the Hungarian Academy of Letters and Sciences, was a far cry from the essays of the young György Lukács and Lajos Fülep, and even from the aesthetic principles of Ady, Babits, and Kosztolányi, who had a similar admiration for Nietzsche. From another perspective, however, the bourgeois radicals of *Huszadik Század* seemed to be less conservative: they approved of industrialization, whereas the philosophers were spokesmen of what in his later Marxist years Lukács was to call Romantic anti-capitalism. With the emergence of the avant-garde, this backward orientation had become obvious even in the sphere of art. While Babits, Kosztolányi, and even Ady were moving from the cult of intentional obscurity of Symbolism and the decorative, adjectival writing of *Sezessionismus* towards a greater emphasis on the verbal elements of syntax, a more Expressionistic style (Kosztolányi translated Imagist verse and discovered the paintings of János Nagy-Balogh, a working-class artist whose work resembled Cubism; and Kassák made more and more works of the international avant-garde accessible to the Hungarian public), Lukács lost touch with contemporary art. Up to 1911 Leo Popper and Irma Seidler helped Lukács understand paintings, but after the death of these two friends, he seemed to take no interest in the visual arts. Paintings became a pretext for him to develop ideological arguments.

A telling example of his growing alienation from the art of recent decades is the value judgement attached to Cézanne's name in his later essays. My first quotation is from an article originally published in 1918:

> "Simmel's historical position could be summarized the following way: he was the Monet of philosophy who has not yet been followed by a Cézanne."[8]

In 1918 Lukács may have been unaware of Monet's later work, the magnificent water lilies painted at Giverny, in which he abandoned the fundamental principle of Impressionism – the accurate transcription of observed phenomena – in favour of an emphasis on tonal harmonies. For him Monet stood for superficiality, whereas Cézanne represented profundity. Less than two decades later he made the following statement:

"Die Porträts von Cézanne sind ebenso blosse Stilleben, verglichen mit der menschlichseelischen Totalität der Porträts von Tizian oder Rembrandt, wie die Menschen Goncourts oder Zolas im Vergleich zu Balzac oder Tolstoi."[9]

It would be an error to assume that Lukács turned conservative after his conversion to the Communist Party of Hungary, in late 1918. The first issue of *A Tett* came out in the same year when the Sunday Circle was established. The characteristic features of the activity of the group centered around Lukács: the speculations about the nature of mysticism, the cult of erotic love, and the neo-Romantic stylization of folklore were all manifestations of an *Art Nouveau* culture. Lukács praised the poetry of Balázs, written in a style reminiscent of Maeterlinck's diction of prefabricated suggestiveness, at a time when Kassák was writing free verse in an idiom comparable to the activist language of August Stramm. The conservative taste of Lukács may have been at least partly responsible for the later conflicts between Marxist aesthetics and twentieth-century art. In any case, it was the basis of the development of the concept of "critical Realism," an ideal that made East-European theoreticians and artists reject innovations which are generally associated with aesthetic modernity.

One of the most violent clashes between the Sunday Circle and the Hungarian avant-garde occurred in 1919. Béla Kun, the leader of the Commune, called *Ma,* Kassák's second journal "a product of bourgeois culture," at a party conference. His statement appeared in print, in *Vörös Újság,* on June 14. In his response published in *Ma*, on July 1, Kassák questioned Kun's competence in art and denied that art had to serve the party and the working class. As a result, the Communist leaders withdrew the permission which made the publication of *Ma* possible. The incident underscored the fundamental disagreement between such Communists as Balázs and Lukács, who tacitly accepted the view that art cannot be autonomous in socialism, and Kassák, who insisted that human creativity was a source rather than a product of social revolution.

At the same time, two friends of Lukács departed from the path he followed. In 1920 Emma Ritoók published a small collection of verse, *Sötét*

171

hónapok (Dark Months), expressing her strong disapproval of the Commune, and Lajos Fülep became a Protestant clergyman in a small village. There may have been personal motives behind their decisions, but their departure also expressed their feeling that the Sunday Circle alienated itself from the traditions of Hungarian culture. In the 1930s Fülep went as far as agreeing with some of the Populist writers' objections to industrial capitalism.

Since Ritoók and Fülep had been the only non-Jewish members of the group, it is possible that their attitude was also motivated by their conviction that the cultural assimilation of their friends had been somewhat imperfect. As is well-known, Lukács's father often emphasized his Hungarian nationalism, but a quotation from a book written by the son of another industrial magnate of Jewish origin may suggest that this attitude cannot be called general. In this autobiographical novel the prosperous father gives the following instruction to the Hungarian tutor of his son:

"You must allow my son, Mr. Szalkay, to remain what he was born, a Jew. And if you must teach him something, then teach him to deal in business and how to make it profitable. Teach him to live here as if he were in a province where one goes to make a profit. Do you know what a *koved* is? It is the Yiddish word for a sinecure, an honourable post for which one gets no pay, or very little. I want no parliamentary representatives, judges, or professors in my family. My son should buy and sell here, but he should not sell himself, for no good will come of it... For have you ever seen a Jew who has gone after *koved* and has ended up well in this country?"[10]

It should be noted that the position taken by this father is rejected in this novel. The author himself had chosen another path: as a critic he insisted on the continuity of Hungarian culture and joined the *Nyugat* movement. Several others followed his example: industrialists Miksa Fenyő and Baron Móric Kornfeld, for instance, made the publication of the same journal possible with their financial support.

Needless to say, what is at issue here is not ethnic, but cultural and linguistic assimilation. Another quotation may shed light on the distinction. One of the most original composers of the twentieth century made the following remark: "my music; produced on German soil, without foreign influences, is a living example of an art able most effectively to oppose Latin and Slav hopes of hegemony and derived through and through from the traditions of German music."[11] Schoenberg was Austrian and considered himself a Jew, but never hesitated to call his work German and even national.

One of the charges levelled at the Jewish capitalists who lived in Hungary around and after 1900 was their reluctance to learn about national traditions. It cannot be denied that Jewish capitalists and intellectuals brought up in the large cities of the Dual Monarchy had a German culture. Not only the Wittgensteins or the Schoenbergs, but also the Kornfeld and Weiss families spoke German at home. This cultural milieu may have contributed to the decision Lukács made around 1911 to stop writing in Hungarian and switch almost exclusively to German. Fülep, on the other hand, never distanced himself from his mother tongue. Their later disagreement may have been rooted in their different attitudes towards language.

When Lukács published his first book of essays, *A lélek és a formák* (Soul and Forms) in 1910, Mihály Babits reviewed it in *Nyugat*. Babits was well-read in philosophy and shared Lukács's interest in metaphysics, but his review cannot be called favourable. The young poet's main concern was the purity of diction, and as a creative artist, he found the philosopher's use of the Hungarian language abusive. Both Babits and Lukács wanted to liberate Hungary from provincialism, yet their intellectual positions were poles apart: for the poet, national tradition was a precondition of culture, and language a precondition of thought; whereas for the philosopher, tradition was international, and language a means to an end, a medium at the service of intellectual activity. In view of the fact that Lukács never made any attempt at the close reading or stylistic analysis of a lyric poem, the charge levelled at him by Babits cannot be dismissed as superficial. What the poet suggested was that the tradition behind the activity of the Lukács circle was not international but German.

For most of the writers of *Nyugat* modernity was closely tied to an escape from the influence of the German culture which dominated Hungarian culture throughout the nineteenth century. Budapest was in competition with Vienna, so the artists living in the Hungarian capital looked for models outside the German-speaking countries. Ady translated Baudelaire and Verlaine, Krúdy drew inspiration from Pushkin and Turgenev, Babits admired Swinburne and Dante Gabriel Rossetti. The reaction against German models was also felt in the other arts: the Gödöllő school of the Hungarian *Art Nouveau* was modelled on the Arts and Crafts Movement, the painter Rippl-Rónai joined the Post-Impressionist group called "*Les Nabis*"

173

in Paris, and Bartók discovered an antidote to the dominance of German culture in the music of Debussy.

Although the superficiality of rapid assimilation and the reaction against Germanic cultural models may have intensified the conflict between different forms of modernity, they cannot be regarded as the only causes of the tension between urban development and cultural innovation.

Capitalism led to inevitable consequences in the cultural life of Hungary. During the Napoleonic wars the country house of Ferenc Kazinczy at Széphalom, a small village in the North-East of the country, had been the centre of literary life; a century later a coffeehouse in Budapest was the meeting place where writers came to discuss politics and culture. Ironically, institutional changes and transformations in the social context of literature were not always complementary. While the consumers of art may have changed, the creative talents continued to come from the traditional classes. In the early twentieth century Hungarian art was sponsored by *nouveau riche* families, but produced by members of what had been the lesser nobility before the revolution of 1848. Many Jewish intellectuals looked upon art as a social equalizer, but with the exception of the poet, novelist, and playwright Milán Füst, none of the major Hungarian writers of modernity came from the Jewish community. The influence of capitalism may have been strong on literary institutions, but the social background of Ady, Krúdy, Babits, and Kosztolányi was not different from that of Berzsenyi, Vörösmarty, Arany, or Madách – to mention but a few poets who dominated the nineteenth century. In contrast to some of their predecessors, all the members of the first *Nyugat* generation had to earn their living, but they often felt ill at ease in the new situation. Major novelists and poets were forced to write *Feuilletons* and *Feuilletonnovellen*. These relatively new genres required a skill at extemporizing. Ady, Krúdy, Kosztolányi, and even Sándor Márai, a younger writer whose first book was published in 1918, had to devote several hours per day to journalism, which often made it impossible for them to concentrate their efforts on writing poetry or narrative fiction.

Cultural preferences were often motivated by a sense of belonging. This *Heimatsgefühl* is inseparable from the evolution of Hungarian literary modernity: the works of Ady, Krúdy, Babits, and Kosztolányi had been conditioned by strong local traditions, and the art of the novelist Zsigmond Móricz was no less deeply rooted in the culture of the peasantry, another traditional class of Hungarian society.

Recent literary scholarship is marked by a growing disenchantment with certain socio-historical clichés. Paradoxically, some Western publications reiterate value judgements which have been partly invalidated by studies revealing novel, hitherto unexplored or neglected aspects of Hungarian culture. A characteristic example is the interpretation of the role of the gentry given in a book published in the United States:

> "The gentry played cards, gambled away its land and fortune, drank to excess, sobbed to gipsy music, and entertained lavishly even after it could no longer afford to do so."[12]

Although there is more than an element of truth in this generalization, it is worth remembering that the devastatingly critical picture of the gentry on which the critic relies was almost entirely drawn by artists who themselves belonged to this class. Just as academic art was represented mainly by Munkácsy, a painter of German petty bourgeois origin, whereas Impressionism was started by Szinyei Merse, and Expressionism was developed by Mednyánszky and Csontváry Kosztka – three painters coming from the nobility – literary modernity was established by members of a class which often resisted modernization. Towards the end of the nineteenth century the gap between bourgeois and artist, *Kulturträger* and *Kunstträger,* had widened, making it almost impossible to draw a clear-cut distinction between the anti-social attitude of innovative artists and the anachronistic values of the gentry. These facts gain added significance, because no similar opposition between artistic and social modernity can be observed in the "Austrian" half of the Dual Monarchy.

I am almost tempted to speak of the co-existence of originality and provincialism in Hungarian culture, provided the latter term is not taken in a pejorative sense. Although Ady's poetry had been called immoral, obscure, and cosmopolitan by some of his right-wing contemporaries, a conservative literary historian, János Horváth, wrote the first book about it. In retrospect, the main thesis of *Ady és a legújabb magyar líra* (Ady and Recent Hungarian Poetry, 1910) is absolutely correct: there is an undeniable continuity between earlier national traditions and Ady's work. The indebtedness of Babits and Kosztolányi to János Arany, the most outstanding poet of the Post-Romantic third quarter of the nineteenth century, is even more obvious; both regarded him as their master from the beginning of their careers. Instead of rejecting the past, they reinterpreted it: while the nineteenth century viewed Arany as an epic poet, a national classic, for Babits

and Kosztolányi he was the author of elegiac and ironic lyrics who anticipated modernity through a rejection of subjective sentimentalism.

Before Kassák made his presence felt in Hungarian culture, Ady had
been the only major poet who sympathized with socialist ideas. Yet even
his work reveals traces of a nostalgia for preindustrial values. *Hazamegyek
a falumba* (I Shall Return to My Village) is only one of those poems which
suggest a rejection of urban civilization. Bartók viewed peasant culture as
an antidote to the kitsch of city life. In *Sons of Death*, an autobiographical
novel by Babits, the hero moves from a rural and cohesive *Gemeinschaft*
to the achievement-oriented *Gesellschaft* of industrial capitalism. The local values of the writer's native Szekszárd, a small Transdanubian town,
are replaced by the internationalism of Budapest. The narrator's perspective is ambiguous: the hero's spiritual education is portrayed as an inexo-
rable process, but the organic community of his early years is presented as
superior to the chaotic world of the modern city. Both *Skylark* and *Golden
Kite/Dragon*, probably the best novels by Kosztolányi, are about provinciality. While the real name of the author's native town has positive connotations (the first part of the compound word "Szabadka" means "free," the
second part is a diminutive), the name of the place in the above-mentioned
books suggests hopeless parochialism ("Sárszeg" literally means "a site of
mud"). There is much irony in these novels, but the final message is that
while cosmopolitanism may lead to civilization, it cannot create culture.
Kosztolányi was a close friend of the analyst Sándor Ferenczi and the first
cousin of Géza Csáth – the author of *Az elmebetegségek pszichikai me-
chanizmusa* (The Psychic Mechanism of Mental Illnesses, 1912), a remarkable early study of complexes – and he relied upon the works of Freud in
his sustained and consistent critique of industrialization.

As early as 1913 Kosztolányi made the following confession:

"What interests me is the Hungarian country-side [...]. It is the land of miracles.
Those who are born there will have a wider horizon than anybody brought up in
a highly industrialized capital. [...] In a world where nothing happens and life
is dominated by drinking wine, playing cards, sadness, and solitude, the soul
will have an inner dimension, a strange compression and intensity of emotions.
Provincial life is always of purely psychic character."[13]

The correspondence with the definition of the gentry quoted above is
striking enough to suggest some ambiguity in the role played by this class

176

in the evolution of Hungarian literary and artistic modernity. It is significant that almost no writer of any distinction was born in Budapest. One of the very few exceptions was Cécile Tormay, a conservative middle-class novelist whose ancestors belonged partly to the Hungarian nobility and partly to the German bourgeoisie. Her second novel, *A régi ház* (The Old House, 1914), suggested that the traditions of the German cities of Ofen and Pesth could make a significant contribution to Hungarian culture only after they were combined with the rural legacy of the Hungarian nobility. Márai, one of the few writers of the next generation with a purely bourgeois background, had even more serious reservations about the relevance of the life of Budapest for Hungarian culture. In his autobiographical work *Egy polgár vallomásai* (The Confessions of a Citoyen, 1934–35) he distinguished between the living law of his native Kassa and the state-made law of the capital. The contrast between the constitutive rules of a gradually developing community and the regulative formulae which serve to conceal the anarchy of a suddenly emerging metropolis is further evidence of the Hungarian writers' reluctance to accept Budapest as an organic part of their country.

In view of this, it becomes clear that Kassák's avant-garde stands in sharp contrast to both the Sunday Circle and the *Nyugat* movement. As a self made man, Kassák could have none of the advantages of provincial traditions. For him the cosmopolitan metropolis was not a source of cultural estrangement, but the basis of transforming culture as a whole. While Ady, Krúdy, Móricz, Babits, and Kosztolányi had a feeling of not quite fitting into the age of industrialization, Kassák was in harmony with his times. His disagreement with the Sunday Circle was partly aesthetic. If we compare the connotative pseudo-symbolism of *A kékszakállú herceg vára* (Bluebeard's Castle, 1911) – the one-act verse play by Béla Balázs which Bartók set to music – with the denotative, conspicuously prosaic diction of Kassák's free-verse poem *Mesteremberek* (Craftsmen, 1914), we can understand why the leader of the Hungarian avant-garde regarded the works of Balázs as mediocre and old-fashioned. The poetry of the solitary ego conflicted with the voice of collectivity, decorative art with functionalism, and Romantic anti-capitalism with a utopian belief in the unity of art and industry.

It is far more difficult to situate the Hungarian avant-garde in relation to the writers of *Nyugat*. Ady reacted with indignation when he received Kassák's first collection of verse, and Babits attacked the new movement in a long review article. Any analysis which tries to underestimate the conflict between the members of the two alternatives of Hungarian literary modernity cannot do justice to the complexity of the picture. Although Kassák had considerable respect for Ady's messianic prophecies, he wished to distance himself from the cult of hidden meaning. For the younger poet the traditional role of the adjective had become suspect.

Kassák's approach to poetic diction was also in conflict with the intentional artificiality of the style of Babits. Both poets insisted on the internationalism of culture, but their attitudes were radically different. Babits adhered to the ideal of a Catholic tradition and spoke of *sui generis* European values, whereas the development of Kassák's Activism implied an attack on an academic, canonical view of culture and anticipated the *Bauhaus* movement, "a Protestant Reformation putting faith in the liberating aspects of industrialization and mass democracy."[14] In the 1910s Kassák's movement seemed similar to German Expressionism. It had grown out of the immense shock which the war produced in the minds, and pleaded with those 'brothers' who felt that a 'new man' and a 'new society' would emerge from the war. After the fall of the Commune, Kassák's activity as a visual artist, the creation of the genre he called *Bildarchitektur,* may have affected his poetic style. The Expressionistic pathos of *Máglyák énekelnek* (Bonfires Are Singing, 1920) was soon replaced by the functionalism of *Tisztaság könyve* (The Book of Purity, 1926), emphasizing the strongly moral connotations of his art. The untitled poems he composed in Vienna in the 1920s manifest an affinity with the German *Dinggedicht* (object-poem) and a preoccupation with a denotative "hardness" that is opposed to the connotative "softness" of Symbolism, decadent Aestheticism, and Secessionism. In his later years, Kassák translated Whitman and Cendrars, expressed reservations about the Romantic lyricism in some of Apollinaire's poems, and preferred the early Imagist work of William Carlos Williams to the poetry of T. S. Eliot, in sharp contrast to Babits, who towards the end of his life felt a great attraction to the Neoclassicism of the American-born British master. Kassák represented a strong reaction not only against the literature of nuance and allusion but also against the Secessionist cult of beauty. He did not seek to please; in his autobiographical poem *A ló meghal a madarak kirepülnek* (The Horse Dies the Birds Fly Out, 1922) he repeatedly used inarticulate utterances. He liked meaningless words because they were free of the associations inherited from the past. He attempted to liberate those energies of language which in his view had been repressed by poets dominated by the legacy of Classical antiquity.

178

Krúdy and Kosztolányi wished to raise narrative prose to the level of lyric poetry: the former made metaphor the structural principle of his style; the latter aimed at the textural terseness of the short poem. By contrast, Kassák's goal was to destroy the very concept of the "poetic," desacralize art, abolish the autonomy and institutional identity of the aesthetic sphere, and end the alienation of the various spheres of human activity from each other. These two attitudes towards the Romantic legacy were irreconcilable.

What united Krúdy and Kassák was a prevailing sense of dislocation from the past. The difference, however, was more important than the similarity between them. Krúdy and Kosztolányi had a nostalgic view of the past, and after 1920 Babits spoke in a similarly elegiac tone about the world lost with World War I. What is more, even Ady was tempted to regard himself as belonging to the old order he often criticized. The triumph over time was conceived by Krúdy, Babits, or Kosztolányi not as a leap into the future, as for the Hungarian Activists, but as a movement into the past. Somehow or other, all the major members of the *Nyugat* circle were attached to the heritage of nineteenth-century Liberal nationalism. By contrast, Kassák preferred to call himself a European poet, reminding his readers that he saw a fundamental difference between European art as represented by Bartók and a reliance upon Hungarian traditions advocated by Kodály. Most representatives of the earlier movement supported the bourgeois revolution of 1918 but became alienated from the Republic of Councils in 1919. After the fall of the latter regime, they distanced themselves from any kind of socialism and interpreted the Treaty of Trianon as a national tragedy. Kassák, on the other hand, moved to Vienna, and never lost his belief in socialism, despite the fact that the leaders of the Communist Party of Hungary banned his journal in July 1919.

Kassák felt no polar opposition between the needs of the creative artist and the values of mass industrial society. He felt at home in a working-class suburb of the Hungarian capital and later wrote his most successful novel about it (*Angyalföld*, 1929), whereas Ady, Krúdy, Móricz, Babits, and Kosztolányi were less pleased with the transformation of Budapest into an industrial metropolis. Ady returned to his village Érmindszent at regular intervals. Krúdy had nostalgic feelings for the *Nyírség*, one of the most backward agricultural regions of the country. Feeling that the past was slipping away from him, Babits turned his back on the present and escaped from the capital to a house on the top of a hill on the outskirts of

Esztergom, a small town in northern Hungary. As for Kosztolányi and Márai, both lived in a district of Buda whose closed community reminded them of the intimacy of Szabadka and Kassa, towns which had been transferred to Yugoslavia and Czechoslovakia after World War I. *Anna Édes* (1926), the last of Kosztolányi's novels, and *Csutora* (1930), an autobiographical novel by Márai, present this district as almost cut off from the rest of the capital.

What distinguished both the major writers of *Nyugat* and the chief representatives of Hungarian Activism from the members of the Sunday Circle was their critique of the language. Kassák's efforts, however, ran counter to the Symbolist exploration of the allusive and associative powers of language. While Kosztolányi's main interest was a kind of *Sprachkritik* and Kassák's goal was to liberate language from the overlays of literary tradition, Lukács ignored the verbal aspect of literary works. The difference between the positions taken by the two Hungarian poets was in their attitudes towards the legacy of Symbolism and in their approaches to literary genres. Kosztolányi's ideal had links with Mallarmé's dictum that poems were made not with ideas but with words. For Kosztolányi language became a human bastion against chaos and nothingness. The world is out there – he maintained – but descriptions of the world are human creations. Where there is no language there is no truth; and we are nothing save the words we use. Viewing himself as a servant and not a master of language, he broke with the idea that language was a medium, and considered a novel to be a work of verbal art, whereas Kassák was convinced that language could be regarded as a medium of expression and style was of no great importance in narrative prose. Because of this, the older writer's fiction has more affinity with the inventions of twentieth-century fiction than Kassák's more conventional narrative works. Kosztolányi's metafictional stories about Kornél Esti, written in the last decade of his life, represent a form of narrative which is "about" its own making, questioning its own practices and presuppositions, and suggesting that any idea we may have of enjoying a shared meaning is sheer delusion. Because of this, they are much closer to the mainstream of the experimental prose of the first third of the twentieth century than any of the Naturalistic novels of Kassák.

As I indicated earlier, World War I, the fall of the Commune and the Peace Treaty of Trianon brought radical changes to Hungarian culture. The impact of these historical events persuaded many that the values of the national past had been touched in their very foundations. A large number of urban centres (Kassa, Pozsony, Nagyvárad, Kolozsvár, Marosvásárhely,

Brassó) were cut off from Budapest. Hungary had become not only smaller, but also less open to cross-cultural influences. The character of the country had changed; the rural areas of the Great Hungarian Plain gained significance. Three of the four modern movements lost their influence after their leaders left Hungary: *Huszadik Század* ceased to appear, the Sunday Circle was dissolved, and Kassák moved to Vienna. A political and social crisis shook the middle class, which turned inward and blamed itself for the failures of the recent past. The supporters of the avant-garde movement were viewed as the adherents of a future that had not materialized. Some felt that the war had made of Modernism a spent force. The very model of urban man had become the basis of a profound ideological cultural dissent, and the belief spread that the lasting forms of culture belonged outside urban civilization. In the summer of 1919 Dezső Szabó published *Az elsodort falu* (The Village Swept Away), a parable directed against both capitalism and socialism. Since its author had published essays both in *Huszadik Század* and in *Nyugat*, and supported Kassák's Activism in the early stage of its development, his novel represented a decisive change of direction and thus anticipated the rise of a new generation. Three years later a collection of poems, *Ibolyalevél* (Violet Leaf), came out. Its author, József Erdélyi, was of peasant origin, and his inspiration came from the oral traditions of his class. Within a few years a Populist movement was organized which involved a strong reaction both against the *Nyugat* movement and against the avant-garde. What is more, it was bound up with a revaluation of the past which made urbanization and artistic modernity seem to be mere episodes in the history of Hungarian culture. While *Nyugat* represented a mixture of cosmopolitanism and provincialism, and Activism a decisive turn toward internationalism, the movement that arose in the 1920s and became a decisive factor in Hungarian culture in the 1930s was bound up with a cult of local traditions.

Needless to say, there were various factors which may have helped the rise of Populism. A few of these had international implications. One of the consequences of World War I was that the belief in progress entered a crisis. Aesthetic modernity seemed to disintegrate soon after it was established. Some of the artists who were among the innovators in the first decade of the twentieth century turned more conservative in the 1910s, whereas others continued to experiment. "Die Moderne spaltet sich, formelhaft gesprochen, in Neue Musik and Klassizismus," as a musicologist wrote about the years in which Richard Strauss stepped backwards from the style of *Elektra* (1908) to the far more tonal writing of *Der Rosenkavalier* (1911), whereas Schoenberg moved further from the less radical language of *Erwurtung* (1909) in the direction of atonal music by composing *Pierrot lunaire* (1912).[15] As is well-known, at the beginning of their careers Bartók and Kodály worked together, but by the 1910s it became obvious that Kodály did not want to break with the traditions of tonal music. Considering the important role Kodály was to play in the Populism of the 1930s, it is important to realize that his aesthetic conservatism may have given support to the Populists who dismissed the legacy of the avant-garde.

Although it would be misleading to overemphasize the connection between the Neoclassicism of the 1920s and the rise of Hungarian Populism, there can be no doubt that the success of such poets as Erdélyi or Sinka was at least partly due to some urban intellectuals' disillusionment with the avant-garde. Babits, who was rather critical of Kassák's internationalism from the very outset, turned more conservative both in a political and in an aesthetic sense after the Peace Treaty of Trianon. Finding the ground giving beneath his feet, feeling the burden of responsibility and detachment, he gave active support to the Populist movement by giving the prize of the Baumgarten Foundation three times to Erdélyi and four times to Gyula Illyés. In his later years Babits realized that he could be a medium rather than a charismatic leader. He was inclined to view art as recreation rather than creation – his *Jónás könyve* (The Book of Jonah, 1939) is a personal adaptation of one of the books of the Old Testament. From a Neoclassical perspective art heavily dependent upon peasant culture seemed to be more acceptable than the subversive, anarchistic spirit of the avantgarde. By the 1920s the reviews published in *Nyugat* were no more favourable to the international avant-garde than *Napkelet,* a conservative journal founded by Tormay in 1923. *Az európai irodalom története* (A History of European Literature, 1934-35), the most sustained effort of Babits as essayist, is an epitome of Neoclassical ideals, an outline of European literary traditions, with a heavy emphasis on Classical Antiquity and the Latin Middle Ages. The last chapters of this highly impressive work make almost no mention of such movements as Futurism, Expressionism, Dada, or Surrealism.

Before World War I Ady, Babits, and Kosztolányi reacted against Positivism. Later Babits and Kosztolányi went as far as rejecting the project of the Enlightenment. They had two different things to say about the way the

Western world was after 1920. For Babits it seemed belated, for Kosztolányi it turned out to be contingent. Modernity involved teleology, so Kosztolányi's distrust of history led to a rejection of the idea of modernity. It is no accident that the author of the stories about Kornél Esti was to exert such a profound influence on the Postmodern writers of the late twentieth century.

Besides the reaction against the avant-garde, the reinterpretation of Hungarian past also paved the way for the Populist movement. The starting hypothesis of some was that at the time of the Turkish occupation the Hungarian inhabitants had been forced to flee the capital, and that in the 18th and 19th centuries (after the end of Ottoman rule) Germans and German-speaking Jews came to live in Pest-Buda. Writers who felt estranged from the foreign culture of the city had a revival in the 1930s. Literary historians supporting the Populist cause reminded the public that as early as 1790 József Gvadányi, the author of *Egy falusi nótáriusnak budai utazása* (A Village Notary's Journey to Buda), contrasted the Hungarian cowboys, shepherds, and horseherds of the lowland with the fashionable cosmopolitans of the capital. Bourgeois liberals dismissed Gvadányi as a provincial opponent of the Enlightenment, but László Arany's declarations of hostility to the rapidly changing society of the capital in his verse novel *A délibábok hőse* (The Hero of Mirages, 1873) could not be called superficial.

There is no doubt that the origins of the Populist movement go back to the nineteenth century. In 1897 a small collection of patriotic poems was published by Géza Lampérth, a poet of no distinction. The book's preface was written by the conservative novelist and literary historian Zsolt Beöthy, who distinguished between rural and urban poetry, and insisted that only the former was acceptable as the expression of national values. One of the last members of the old Liberal generation, the seventy-one-year-old Pál Gyulai was quick to point out that folk culture "may be one of the main sources of national poetry, but should not be identified with it."[16]

In the first two decades of the twentieth century *Nyugat* and Kassák's Activism seemed to invalidate Populistic efforts, but soon an undercurrent in favour of rural values set in. In some cases the advocates of the resurrection of the Hungarian village could find support from anti-Semites who lived in the neighbouring countries. Karl Lueger used the word "Judapest" on occasion, and the Romanian Octavian Goga made the following remark in 1913: "Die ungarische Nationalliteratur hat in der Dichtung mit Petőfi und Johannes Arany, in der Prosa mit Mikszáth ihre Ende gefunden und hat der Budapester jüdischen Nationalliteratur Platz gemacht, die in unseren Tagen herrscht."[17]

Although the Hungarian Populism of the interwar period was inseparable from an occasional distrust of foreign influences, it would be a gross simplification to associate the movement with anti-Semitism. Its definition must be made on a much more general basis. The Commune of 1919 and the Peace Treaty of Trianon represented not only a historical break but also a cultural rupture. The rise of Populism was possible only because the legacy of bourgeois Liberalism became discredited when it proved to be too weak to resist totalitarian dictatorship. The consequences of this crisis were not only a highly convincing critique of the superficially international mass culture of Budapest and a reassessment of folklore, but also a disturbance in the continuity of artistic modernity and an unfortunate dichotomy between the values of urban and peasant culture.

The growing discrepancy between the aesthetics and the style of Bartók and Kodály is symptomatic of the state of Hungarian culture after World War I. While the composer of *Music for Strings, Percussion, and Celesta* (1936) "se situe parmi les 'cinq grands' de la musique contemporaine aux cotés de Stravinsky, Webern, Schönberg et Berg,"[18] as a major composer of the second half of the twentieth century wrote, Kodály could be considered a late Romantic whose works could serve as a pretext for the justification of various forms of conservatism.

The political significance of Populism cannot be questioned. In the aesthetic sense, it accompanied a revival of nineteenth-century ideals, but it also had some continuity with the developments of the early twentieth century. Three of its immediate antecedents are of special significance.

The first among these is bound up with the fact that the modernity of *Nyugat* was closely tied to the traditions of preindustrial classes. In the case of Móricz, these traditions belonged to the peasantry, so for him it was easy to turn towards a Populistic interpretation of culture in his later years. His best short story, *Barbárok* (Barbarians, 1931) is reminiscent of the style of folk ballads, and *A boldog ember* (The Happy Man, 1935) is based on interviews with a poor peasant, so it represents an attempt to make documentary acceptable as literature, an effort characteristic of interwar Populism.

The difference between the social backgrounds of the creators and consumers of early-twentieth-century modernity also involved a contradiction

184

between the values of the bourgeois and the artist. For Ady this tension involved occasional clashes with his sponsors. The post-war generation of the 1920s viewed the problem as unsolvable. Sándor Márai's best work, *The Confessions of a Citoyen*, presents the anarchism of a *Kunstträger* and the civilized attitude of the *Kulturträger* as irreconcilable alternatives.

The third of the phenomena that made the rise of Populism possible was the proliferation of cheap journalism, fiction, and drama which alienated many artists from the mass culture of Budapest. László Németh, who started his career with essays assessing the achievement of Proust and Joyce and emphasizing the artistic flaws in the novels of Móricz and the aesthetic conservatism underlying the verse of Erdélyi, soon became the most violent critic of the superficiality of the values of the Hungarian bourgeoisie. His long pamphlet *Kisebbségben* (In Minority, 1939) is an attempt to present urbanization as alien to Hungarian culture.

Populism made an undeniable contribution to Hungarian culture through its criticism of mass culture. It raised folklore to the status of high art and modified the concept of literature by making non-fiction a canonical genre. It also changed the wider context of Hungarian culture by calling attention to its similarities with the cultures of other nations in Eastern Europe. In his review of *A History of European Literature* Németh reproached Babits for his exclusively Western concept to culture. His criticism was absolutely justifiable. The modernity of *Nyugat* was inseparable from the idea that Hungary belonged to Western Europe. Ady occasionally spoke of common sorrows of Slavs, Romanians, and Hungarians, but for Babits tradition meant mainly the legacy of Western Europe. The Peace Treaty of Trianon, the loss of more than two thirds of the country, and the emergence of Czechoslovakia, the Southern Slav state, and a greater Romania that included Transylvania made intellectuals aware of the Eastern neighbours of the country.

Yet the new focus proved to be not only broader but also narrower. None of the Populists could compete with Kosztolányi's polylingualism; for them the usable past was much more local, both in time and space. The loss of old illusions also involved the creation of new ones. Some Populists were inclined to believe that Eastern Europe could follow a path different from that of Western urbanization. Among the models to be rejected were the legacy of the avant-garde. Having returned to Budapest in 1926, Kassák found himself in a changed world. After some unsuccessful attempts at continuing his activity, he even made a compromise with the spirit of the times. His more traditional verse, written in the 1930s and later, represents not only a stylistic change but also an artistic decline.

Undeniably, there were some attempts at a synthesis of modernity and Populism. Attila József learned not only from Kosztolányi and Kassák but also from Erdélyi, but he was an exceptional and even solitary figure. No other major literary talent followed his example. In music, the decline was conspicuous: hardly any original composer emerged until Communism ruled out the very possibility of innovation. In the visual arts discontinuity may have been somewhat less obvious, although the institutionalization of the avant-garde was delayed by almost half a century. The political Establishment supported first the Neoclassicism of the "Roman School," then (after 1945) the eclectic style called "Socialist Realism," so continuity with Kassák's Activism could only be reasserted in the form of counterculture.

Although the Populism of the 1920s and 1930s was not without antecedents and significant achievements, it led to a fatal division between urban and rural values, high art and popular culture. By the time of World War II Hungarian culture seemed to be more archaic than it had been before World War I. In poetry and in the visual arts there was some continuity, but culture as a whole had stopped on its way towards becoming an institution supported by the bourgeoisie. Bartók had no successor in music, and the initiatives of Krúdy and Kosztolányi were not taken seriously by other prose writers, so that the representative Hungarian novel of the twentieth century remained unwritten. *Tündérkert* (A Garden of Fairies, 1922), by Móricz, or *Iszony* (Revulsion, 1947), by László Németh, are fine works but are marked by Conservatism in the aesthetic sense. The former is an attempt to revive the tradition of nineteenth century Realism, whereas the latter is a somewhat belated example of the psychological novel. The narrative prose of the avant-garde and the Populist movement is second-rate by comparison. Kassák's Expressionistic novel *Tragédiás figurák* (Tragic Characters, 1919) or Sinka's autobiography *Fekete bojtár vallomásai* (The Confessions of a Black Shepherd, 1944) represent the outmoded view that language plays a far less important role in prose than in verse.

After 1945 Communism increased the gap between Hungary and Western culture. The artists active in the decades following 1956 could not rely on a consistent tradition of modernity; their task was not only the restoration but also the creation of the tradition of the modern. Péter Esterházy, the most significant literary talent born in the Communist era, is not only a representative of the Postmodern condition but also a follower of Kosztolányi, the best Hungarian writer of the early twentieth century. The distance between these two writers is smaller than that between the significant artists of the early and late twentieth century in France, Britain, Germany, or the United States. This would suggest that notwithstanding the significant achievements of the early twentieth century, it is hardly possible to speak about a consistent tradition of modernity in Hungarian culture.

Notes

[1] Gyula Krúdy, *Pesti Album*. Budapest: Franklin-társulat, 1919, 17.

[2] Allan Janik–Stephen Toulmin, *Wittgenstein's Vienna*. New York: Simon and Schuster, 1973, 39.

[3] William M. Johnston, *The Austrian Mind: An Intellectual and Social History 1848–1939*. Berkeley: University of California Press, 1972, 6.

[4] Mary Gluck, *Georg Lukacs and His Generation 1900–1918*. Cambridge, Massachusetts: Harvard University Press, 1985, 23.

[5] Stephen Spender, *The Struggle of the Modern*. London: Hamish Hamilton, 1963, 71–78.

[6] Perry Anderson, "Modernity and Revolution," *New Left Review* 144 (1984), 112–113.

[7] Suzi Gablik, *Has Modernism Failed?* New York: Thames and Hudson, 1984, 16.

[8] György Lukács, *Ifjúkori művek 1902–1918*. Budapest: Magvető, 1977, 147.

[9] Georg Lukács, *Probleme des Realismus*. Berlin: Aufbau, 1955, 129.

[10] Lajos Hatvany, *Urak és emberek*. Budapest: Szépirodalmi, 1980, 91.

[11] Arnold Schoenberg, *Style and Idea: Selected Writings*. Berkeley: University of California Press, 1984, 173.

[12] Mario D. Fenyo, *Literature and Political Change: Budapest 1900–1918*. Philadelphia: The American Philosophical Society, 1987, 16.

[13] Dezső Kosztolányi, *Írók, festők, tudósok: Tanulmányok magyar kortársakról*. Budapest: Szépirodalmi, 1958, Vol. II, 333–334.

[14] Charles Jenks, "Postmodern vs. Late Modern," in Ingeborg Hoesterey, ed., *Zeitgeist in Babel: The Postmodernist Controversy*. Bloomington, Indiana: Indiana University Press, 1991, 12.

[15] Carl Dahlhaus, *Die Musik des 19. Jahrhunderts*. Wiesbaden: Akademische Verlagsgesellschaft Athenaion, 1980, 282.

[16] Pál Gyulai, *"Első könyvem," Kritikai dolgozatainak újabb gyűjteménye*. Budapest: Magyar Tudományos Akadémia, 1927, 375.

[17] Julius von Farkas, *Der Freiheitskampf des ungarischen Geistes 1867–1914: Ein Kapitel aus der Geschichte der neueren ungarischen Literatur*. Berlin: Walter de Gruyter and Co., 1940, 208.

[18] Pierre Boulez, *Relevés d'apprenti*. Paris: Seuil, 1966, 304.

The Permanence and Mutability
of Aesthetic Values

This is an expanded version of a paper I read at Indiana University on 5 April 1997. The topic of the conference – "Hungarian Contributions to Scholarship" – suggested a synthetic approach. My decision was to discuss the Hungarian contribution to Comparative Literature studies with a special focus on a book that exerted a profound influence on literary opinion in Hungary during the decades following its publication. In preparing the fuller presentation published here, I have decided to omit the introductory section and give a somewhat lengthier analysis of what may be regarded as the most important history of European literature published in Hungarian.

It is common knowledge that among the larger works that attempt synthesis and take panoramic views on Western literature there are two that still continue to play a major role in the formation of literary taste in Hungary. The first is *A History of European Literature* (1935) by Mihály Babits, one of the major Hungarian poets and prose writers of his age, and the second *A History of World Literature* (1941) by Antal Szerb, essayist, critic, novelist and short-story writer. This essay is devoted to the first of these two works. On another occasion I will examine the later work, which is a much more ambitious undertaking but heavily indebted to its predecessor in the sense that it is based on the idea that literature is a closed concept. Since Szerb does not act critically in relation to Babits (he refrains from problematizing the distinction between literature and nonliterature), his work can be read almost as a commentary on its predecessor that leaves most of the ideals of the poet-essayist unchallenged. Although the title *A History of World Literature* would suggest an extension of scope, it does not attempt to move beyond the Eurocentrism that is more justifiable in the work by Babits. Because of this, some of the remarks made in the following pages may apply to both works.

l. The Concept of World Literature

What is the justification for writing a comparative history of literature? When asking this question, Babits expressed his conviction that in his age national literatures tended to keep a growing distance from their common legacy. "World literature is a unified, coherent process, blood circulation on a monumental scale," he wrote at the beginning of *A History of European Literature*. "It existed a long time before Goethe recognized its existence and gave it a name; it is much older than national literatures." In the 1930s such an opening statement had obvious political implications. "It is not a modern task to draw the picture of world literature as a traditional unity. If someone tries to do this today, he or she has to bear in mind that such an effort is conservative, even reactionary. The power of European tradition is declining; the different nations insist on continuing their fights in the field of human spirit, looking at each other with hostility; our literary culture seems to disintegrate."

It would be a simplification to assert that in drawing the distinction between national and world literature, Babits simply ignored the cultures of other continents. He never denied the artistic value of works composed outside Europe but viewed them as the manifestation of various national literatures. World literature was not born in Europe, he added, and it certainly extended to other continents. His criterion was not geographical when he maintained that more readers had a first-hand knowledge of the works of Dante, Shakespeare, or Goethe than of the poetry of any other continent. Although his focus on Europe may seem unjustifiable from the perspective of the late twentieth century, his emphasis on the international character of literature was exceptional rather than typical in 1935. His taste was "Catholic" in the original sense of the word, and his attack on provincialism was comparable in strength to those made by Ford Madox Ford, Ezra Pound, and T. S. Eliot in the English-speaking countries, Valery Larbaud in France, or Ernst Robert Curtius in Germany. His goal was that of the curator of an imaginary museum, who would strip works of their local origins and estrange them from their original functions.

The sharp distinction between local and universal values is perceptible throughout his work. "It was a national event rather than a phenomenon of world literature," he remarks about the first performance of *Hernani*. "The battle was won by the Romantics, but the liberty it led to was not too meaningful outside France." Assimilation is viewed as a sine qua non of world literature. St. Paul is more central to this ideal than Moses because he was a Roman citizen who relied on Hebrew culture and used the Greek language. It is assumed that world literature from its earliest phase was governed by synthesizing multicultural sources.

> The great literature of ancient Rome was not developed by the representatives of some 'national spirit.' The 'true Romans' who were intolerant, isolated themselves from alien forces, and wished to create a culture deeply rooted in local traditions. [...] The glory of literature in Latin was the result of the activity of writers who were the most brilliant spokesman of the alien spirit of Greece.

The Hungarian author's vision of culture has been compared to that of T. S. Eliot. Although the American-born poet-critic is not mentioned in *A History of European Literature*, there are undeniable similarities between the arguments made in *Tradition and Individual Talent* and in the book written by the Hungarian author. Both Eliot and Babits were convinced that the European legacy was in principle accessible to mankind as a whole, whereas national literatures had more limited scope and relevance. From our vantage point such a position may seem Eurocentric. Babits makes occasional references to Asian cultures – when introducing the genre of the "novella," for instance, he mentions the *Panchatantra* and the *Arabian Nights* – yet he takes it for granted that world literature is identical with European literature. It was born in ancient Greece; its tradition was continued later by writers who used Latin; and the legacy of the Christian Middle Ages was further developed by authors who used languages related to Latin. Although it is true that Babits admitted that later other linguistic communities also joined the tradition – otherwise it would have been impossible for him to include literature written in his native language – his conception seems somewhat limited if compared with the canon outlined in *The March of Literature* published three years later by Ford Madox Ford. Ford was the Hungarian author's senior by ten years, yet his book reflects a taste that may be called less dated. Although his treatment of the twentieth century is as scanty as that of Babits, his early chapters on Chinese poetry reveal his closer association with the avant-garde.

190

In any case, a criticism of the nationalist approach to literature and Eurocentrism are the two main characteristics of *A History of European Literature*. "For the historian of a national literature nation may have greater significance than 'literature." This statement suggests that for Babits only a work of the greatest artistic value can aspire to a status in world literature. This assumption reflects a strongly canonical view.

> Minor literature is attached to time and space. For world literature only great individuals are of interest, who respond to one another through ages and countries. Only the greatest belong to world literature. [...] Those who continue the work of their predecessors and shake hands above the different nations.

A close reading may reveal a self-contradiction in such an approach. On the one hand, world literature is defined as continuity; on the other hand, it represents a canon of works of timeless aesthetic value. The texts central to this canon ask for slow reading. The reader can go back to them with increased insight and appreciation. "One has to stop at individual lines and drink them drop by drop, as one enjoys good wine," he remarks about Shakespeare. Such semantic plenitude is rare in works composed in more recent periods. When asking for the reason for this decline, the following answer is offered: "The most likely explanation must be found in the higher culture and more refined sensibility of an earlier age that for us is no longer understandable and credible. In the last three centuries literary culture has never ceased to decline, despite some wonderful moments of recovery."

The adherents of the Neoclassical ideal of a timeless canon often tend to be nostalgic. Babits was firmly convinced that the interwar period was marked by cultural decline. When describing the age of Horace, he raised the following questions: "What could have become of mankind if the culture of the nineteenth century had not fallen suddenly into the extreme darkness of the present age? And what achievements could have been made if Roman culture had continued to develop undisturbed?"

History is not regarded as distinct from a critical evaluation, but the unfolding of European literature is not presented as a history of progress towards the achievement of certain ends. Unlike Hegel or Burckhardt, Babits was reluctant to find in all aspects of the Renaissance an improvement on the Middle Ages. Deeply concerned about the disintegration of the unity of world literature and a collective loss of memory, he could not believe in what was usually called the Enlightenment project. This attitude may have developed as a result of the experience of World War I, the short-lived Hungarian Commune of 1919, and the Trianon Peace Treaty. In any case, after the 1920s Babits had become increasingly skeptical of cultural progress. It was a strong fear of a cultural decline that made him a supporter of a supranational canon.

The reader may be insensitive to the greatness of some works but aesthetic values are immanent. Such a preconception underlies the narrative of *A History of European Literature*. The very concept of literature seems unchanged since Homer. Dada is characteristically dismissed as a Romantic experiment and "mere illusion" at the end of the introductory section of the book. By ignoring popular culture, oral literature, and folklore, Babits seemed reluctant to admit that the ontic status of the literary work is variable.

The clear-cut distinction between national and world literature is further elaborated at the beginning of the first historical chapter. "The history of a national literature opens with folklore, i. e. collective and anonymous experiments. No comparable start characterizes world literature." Writing at the time of the rise of Populism in Central and Eastern Europe, he dismissed the idea that high culture could draw inspiration from folklore and rejected the cult of the "primitive" advocated by the avant-garde. In his view the evidence for the universality of the *Iliad* and the *Odyssey* was that they were praised, preserved, and canonized in a very early period. Their style and structure are so sophisticated, Babits argued, that they cannot be viewed as the products of some "primitive" culture. They can be appreciated only by a literate public. Last but not least, a further proof of their supranational character is that their narrator is reluctant to sympathize with any of the communities involved in the war of Troy related by him.

As is well-known, Neoclassicism was one of the dominant movements in the arts of the interwar period. After 1920 Babits became a major representative of this trend, and *A History of European Literature* was written with the purpose of justifying the relevance of international Neoclassicism in a Europe divided by World War I. At a time when the relevance of the Classical heritage for the cultural life of the day was increasingly questioned by the advocates of the avant-garde and by the Populists, he drew attention to the culture of ancient Athens and Rome, as well as to the Latin Middle Ages. He was born into a society in which lawyers and doctors, clergymen, politicians, civil servants, and even bankers read Virgil and Horace, Livius and Tacitus, Cicero and Seneca, and sometimes even the Greek authors, as a matter of course in the original. The type of secondary school called "gymnasium" in which he studied and later worked as a professor convinced him that Graeco-Roman Antiquity represented the core of the canon. As a young instructor he published an essay in the yearbook of the gymnasium of Fogaras, arguing that education was closely tied to articulation, so the study of rhetoric was indispensable for culture. Later he felt dismayed at seeing that the knowledge of classical languages was declining at an alarming rate. He viewed the historian as a kind of curator, the keeper of the canon, and insisted that world literature was at least in part a matter of accessibility. Greek and Latin were used by authors with very different ethnic backgrounds; hence their universal character. It was Protestantism that placed a high priority on the Old Testament and constituted a movement that helped the rise of national cultures versus the common European legacy. National cultures as such have limited relevance in so far as they are accessible only to their own interpretive communities. That is the message of the chapter on the Bible in *A History of European Literature.*

> I have nothing in common with the Old Testament. I feel the lack of openness and hothouse atmosphere of a self-centred race in the barbaric tales about Moses, the partriarchal family and business relations, the strong sensualism of the love lyrics, the inhuman patience of Job, the fits of anger of the prophets, the national attachment to God, and the cynical skepticism of the Preacher.

Babits can be criticized, and has been, for taking a cultural rather than religious interest in Christianity. He undoubtedly failed to see that many passages in the Old Testament could be interpreted as foreshadowing passages in the New Testament. The statement just quoted is certainly in contradiction with the long and distinguished tradition of emphasizing the unity of the Bible. Readers of Hegel or Northrop Frye may dismiss the Hungarian poet's approach as irrelevant. Whatever the weaknesses of his reading of the two Testaments, it was inseparable from his opposition between world literature and national literatures. Although Babits was indebted to the legacy of Romanticism, he rejected the idea that literature was the expression of "Volksgeist." For him the individual represented values more fundamental than any community. His conception was marked by a profound self-contradiction: the Platonic ideal of unchanging aesthetic values was undermined by a reader-response orientation. The tacit assumption underlying the narrative of *A History of European Literature* is that the creative artist has the best qualifications to give a valid interpretation of

193

the legacy of his art. This starting point resembles that of Pound, T. S. Eliot, and some New Critics. Somewhat paradoxically, the significance of this work for scholarship is related to the fact that it reflects the views of a European poet-novelist on the international literary canon. One of the features common to *The March of Literature* and *A History of European Literature* is that they can be read both as pieces of historiography and as spiritual autobiographies. Their influence on historical works is at least as important as their influence on literature. This makes it understandable why Babits calls Pindar local in time and space in contrast to Alcaeus, although Pindar's works have survived and Pindaric odes often served as sources of inspiration for poets who rejected the more didactic tradition of Horace.

No one can accuse Babits of having failed to warn his readers that his criteria for selection were subjective. Needless to say, he is willing to accept some results of philological research – he admits, for instance, that the *Iliad* is a much earlier work than the *Odyssey*, so the two epics must have been written by different poets –, but he insists that no history of world literature could be written by a Positivist scholar. "World literature lives in its readers; and I am trying to describe how it lives in me."

To write a history of European literature is an impossible task for one person, yet only the unified perspective of a single individual can make world literature appear as an organic whole. This paradox serves as an excuse for the Hungarian author's admissions of the limitations of his reading. Not knowing Portuguese and finding the available translation weak, he was unable to read the epic by Camões, and a similar language barrier made it impossible for him to pass a value judgement on the plays of Lope de Vega and Calderon.

2. The Historian's Perspective and Narrative Rhythm

One of the characteristics of *A History of European Literature* is that its author does not remain faithful to the principles laid down in the introductory section. At the outset he insists that in reading literature only firsthand knowledge and experience counts. When introducing the eighteenth century, he contradicts himself:

since I cannot say much new about this century, I shall try to be a conscientious chronicler. New things can be said only about what is capable of constant renewal. In England *Pamela* appeared, a novel by Richardson. Who would be able to say anything new about *Pamela*? Certainly not someone who has not read it. [...] Once I glimpsed into it. It must be infernally boring, and the same could be said about the other works of Richardson. [...] 'Who has read Klopstock's *Messiah*?' That question was often asked when I was a young student. Let me confess that I have not read it.

Fortunately such lapses are quite rare. In fact, Babits goes out of his way to define the three perspectives used in his narrative. Works read in the original often receive a stylistic analysis. Such strict scrutiny can be observed in the passages devoted to the author's favourite poets. Similar to Valéry or Heidegger, Babits has a strong temptation to regard prose as inferior to poetry. Great prose stylists often seem to have escaped him. The three sentences on Joyce in the final chapter do not go beyond a fairly unoriginal reference to interior monologue, and Fontane or Henry James are not even mentioned. Yet there are some exceptions. "Carlyle is primarily a voice," Babits observes and his characterization of the uniqueness of the language of *Sartor Resartus* is more than apt.

A less careful scrutiny is used in the case of texts inaccessible to the author in the original language. When comparing Byron and Pushkin, he makes the following statement about the Russian author: "my feeling is that he is more authentic than his master, despite the fact that unfortunately I do not know the music of his verse in the original." While it is quite understandable that the readers are frequently warned of the gap between original text and translation, it is somewhat surprising that translators are characterized as useful transmitters and fertilizers rather than artists in their own right, especially in view of the fact that Babits himself was a major translator. The translator is compared to a bee, whereas original works are called flowers. In order to demonstrate his point Babits invokes the example of August Wilhelm Schlegel, a mediocre poet but an extremely influential translator of Shakespeare.

A third narrative modality can be detected in the passages in which Babits admits that he has not read a certain work. This distance is especially felt if the work in question was written in a language known to the author – as in the case of the book entitled *Paroles d'un croyant* by Félicité de Lamennais. The three different perspectives share the idea that history can be written only on the basis of a dialogue between past and present. That explains why generic classification is reinterpreted in the light of later developments. It is suggested, for example, that the odes of Horace could be read as songs in the twentieth century. For the same reason, modernity is treated as a questionable and ambiguous term. The mechanistic materialism of Lucrece was modern yesterday. Today it seems limited and outmoded. When comparing Dante's *Vita nuova* and Boccaccio's *Fiammetta*, Babits points to the vulnerability of a twentieth-century perspective: "The later work is closer to the taste of the modern reader – which should not be taken as a favourable value judgement." On other occasions it is suggested that the antecedents of later developments do not necessarily correspond to great artistic achievements. "It is by no means true that the good always paves the way for the future." This remark is made about *Manon Lescaut*, which Babits considers to be a conservative novel. "It is certainly true that 'modernity becomes obsolete faster than anything else.' It bears the stamp of the age." Ironically, this generalization applies to some judgements formulated by Babits himself, such as to his claim that in the middle of the nineteenth century the works of Musset seemed to represent modernity, in contrast to those of Tennyson, whereas later the verse of the English poet proved to be of more lasting value. The conclusion is inescapable that comparative value judgements about works written in different languages are especially vulnerable, and modernity is a matter of perspective: for Taine Musset, for Babits Tennyson seemed to represent it; in our age both authors may seem equally distant.

A History of European Literature consists of two halves, which were originally published in separate volumes. The self-contradictions of the work are closely related to this division and testify to the author's growing awareness of the difficulties of writing such a synthetic work. The first half starts with the *Iliad* and ends with the late eighteenth century, whereas the second covers the period between 1760 and "the present age." Babits was perfectly aware of this disproportion. The only explanation he could offer was that the narrator of world literature could not help slowing down when he came to discuss the literature on which he had been brought up.

Narrative rhythm is not the only factor that reveals a shift in focus. Part one starts with Homer, part two with Ossian. In the former timeless aesthetic value seems to be the governing principle, whereas in the latter it is reception that is decisive. This dichotomy raises important and difficult theoretical questions. How is it possible to distinguish between interpretation and that which is interpreted? How is the identity of a literary work explained over time? To what extent is the canon of world literature vulnerable to historical changes? The inconsistencies of *A History of European Literature* are closely related to its author's inability to find satisfactory answers to these three questions.

While in the first half of the work the output of a given author is usually treated as a unit, in the second half chronology is observed. Goethe's career is discussed in eight different chapters. Although works are personalized throughout the book in the sense that the status, significance, and value attached to them is bound up with the idea that every poem, play, or novel is the product of a particular individual's compositional activity, in the chapters on the nineteenth-century individual careers are deconstructed for the benefit of emphasizing paradigm shifts marked by the rise and fall of such movements as Romanticism or Realism.

Today world literature and Hungarian literature are taught as separate subjects in different departments of the Hungarian universities. Babits would be unhappy with such a division. *A History of European Literature* is an attempt to discuss Hungarian literature as an integral part of an international historical process. Insofar as the subject of the work is the image of world literature as it appears to the author, the goal is met; but to the extent that the criterion is international reception, the inconsistency arises that some works are included on the basis of the author's belief in their artistic value. The poetry of Dániel Berzsenyi (1776–1836) is a case in point. "Unlike Byron, Berzsenyi is never turgid; in contrast to Chateaubriand, he is never posing. We Hungarians happen to know a great poet from the years which for others may be associated with the cloak of a Lord and the tie of a 'vicomte.'" Babits felt despair at seeing that Hungarian literature was not known to the rest of the world. His lines about the late poems of Vörösmarty express resignation, perhaps even helplessness: "His last poems are certainly among the greatest achievements of nineteenth-century lyric. Yet they represent a literature 'unknown' to Europe. There can be neither excuse nor consolation for this."

For T. S. Eliot Dante, for Harold Bloom Shakespeare stood in the centre of the Western canon. Babits translated both the *Commedia* and *The Tempest*, yet in *A History of European Literature* he gave more space to the works of Goethe than to those of the two other poets. The chapter entitled "Intermezzo about Goethe" is not only the summary of earlier assessments of the works but also an emphatically subjective homage to the author whose output is the embodiment of world literature in the sense that it is encyclopaedic in genres and sources of inspiration. For Babits Goethe is an author who deserves special attention because he worked within a medium pre-shaped by many traditions.

3. The Loss of Narrative Teleology

The study of Goethe's works led Babits to the conclusion that the main challenge to the ideal of a Western canon came from Romanticism. Accordingly, this movement is given a more detailed analysis than any of its counterparts. It is significant that Kleist, an author rejected by Goethe, is presented as one of the most profound exponents of Romanticism, and special emphasis is placed on his poem *Germania an ihre Kinder*. Babits observes,

> it is a frightening poem, and unfortunate is the people which includes it in the curriculum. Are we still within 'European' literature? Undoubtedly, it is inseparable from Europe. Nationalism, the intellectual current that not only tolerates but even produces such voices, is definitely European. It is not the property of Germans, since it was born elsewhere. It is a European trend, although it divided the European spirit and may succeed in breaking it into tiny and barbaric national 'cultures,' Yet the poet who represented this frightening trend with so much barbaric sincerity should not be blamed, for he stood for Europe.

Romanticism for Babits is a term to be evaluated heuristically, one that is inseparable from the paradoxical nature of history. He seems critical of the antiquated concepts of periodization and influence, never falls prey to the aberration of calling certain authors more or less "Romantic," and refuses to accept the idea of an eternal clash between Classical ideals and their Romantic rejection, in sharp contrast to his "Geistesgeschichte" contemporaries. "To break free from Classicism, we have to turn to the Classics," he wrote. Another remarkable feature of the chapters on the nineteenth century is that Realism is not defined as a reaction against Romanticism. Instead, a gradual transformation is described, a shift from the local colour of the distant to that of the familiar. While Romanticism is characterized as a movement inspired by the tension between the cult of local values and the universal characteristics of the imagination, Realism is called a more one-sided trend that undermined the unity of European culture. "Realism was one of the causes of the gradual disintegration of European literature into separate national literatures. An emphasis on local colour and partial truth may easily lead to division and national selfishness."

This change seems counterbalanced by another teleological process leading to the cult of l'art pour l'art. This development makes it possible for Babits to condemn sentimentalism in Dickens, didacticism in George Eliot, Tolstoy, and even Dostoyevski. While trying to sustain the illusion that towards the end of the nineteenth century literature was moving in a specific direction, Babits cannot help realizing that this preconception could easily result in the exclusion of significant works. "How deeply divided the leading intellectuals had become!" he exclaims. Afraid of getting lost in details, he decides to discuss the major works published in the 1870s strictly observing their chronological order. The conclusion of this long chapter is that Naturalism seemed to be decisive in the short term but its opponents proved to be the winners in the end. Still, he is not quite satisfied with this solution, as is clear from the opening of the next chapter:

History as history cannot be continued from this stage. It is no longer unified. Is it possible that our lack of perspective makes it chaotic? Literature is a matter requiring some distance. In its absence only individual works are perceptible.

The history of European literature is related in the form of the narrative of a journey. At the end of this journey Babits noted that texts are not literature as such, they can only become literary works. What is close in time can be described only in a very subjective manner.

When I started reading, Naturalism was triumphant. Attempts at a revival of the Romantic legacy were not yet known to us. [...] One of the characteristic writers of the age was Maupassant [...]. Although I was only eleven years old when he died, I read his short-story collections as the embodiment of what was 'contemporary.'

In some respects, this subjective interpretation seems highly relevant today. The analysis of an immense dialogue between Tolstoy and Nietzsche, for instance, reveals that Babits had exceptional insight when reading authors of the later nineteenth century. In other respects, however, the last chapters of his work confirm the truth of his conclusion that contemporary literature might be a self-contradictory concept. Swinburne's works are given a more detailed analysis than those of Mallarmé. While Anatole France, Oscar Wilde, and G. B. Shaw are overrated, and although his brother's works were read by Babits in his formative years, Henry James is not even mentioned. Although none of those born after 1880 – Martin du Gard, Joyce, Woolf, Giraudoux, François Mauriac, Julien Green, Malraux – could be called insignificant, the treatment of the early twentieth century is sketchy. Except for the derogatory allusion to Dada at the beginning of the work and an equally offhand mention of "erratic experiments" in the final section, avant-garde movements are excluded and the literatures of the Americas and the smaller European nations are ignored. The New World is represented only by Washington Irving, Emerson, Thoreau, Longfellow, Poe, and Whitman – Dickinson is merely glossed over in the penultimate paragraph among those regretfully left out. No twentieth-century Spanish or Latin American author is discussed, and Sienkiewicz is the only non-Russian Slav whose name appears in the book. His disregard for such writers as Unamuno, Kafka, Reymont, and Faulkner is as surprising as the exclusion of the ancient Chinese and Japanese poets and the representatives of Futurism and Expressionism, since the works of all these authors had been translated into Hungarian by his contemporaries.

Still, such weaknesses are probably found in the final chapter of most, if not all literary histories. Given the scope of the book, *A History of European Literature* has to be regarded as one of the pioneering attempts at a synthetic approach to the Western canon. The shift from a Platonic concept of immanent aesthetic values to a profoundly historical view is the result of a serious inquiry into the workings of literature. The distinction between timeless values and reception, or a shift from the former to the latter, is by no means a simple polarity or a sharp antithesis. One thinks of it as a passage, transition, or transformation rather than as a sheer opposition. Although the narrative is based on a chronological sequence, it would be erroneous to believe that Babits equates history with linearity. As he constantly reminds his reader, the major poet lives not in the present but in the past and the future. He avoids not only the naive Platonism to be found in the works of such interpreters of European literature as Curtius but also the temptation of subordinating literature to history. Such moments of recognition as between Homer and Virgil, Virgil and Dante, or Dante and Goethe are retrospectively reinterpreted as central articulations in the history of literature. Unlike his comtemporary Dezső Kosztolányi – who endorsed a more open concept of literature but assumed that literary works stood by themselves and could be examined in isolation – Babits associated literariness with intertextual relations. Goethe is in the centre of his canon because the author of *Faust* never ceased to recognize himself for what he was in relation to his precursors and open new territory, which was to be conquered by other poets than himself. Historicity turns out to be a characteristic innate to literature, which has nothing to do with political events. *Weltgeschichte* and *Weltliteratur* are equal parts in a dialogue of great complexity. The relationship between them is both a discontinuity and a continuity. The end of the passage on Chénier can be taken as a clue to understanding the methodological importance of *A History of European Literature*:

> His rhymes, and the modality of his verse, had more influence on the future of Poetry than the world Catastrophe which cut his life short. [...] Literature, as organic life, has an inner logic that cannot be broken by any crisis. [...] Those who try to explain literary phenomena with reference to contemporary events are mistaken.

A History of European Literature is a spiritual journey. Its starting point is a Platonic belief in the timelessness of aesthetic values; its end is an acceptance of mutability as a consequence of an unfinished dialogue between past and present. In the first half the guiding principle may remind one of what E. H. Gombrich represented in art history in recent decades, when he maintained that the "history of art [...] is rightly considered to be the history of masterpieces,"[1] while in the second half it is admitted that certain works that once seemed unquestionably significant, later proved to have no lasting value. The supremacy of creative activity has been replaced by that of reception. The example of Macpherson has led Babits to the insight that the notion of the canon rests on the definition of the literary work as fixed for all of time. In contrast to such countries as Russia, Bohemia, or the United States, Hungary had no school of textual analysis in the early twentieth century, and this absence made it relatively easy for Babits to reject the idea that the work-concept was fixed. The assumption underlying the later chapters of *A History of European Literature* is that it cannot be argued that literary works, once created, are fully formed and permanently existing entities, unchanging continuants, since the meaning of a work of verbal art is to be found in its interpretive experiences. Once an essentialist concept of literature appears vulnerable and canonic status seems a matter of perspective (the result of temporal process), the canonic work has to be regarded as an ontological mutant that cannot be viewed as existing outside history. Although *A History of European Literature* has undeniable weaknesses, lacunae, and idiosyncrasies, a shift to a contextual view of the literary work and a questioning of the permanence of the canon in the later chapters of the book are worthy of consideration in so far as they anticipate a thesis formulated in more recent decades. As Paul de Man wrote in a passage previously cited, "Despite its irrestible tendency toward canon formation," "literature is noncanonical, the critique or, if you wish, the deconstruction of canonical models."[2]

Notes

[1] E. H. Gombrich, *Ideas and Idols: Essays on Values in History and in Art.* Oxford: Phaidon, 1979, 152.
[2] Paul de Man, *Romanticism and Contemporary Criticism: The Gauss Seminar and Other Papers.* Baltimore and London: The Johns Hopkins University Press, 1993, 191.

Bartók's Place in Cultural History

Judit Frigyesi: Béla Bartók and Turn-of-the-Century Budapest.
Berkeley – Los Angeles – London: University of California
Press, 1998, 357 pp.

A literary historian is not qualified to comment on a work by a musicologist unless it deals with literature as much as with music. The author of
this book attempts to situate Bartók's music in cultural history. She aims
high – perhaps a little too high – but the book undeniably has a much wider
horizon than most, if not all, full-length studies of the works of the greatest
Hungarian musician of the first half of the twentieth century.

Her analyses of Bartók's compositions are impeccable. The closer we
are to the structural examination of specific pieces of music, the more convincing the arguments are. The emphasis on the "variational technique"
(251) seems her overriding concern. This is an excellent starting point, for
it helps us understand "the developmental process of the music" (261), "thematic relations," "the dialectic of unity and utmost opposition" (281), which
may involve a recapitulation that "appears to be the result of a gradual process
and yet strikes the listener as something unexpected" (273). The composer's
ability to transform material is demonstrated with rare sensibility. It is a pity
that this production-oriented train of thought is not supplemented by a study of
actual (recorded) performances. There is one exception: the assessment of the
recordings of the remarkable Mária Basilides (accompanied by Bartók himself) in a brief yet highly pertinent note (330–331).

It might be a slight self-contradiction that although the reconstruction
of the goals of the artist is brought into question, the focus is on "Bartók's
artistic decisions" (119). Fortunately, during the actual analysis of Bartók's
works structural relations are interpreted with references to the listener's
experience. This is quite evident in the discussion of the *First Piano Concerto*: "the many themes derived from the introduction become gradually
more and more distanced from their common thematic origin [...]. Be-

cause the technical aspects of these themes change very gradually, the listener experiences each change of character as surprising and yet somewhat unavoidable" (137). What the reader may miss is research into the history of the reception of the works. László Somfai has set an example for such an investigation with his comments on interpretive traditions in his *Béla Bartók: Composition, Concepts, and Autograph Sources* (Berkeley: University of California Press, 1996). "Wirkungsgeschichte" is an integral part of cultural history; the analysis of different interpretations could be as instructive as the investigation of how Bartók's legacy has survived in the music composed during the more than five decades since his death.

In contrast to the chapter on the *First Piano Concerto*, in the case of *Duke Bluebeard's Castle* the author adopts a different perspective by making perceptive comparisons with works by Ernő Dohnányi, Zoltán Kodály, Leó Weiner, and even with other pieces by Bartók. The discussion of Bartók's opera may be the best part of the book, containing illuminating pages on the conceptualization and notation of rubato.

The detailed analysis of the two selected works serves as a solid basis for more general remarks about Bartók's musical style. Among these the most important are related to the composer's interest in folk music. Although some of the criticism levelled at Schönberg's preconceptions may be too harsh and some readers could ask for a more substantial comparison with Stravinsky, the parallel drawn with the second Viennese school leads to a conclusion that deserves special attention: "The theory Bartók devised for his folklore-based style is no less artificial than Schönberg's and Webern's thesis claiming the universal necessity of twelve-tone music. Similar to theirs, Bartók's concept intellectualized a highly personal artistic style in a manner that could be seen as part of a common European aesthetic tradition. [...] In fact, it would be misleading to say that Bartók's aim was to integrate elements of folk music or even to organically derive the new style from it. What he wanted to achieve was a profound understanding of the material of music" (108–109). The argument that Bartók's position has to be given a historical interpretation is further strengthened by an approach to "gypsy music" that is entirely free of dogmatism. Relying on the works of Bálint Sárosi, Judit Frigyesi admits that the composer criticized "gypsy music" "with the enthusiasm typical of a new convert" and views its sharp separation from "peasant music" as belonging to the paradigm Bartók "created for himself" (245).

When focusing on organicism, Judit Frigyesi has put her finger on issues of vital importance. Bartók's idea of a natural "Weltanschauung" that has not been corrupted by urban civilization is undoubtedly part of a Romantic legacy. What may be problematic in the author's line of argument is a consequence of a somewhat loose terminology. "Romanticism" and "Modernism" are used without paying attention to the continuing debates over their definition. Once again, there may be a self-contradiction. On the one hand, the author remarks that "it is always difficult and sometimes foolhardy to reconstruct the purpose of an artist" (2), on the other hand, she is reluctant to examine the relations between the composer's declarations and the impact of his music. In view of the predominance of the organicist view of art since the later eighteenth century, it is not easy to accept the claim that "the revival of the organicist theory means less the continuation of prevailing concepts of art than a break with them" (90). In so far as Bartók regarded peasant culture as organic, his position was in perfect harmony with the legacy of Romanticism. Webern admitted that his organicist conception, the idea that there was no sharp distinction between products of nature and those of art, was inspired by Goethe's morphological worldview.[1]

The author's thesis that Modernism subscribed to an organicist aesthetics has been questioned by John Neubauer,[2] a cultural historian whose earlier works stress the problematic ideological implications of the biologistic approach to art and history.[3] The book widely regarded as the most thorough historical study of the subject, Lotte Thaler's *Organische Form in der Musiktheorie des 19. und beginnenden 20. Jahrhunderts* (München – Salzburg: Katzbichler, 1984), traces the organicist music theory from Adolf Bernhard Marx through Hugo Riemann to Heinrich Schenker and Hans Mersmann. This continuity was not broken before the rise of the avant-garde. Marinetti's insistence on the beauty of the machine made its influence felt throughout Europe, including Hungary. In 1915 Lajos Kassák started his first Activist journal, *A Tett.* By consensus his free-verse text *Craftsmen* (1915) is regarded as bringing a paradigm shift in Hungarian literature. His movement meant a serious challenge for *Nyugat.* One of the fundamental differences between the aesthetics represented by the leading contributors of the two periodicals was that the first group accepted the ideal of organic form whereas the second rejected it.

Except for some passing references, nowhere does Frigyesi's book deal with the Hungarian avant-garde. This may be a serious weakness. While with the exceptions of Kosztolányi and his cousin, Géza Csáth, the most original writers associated with *Nyugat* never wrote about Bartók and neither the poet Ady nor the philosopher Lukács expressed any interest in modern music, the composer found some of his strongest supporters in Kassák's circle. What may be even more important is that the representatives of this avant-garde movement tended to view Bartók's music as a manifestation of their aesthetics. It would be interesting to know the reasons for this. The question could be asked whether the spokesmen of the avant-garde associated internal repetitions with the inorganic, in the same way as Furtwängler, a late Romantic representative of the tradition surveyed by Lotte Thaler – who regarded the great artwork as a "living organism" or "organic development" (Werden)[4] – was inclined to associate Bartók's music with "construction" (das Konstruierte), on the basis of the composer's instruction on the exact duration of his pieces,[5] and perhaps also under the impact of what has been called "the motoristic drive" in the first movement of the *First Piano Concerto*,[6] a work that had its first performance with Furtwängler as conductor. Of course, it is quite possible that both the German conductor-composer's reservations about Bartók's music and the avant-garde admiration for it may be considered partial misinterpretations due to a failure to understand Bartók's rubato performance.

How can we define the relations between Modernism and the avant-garde? This question leads to issues that need a different competence from that of the analyst of musical compositions. Judit Frigyesi insists that Bartók's work has to be examined in the context of his age. This is a very important thesis, but my impression is that the early twentieth century was a more complex period than suggested in this book.

In some respects, the panoramic character of the investigation is combined with remarkable subtlety of perception. The author avoids a serious pitfall by translating "faj" as "ethnicity" and not as "race," and she is no doubt right in arguing that Bartók's interest in folk music was inseparable from his desire "to arrive at a higher level of simplicity": "Simplicity was both at the beginning and at the end of the road in the development of artistic expression" (98–99). No less convincing are the parallels between the composer's interest in peasant culture and the inspiration drawn from peasant architecture by secessionist artists or between the forgeries of Kálmán Thaly and Ady's imitations of songs sung by poor fugitives in the late seventeenth and early eighteenth century. Problems start when the value-judgement implicit in such a phrase as "the sickness and corrupt selfishness of Hungarian society" (168) is not supported by a thorough analysis.

The idea that the "road to modernization and democratization" (92) was the same may involve a tacit acknowledgment of the Marxist preconception that the superstructure is a reflection of the base. Sometimes Marxist clichés occur in the characterization of Hungarian society and literary works are given a rather simplistic treatment. In one case a psychologically motivated detail is taken out of context. In another a bitterly grotesque parody of the 1848 revolution is misinterpreted: "For Arany, the portrayal of Toldi would not have been complete without a scene of dancing and drinking – but in the *Gypsies of Nagyida*, another of his epic poems, he caricatured the *verbunkos* mania" (58–59). We have seen many cases of the literary misappropriation of musical works. It seems that a musicologist's readings of literary texts can be no less irrelevant.

Let us turn to an even thornier question. Throughout its long history Hungarian nationalism had many versions. It is absolutely justifiable to criticize Dezső Bánffy, whose government introduced chauvinistic measures between 1895 and 1898, but it is advisable to be careful with generalizations, even when speaking about such a class as the Hungarian aristocracy. We could mention, for instance, Miklós Bánffy, another member of the same Transylvanian family, who was appointed by the Hungarian prime minister to exercise control over the Budapest Opera House in the years 1912–1918. Tibor Tallián has collected the evidence suggesting that it was thanks to the support of this aristocrat and politician that *The Wooden Prince* was performed.[7] Some members of the old ruling class resisted chauvinism, and some versions of nationalism were not necessarily incompatible with Bartók's outlook. It is an exaggeration to maintain that "Bartók selected the folk-music sources of his Hungarian national music in such a manner that his folklorism could not be used to support the nationalism of the political establishment" (21). It is not quite easy to endorse the following declaration: "The claim that features of Hungarian peasant songs could be traced back before the conquest of Hungary challenged the traditional view of the conquest as the very moment of the nation's birth – the origin of everything truly Hungarian" (79). Some of the literary texts that Bartók had to read in secondary school tied national identity to pre-conquest times. In *A Short History of Hungarian Literature* (*A magyar irodalom kistükre*, 1896), a work that "served for almost half a century as a kind of secular Bible, a paragon of style and a measuring rod in secondary schools and especially for conservative instructors," the criteria of being Hungarian were "traced back to the nomadic ancestors of the steppe in the Volga region." Zsolt Beöthy, the author of the book, was a highly influential ideologue of the "gentry" class and an advocate of the organicist interpretation of culture.[8]

No cultural historian starts from scratch. In this book an astonishingly large number of sources is cited but sometimes the selection is arbitrary. Two books published in America on the intellectual life of early twentieth-century Budapest could have been consulted: *Literature and Cultural Change: Budapest, 1908–1918* by Mario Fenyo (Philadelphia: The American Philosophical Society, 1987), the only monograph on the journal *Nyugat* available in English, and *Béla Balázs: The Man and the Artist* (Berkeley, CA: University of California Press, 1987), a 550-page-long biography by Joseph Zsuffa. Among the Hungarian sources that could have inspired the author to develop a more nuanced interpretation, the special issue of *Huszadik Század*, entitled "The Jewish Question in Hungary" (1917) deserves mention, together with those works on Lukács which do not neglect the philosopher's texts written in German. As is well-known, in his later years Lukács became a Marxist philosopher. His inclination to social prophecy cannot be ignored when reading his early works. "The weaknesses of the later work are already present from the beginning," as Paul de Man observed. "The roots of Lukács's later dogmatic commitment to Realism are certainly to be found" in the works written in the first two decades of the twentieth century.[9] If this interpretation is correct – and much evidence could be cited to prove the young philosopher's conservative taste – it may be questionable to associate Lukács with artistic Modernism.

From a Postcommunist perspective some of the sources cited in this book seem dated. This makes some interpretations vulnerable, especially in the case of second-hand references. Zoltán Horváth's book on turn-of-the-century Hungary was published in 1961, a few years after the revolution of 1956 was crushed. Although it still has some validity, its fairly dogmatic Marxist approach – characterized by such clichés as "Horthy Fascism," "a half-feudal society," and "a never completely finished bourgeois revolution" – has been long surpassed. Judit Frigyesi calls him a "historian," in contrast to the author of the "Afterword" to the second edition, who tried to warn the reader by calling him "a publicist rather than a scholar."[10] To derive second-hand information from this work implies that one accepts the preconceptions of its author. In a similar way, it may lead to distortions if, in order to characterize Ady's poetry one makes use of a book published in 1949, the darkest phase of Communism, written by József Révai, the cultural dictator of the period.

In any case, some of the generalizations in this book are in conflict with the results of recent scholarship. Krúdy, Ady, Móricz, Babits, and Kosztolányi insisted so much on their close ties with their literal and spiritual ancestors that it is one-sided to assert that "all members of this generation found themselves opposing the ideas they had inherited from their parents" (2). Furthermore, some literary works are described in contradiction with cultural and literary history. Three nineteenth-century authors: Vörösmarty, Széchenyi, and Madách are compared in one sentence: "His dark images were preceded by Széchenyi's vision of the country as a barren and deserted fallow land, and this topic was explored in Imre Madách's *Tragedy of Man*" (67). Since the lyrical drama last named has no more than one hardly perceptible allusion to Hungary, and this reference is to the fifteenth-century warrior János Hunyadi, it is difficult to understand the statement. In a later chapter *The Tragedy* is given a fanciful interpretation. The hero's decision not to commit suicide is explained in the following way: "He chooses to live, not out of fear of death and not even simply because of his love for life but because he understands that spirit is not possible without life" (189). Readers familiar with the text will know that Adam's desire is to make the history of mankind impossible. When Eve tells him that she is pregnant, he falls on his knees, acknowledging God's victory: "Lord, you have conquered."

One of the reasons why it is difficult to make interarts comparisons is the lack of a common terminology. The reader of this book will be uncertain whether "symbol" is a synonym for "representation" or "expression" (266), or – if the answer is "no" – how these concepts may be related. Of course, such problems of terminology also apply to many other scholarly studies. Musicologists have a language of their own for structural analysis, but when they attempt a semantic interpretation they often borrow terms from literary criticism. The rather loose use of such words and expressions as "lyricism," "dramatizing" (244), "musical metaphor" (253), or "musical symbol" (260) may be open to question. In general, "metaphor" and "symbol" are used too often and somewhat vaguely. "Love thus becomes the metaphor for life" (217). Shortly after this statement there is the subtitle "Woman as the Metaphor for Life" (218), and later the following sweeping generalization is made: "in Hungarian modernist literature the act of 'seeing' is a metaphor for love" (261). At the start of the splendid analysis of *Duke Bluebeard's Castle* one finds the following sentence: "Night is the symbol of coldness and emotionlessness, and it is the symbol of fiery love. [...] Furthermore, night is the traditional symbol of womanliness [...], but also the symbol of the mystery of existence [...]. And finally, total darkness is the symbol of wholeness" (228–229). A literary historian would prefer to connect the libretto to *Csongor and Tünde*, a verse play by Vörösmarty, in which Night has a monologue. Both Balázs and Lukács admired this work and Weiner composed incidental music for it that was performed in 1915, three years before Bartók's opera.

When a term is undefined, in some cases it may be used too vaguely, whereas in other cases its field of relevance may be too restricted. This is true of the use of the term "romantic." When it is declared that "the underlying aim of the Viennese was essentially romantic: to attain the maximum potential of art in expressing truth" (39), the reader may wonder whether this statement is about a feature that is specific to Romanticism. On the other hand, the consequences of the Romantic philosophy of language are not considered, although they could support the claims for organicism. In sharp contradiction to Wilhelm von Humboldt's view of language as organism, it is asserted that already "at the middle of the nineteenth century, artists and critics of art proclaimed that 'the great mystery of being' was not expressible in the logical framework of language" (33). One of the distinguishing features of Romantic literature was the separation of logical structures from language, a separation that played a major role in the language-based cultural relativism of Kosztolányi, Bartók's only major Hungarian literary contemporary whose essays on language are significant.[11]

Western publications that contain texts in Hungarian are always marred by innumerable misprints. Judit Frigyesi must have taken great care to avoid this danger, and in this respect her book is a complete success. Considering the vast literary material covered, it is amazing how few inaccuracies occur. However, the information given about a photograph from 1930, showing the participants of a *Nyugat* evening (86), is not quite correct. Those familiar with Ady's work will know that *New Poems* (*Új versek*, 1906) was not the poet's first but third verse collection (322). Not much more important is to observe that the writer and translator Marcell Benedek is called Jewish (82), whereas Béla Balázs is characterized as "German on his mother's side" (48), although Benedek's father, Elek Benedek de Kisbacon (1859–1929), the author of short stories based on folk-tales mostly collected by himself, came from the Transylvanian nobility, and Balázs's mother was Jenny Levy. Somewhat more embarrassing is the hypothesis about Bartók's contacts with literary Modernism: "He consistently allied himself with the circles whose ideals came closest to those of the radicals before the war (that is, with the literary circles that formed around the journals *Nyugat* (West), *Szép Szó* (Beautiful word), and *Ma* (Today) and not with the mildly right-wing and somewhat racist 'village-movement'" (7). Of the three periodicals, one belongs to the pre-war period. The first issue of *Ma* was published in 1916, and *Szép Szó* (1936–9) was the organ of a later generation. As to the "village movement," some of its representatives (József Darvas, Ferenc Erdei) were Communists.

The last example suggests that Judit Frigyesi's familiarity with Hungarian literary scholarship is uneven. She is perfectly aware of the fundamental shortcomings of the poetry of Balázs, but her treatment of Ady's verse suggests that she does not speak the language of literary history. "The positive message of Ady's art, embracing the entire society, cannot be overestimated" (103–4), she writes. Her task is certainly very difficult, because the "literature on Ady in English is minimal," but her complaint that "he is far from being extensively studied by modern scholars in Hungary" (14) may be correct only if we add that more has been written on Ady than on any other Hungarian writer of the twentieth century.

History is inseparable from reinterpretation. Frigyesi is aware that Ady's poetry "lost something of its appeal for the following generations" (172), and "few in Hungary choose him for their favourite poet" (195). What she could have added is that Ady's works were distorted by the Communists, and this is one of the reasons why his reputation declined in recent years. Although it is quite possible that he will make a come back in the future, today the legacy of Babits and Kosztolányi seems more powerful. When Debussy set *Pelléas* to music, Maeterlinck was much more famous than the "musicien français." Although Ady may be a greater poet for Hungarians than Maeterlinck for the French-speaking audience, it would be pointless to deny that today Bartók's works internationally are far more admired than Ady's verse.

Frigyesi loves Ady's poetry and makes valuable observations about the poems she discusses. Her selection is subjective; it does not do justice to the complexity of the work as a whole. Readers unfamiliar with Hungarian literature will not realize the apparent contradiction between the harsh criticism directed against the poet's conservative contemporaries and the praise for the "foundational study of Ady's symbolism" written by the conservative scholar János Horváth (323). Ady made the following statements in *Új Idők*, a conservative weekly edited by Ferenc Herczeg, in 1908: "I have nothing in common with the so-called modern Hungarians, my alleged rebellion is not a rebellion. [...] I know nothing about the revolution which is attached to my name."[12]

One of the merits of the chapter on Ady in Frigyesi's book is the special emphasis laid on the devotional lyrics that were neglected in Communist Hungary. Unfortunately, no attention is paid to the poet's attraction to the Calvinist concept of predestination, the legacy of Protestantism in Hungarian literature, or the quotations in Ady's works from the late-sixteenth-century Hungarian translation of the Bible. Because of this, the claims that for Ady "God is an entirely secular concept" (183), and the "particular form of mysticism in Ady's poetry comes especially close to the spiritual thinking of East European Jews" (186) seem exaggerated.

Jews played a highly significant role in the intellectual life of Budapest in the early twentieth century and it is very fortunate that this book pays a special attention to their contribution to culture. *Nyugat* was sponsored by industrial magnates of Jewish origin. There is much truth in the statement that "Ady's most faithful supporters and closest friends were two Jews, Béla Reinitz and [...] Hatvany" (82), but the whole truth is more ambiguous. In the above-mentioned article Hatvany is ridiculed, and the sentence "I have nothing in common with those who have failed to learn the Hungarian language"[13] may contain a criticism of some assimilated Jews.

Sensitive issues cannot be discussed if we paint in black and white. "I have nothing to do with those who have read some German books in a cheap edition and now want to bring salvation to Hungarian literary art at that low price."[14] These words may suggest a kind of inferiority complex, but also dissatisfaction with the German culture of some Hungarian Jews. Because of the tensions inside the *Nyugat* circle and in Hungarian cultural life, "Költés és való" (Poetry and the Real), an article by Ignotus, published in 1926, can hardly be taken as a text that "represents the aesthetics of the movement in general" (90). Born in 1869, Ignotus was older than those who introduced innovations into Hungarian verse and prose; his taste was more conservative. In 1919 he left Hungary and by 1926 his position had become marginal. Shortly after his above-mentioned article was published, his name disappeared from the title page of the journal.

Bartók's place in Hungarian culture cannot be defined unless we deconstruct the idea of a monolithic Modernist movement. On 11 August 1913 Ignotus gave a lecture in the Society for Adult Education. The text appeared in *Nyugat* under the title "World Literature." A short quotation will give an idea of predictions made by its author: "The whole world is but one city – and nothing can change this. [...] one language will be raised to the language of world literature."[15] Whatever the legitimacy of this prophecy, it is a far cry from Bartók's ideal of the uncorrupted rural community, Ady's poem *I Return to My Village* (1907), or the following confession (already cited) made by Kosztolányi in 1913: "What interests me is the Hungarian country-side [...]. It is the land of miracles. Those who are born there will have a wider horizon than anybody brought up in a highly industrialized capital. [...] In a world where nothing happens and life is dominated by drinking wine, playing cards, sadness, and solitude, the soul will have an inner dimension, a strange compression and intensity of emotion. Provincial life is always of psychic character."[16]

Judit Frigyesi believes that there are links between Bartók's ideas and the philosophy of Lukács. I am not sure the evidence she provides is entirely satisfactory. The composer is not even mentioned in the vast collection *Ifjúkori művek (1902–1918)* (Budapest: Magvető, 1977). As far as the relations between *Nyugat* and the philosopher are concerned, although he published several essays in the journal, his interests were somewhat at odds with the aims of Ady, Babits, and others, whose effort was to go beyond German culture. In any case, it is not the whole truth that "Hungarian modern art was deeply rooted in the same philosophical tradition as the art of Schoenberg" (23). Strong as the impact of German culture had been throughout history, Hungarians did their best to liberate themselves from it from the early Middle Ages. Art Nouveau architects turned to Ruskin and the Pre-Raphaelites, painters to the French Impressionists, Ady to Baudelaire, Verlaine, and Rictus, Babits to William James and Bergson, Swinburne and Wilde, Krúdy to Turgenev, and Kassák to Whitman and Apollinaire for inspiration.

In 1910 *Nyugat* published a review of *Soul and Form* by Lukács. One may call it unjust but it clearly shows the fundamental difference between the positions of the most important creative talents associated with *Nyugat* on the one hand and the circle of Lukács on the other. "I have to admit that these ideas are entirely German," Babits wrote. "He is afraid of calling a spade a spade. We cannot overcome our aversion to this modern, affected German terminology [...]. This culture is typically German or rather Viennese."[17] Eight years later Kodály expressed similar views in his obituary of Debussy, published in *Nyugat*, and in 1921 Bartók emphasized the significance of the French composer's works in such terms: "when Kodály called my attention to the works of Debussy, I was astonished to see in his works the presence of pentatonic melodies that were comparable to our folk music."[18]

All in all, one has to admit that a reader familiar with Bartók's music but ignorant of Hungarian culture may find much information in this book that can help the understanding of the compositions. The shortcomings are related to the inconsistencies. The author is aware how "difficult it is to draw connections between poetry and music," (193) but she has less respect for the internal laws of literature than for those of music. The ambiguity of her attitude is quite apparent in her judgment on the text of Bartók's opera: "Balázs's neglect of the language reflects his belief in the superiority of the concept over verbal expression. […] the play became really functional as a libretto" (290–291). Once we admit that the play has an "oversimplified pseudo-folk style," it is hardly possible to assert that "the underlying thought is perfect and brilliant" (292). If the author believes that Ady's poems "resist translation" (177), yet she cannot resist the temptation she herself regards as dangerous, she cannot complain if her reader is not happy with her translations. A musicologist cannot be expected to write poetry, yet what is poetry in one language cannot be transformed into versions that are not poetry in another language. It is one thing to insist that Ady's poetry made a great impact on Bartók, another thing entirely to convince a reader ignorant of the Hungarian language of the high artistic quality of Ady's verse. Judit Frigyesi has succeeded in reaching the first goal, but failed to achieve the second objective.

Notes

[1] Anton von Webern, *Wege zur neuen Musik*. Wien: Universal Edition, 1960, 10.

[2] John Neubauer, "Overtones of Culture." *Comparative Literature*, Vol. 51, No. 3, 243–54.

[3] John Neubauer: "Morphological Poetics?" *Style* 22, 1988, 263–274; "Organic Form in Romantic Theory, The Case of Goethe's Morphology." Larry H. Peer, ed.: *Romanticism across the Disciplines*. Lanham: University Press of America, 1998, 207–230.

[4] Wilhelm Furtwängler, *Ton und Wort: Aufsätze und Vorträge 1918 bis 1954*. Wiesbaden: F. A. Brockhaus, 1966, 12, 186, 215; *Briefe*. Wiesbaden: F. A. Brockhaus, 1965, 214; *Aufzeichnungen 1924–1954*. Zürich: Atlantis, 1996, 77, 142; *Gespräche über Musik*. Siebte Auflage. Zürich: Atlantis, 1958, 40.

[5] Wilhelm Furtwängler, *Vermächtnis: Nachgelassene Schriften*. Dritte Auflage. Wiesbaden: F. A. Brockhaus, 1956, 38; *Aufzeichnungen*, 288.

[6] Halsey Stevens, *The Life and Music of Béla Bartók*. Revised edition. London-Oxford-New York: Oxford University Press, 1964, 233.

[7] Tibor Tallián, "A gróf szolgálatában: Bánffy Miklós az Opera élén (1912–1918)." *Protestáns Szemle* 55 (1993), 189–197.

[8] G. Béla Németh, *A magyar irodalomkritikai gondolkodás a pozitivizmus korában: A kiegyezéstől a századfordulóig*. Budapest: Akadémiai, 1981, esp. 201–204 and 379–380.

[9] Paul de Man, *Blindness and Insight: Essays in the Rhetoric of Contemporary Criticism*. 2nd ed., rev. Minneapolis: University of Minnesota Press, 1983, 52, 55.

[10] Péter Nagy, "Utószó." Zoltán Horváth, *Magyar századforduló: A második reformnemzedék története (1896–1914)*. Second edition. Budapest: Gondolat, 1974, 623.

[11] I have published several essays on the topic: "Organic Form and Linguistic Relativity." *Proceedings of the Xth Congress of the ICLA*. New York: Garland, 1985, Vol. III, 233–239; "Dezső Kosztolányi." George Stade, ed., *European Writers: The Twentieth Century*. Vol. 10. New York: Scribner, 1990, 1231–1249; "Kosztolányi nyelvszemlélete." Ernő Kulcsár Szabó – Mihály Szegedy-Maszák, eds., *Tanulmányok Kosztolányi Dezsőről*. Budapest: Anonymus, 1998, 259–271.

[12] Endre Ady, "A duk-duk affér." *Ady Endre publicisztikai írásai*. Budapest: Szépirodalmi, 1987, 656.

[13] Ady, "A duk-duk affér," 656.

[14] Ady, "A duk-duk affér," 656.

[15] Ignotus, "Világirodalom." *Nyugat* 1913, 275–276.

[16] Dezső Kosztolányi, *Írók, festők, tudósok: Tanulmányok magyar kortársakról*. Budapest: Szépirodalmi, 1958, Vol. II, 333–334.

[17] Mihály Babits, *Esszék, tanulmányok*. Budapest: Szépirodalmi, 1978. Vol. I, 158–159.

[18] Béla Bartók, *Írásai*, Vol. I. Budapest: Zeneműkiadó, 1989, 33.

The Literature of the Holocaust in Hungary

"Durch sein Gedicht stiftet der Dichter Gedächtnis."
(Hans-Georg Gadamer)

In a short article published in 1974 János Pilinszky, the greatest Hungarian poet of the decades following World War II, argued as follows: "What I find unique in Radnóti's life can be expressed only by the unfortunate expression 'situational congeniality'. In his case talent – which is responsible only for a few per cents of the achievement of a so-called creative man – was supplemented by a tragic situation that was not foreseeable from the perspective of the beginning of the poet's career. His early verse contained some surrealistic elements. The perfectly bucolic lyrics which followed were totally unexpected. He seemed to be destined to compose idylls in a Latin tradition about a paradise lost and regained."[1]

There are poetic exaggerations in this statement, but the problems raised are by no means negligible. The questions as to how Radnóti's life may affect the reception of his works and how the avant-garde and Neoclassicism are related in his poetry are crucial for any historian of literature.

1. The Impact of the Poet's Tragic Fate on the Perception of his Works

Although no reader of Radnóti's poetry can ignore the sad end of the poet's life, an awareness of his death may be also an obstacle to a proper understanding of his works. In *Hesitant Ode* (composed on 26 May 1943) the speaker seems to warn the reader not to devote too much attention to his personal destiny, "for I'm worth no more than the value of the word / in my poem." After Radnóti's achievement became sanctioned as a monument of anti-Fascist literature, literary historians came to realize the draw-

216

backs of such a canonization. As early as 1964 István Sőtér remarked in a lecture on Radnóti delivered in Paris that "not even the most moving tragedy can grant exceptional significance to a work,"[2] and some members of the next generation (Miklós Szabolcsi, Géza B. Németh, and others) made attempts to develop an immanent approach to the poems.

If we ask the question as to how Radnóti's output is viewed in Hungary today, we are confronted with several paradoxes. It is difficult not to see the discrepancy between works about Radnóti published in the West and in Hungary. On the one hand, in the last decades more translations of his verse and prose were published than of the works of any other Hungarian author; on the other, it would be almost impossible to name any middle-aged or young scholar working in Hungary who could be called a specialist of his poetry. Since his name was hardly mentioned by the participants of the conference on Hungarian lyrics between the two wars held in Pécs in 1991,[3] one may have the impression that by general consent Radnóti is not regarded as one of those few who revitalized Hungarian poetry in that period. In the last twenty years or so fewer and fewer undergraduates decided to write their thesis on his works at Eötvös University, and when I inquired at the other faculties of humanities, most of my colleagues spoke about a similar situation. While in the 1950s the poet-critic László Lator had to defend Radnóti against the charge of pacifism made by István Király, in the 1990s the young generation seems to have turned away from the works of the author of *Razglednici*. Neither the disciples of G. Béla Németh nor the youngest generation of critics have published any major essay on Radnóti. The interpretation of individual poems is lacking, the methods of structuralism or hermeneutics have not been applied to them, and no comprehensive appraisal of the historical position of Radnóti's verse was made in the last decades.

It would not be a far-fetched conclusion that there is to date no adequate book on Radnóti. The latest and by far the most serious scholarly monograph was published in New York in 1986. The almost 800-page-long volume by Emery George deserves the highest praise, but only as a highly meticulous analysis of the foreign sources of Radnóti's poetry, not as an interpretive and evaluative study of the original texts themselves.

It would be easy to continue the line of paradoxes. Most readers agree that Radnóti's best poems were written at the very end of his life during the months spent in a forced labour camp, when he had no hope that the lines jotted down by him would be read by anyone. Contrary to the expectations one might have, the tone of several late poems is idyllic rather than tragic. Because of this, it cannot be taken for granted that Radnóti's posthumous collection can be read as the voice of a collective fate. Even more difficult is to argue that the foreshadowing of the Holocaust can be glimpsed in his earlier volumes. While a canon of Holocaust literature has emerged as a result of several studies of the works treating the persecution of Jews during World War II, an attempt to interpret Radnóti's achievement as belonging to such an international canon might run the risk of excluding the majority of his poems.

To be sure, some of the usual objections against the concept of Holocaust literature are irrelevant for readers of the Hungarian author. "There is no such thing as a literature of the Holocaust, nor can there be. The very expression is a contradiction in terms. [...] A novel about Auschwitz is not a novel, or else it is not about Auschwitz."[4] This statement made by Elie Wiesel can apply only to post-Holocaust works which cannot claim the kind of authenticity of texts written by victims during the persecution. The diaries kept by those who suffered have a documentary value lacking in the memoirs called eyewitness or survivor accounts. Post-Holocaust literature may have a degree of illegitimacy, since there is a danger of pretense in the exploitation the pain of others. Only those texts may belong to the exceptions which have an unquestionably high aesthetic quality. In such cases it would be misleading to speak of an imaginative misappropriation of atrocity. The works of Celan or Pilinszky are obvious examples.

The poems composed by Radnóti in the forced labour camp are less original than *Todesfuge* or *Apocrypha*, but they have an additional documentary value: they represent an unexpected legacy to us from the dead. This aspect of his works gives them a significance supplementing and possibly even surpassing their contribution to Hungarian literature.

Speaking about the literature of the Holocaust, several distinctions can be made. First of all, some texts were written in Hebrew or Yiddish, others in some languages used by assimilated Jews. A third type is represented by Celan. He used the language of Hölderlin, Nietzsche, and Heidegger – whose works had made a decisive impact on his idiom –, thus proving that the German language was not irreparably polluted under Hitler, but occasionally he mingled German with Hebrew and/or Yiddish, as in such pieces published in the volume *Die Niemandsrose* (1963) as *Die Schleuse* or *Benedicta*.

Radnóti did not possess a poetic idiom comparable to Celan's. Another difference between their works is that while the Hungarian poet put a heavy emphasis on Classical prosody, his German successor relied on the long tradition of Jewish lamentation. The artistic goals and the conceptions of

218

language of the two poets were poles apart. Radnóti set himself the task of glorifying language by reworking traditional forms, Classical prosody, and such genres as eclogue, verse epistle, or hymn, whereas Celan's ambition was to deconstruct and even eliminate language and traditional forms of structural organization. The Hungarian poet's desire was to purify diction violated by some; his German colleague viewed accepted usage as a veil that had to be torn apart in order to get at the things (or Nothingness) behind it. For the former expression meant the recreation of the past, for the latter the undermining of rhetoric. These two possibilities also preoccupied other writers and were defined by Samuel Beckett in a letter written in 1937. The first he called "eine Apotheose des Wortes." The characterization of the second is from the passage previously cited: "Grammatik und Stil. Mir scheinen sie ebenso hinfällig geworden zu sein wie ein Biedermeier Badeanzug oder die Unerschüttichkeit eines Gentlemans. Eine Larve. Hoffentlich kommt die Zeit, sie ist ja Gott sei Dank in gewissen Kreisen schon da, wo die Sprache da am besten gebraucht wird, wo sie am tüchtigsten missbraucht wird. Da wir sie so mit einem Male nicht ausschalten können, wollen wir wenigstens nicht versäumen, was zu ihrem Verruf beitragen mag. Ein Loch nach dem andern in ihr zu bohren, bis das Dahinterkauernde, sei etwas oder nichts, durchzusickern anfängt – ich kann mir für den heutigen Schriftsteller kein höheres Ziel vorstellen."[5]

This description is of a later paradigm in the history of poetic diction than the one Radnóti represented. Post-Holocaust literature at its best is related to a poetics of silence. The following untitled poem from *Atemwende* (1967) clearly shows how an allusive treatment of the Holocaust may go together with a cult of the unspoken:

"STEHEN, im Schatten
des Wundenmals in der Luft.

Für-niemand-und-nichts-Stehn.
Unerkannt,
für dich
allein.

Mit allem, was darin Raum hat,
auch ohne
Sprache."

Radnóti seems to have been the only important poet of the Holocaust to distance himself from the traditions of Jewish culture. Yitzhak Katznelson used hexameters in his *Song of the Slaughtered Jewish People*, but his long poem was compozed in Yiddish. While in most Post-Holocaust works there is a profound dissatisfaction with either non-Jewish culture or poetry, both are absent from Radnóti's works. He never cut himself off from the Latin authors he studied at school, but relied upon them even after his tragedy had liberated him from the modish eclecticism to which several members of his generation were attracted.

The growing awareness of the threatening impact of the Third Reich made its influence felt in at least two ways in Hungary. Writers and artists looked for accepted forms of expression with the intention of trying to reach a wide audience. At the same time, they wanted to rely on well-established traditions which individuals could find helpful in the defense of their personalities. Both tendencies contributed to the rise of Neo-classicism. Along with Radnóti, Zoltán Nadányi, Jenő Dsida, Sándor Weöres, and Zoltán Jékely are generally regarded as the main representatives of this trend in the 1930s.[6] The Populists also turned to the past, but they drew inspiration mainly from the "Lebensbilder" of Petőfi, whereas Radnóti studied the Romantic recreation of Latin idylls and found a justification for his eclectic approach to culture in Biedermeier art, the topic of several books published by Béla Zolnai, one of the professors whose lectures the poet attended at the Ferenc József University in the early 1930s.

The poems of Radnóti's formative years are generally considered to be mediocre. One of the perceptive critics of the older generation described his response to them in the following way: "What I saw in them was studied unease, [...] a mannered approach. I was made nervous by [...] the constant idyllic pose, the loud smacking kisses and even more so the acting [...]. Who could have thought that it was posssible to arrive from this stage at greatness in poetry?"[7] Radnóti himself was aware of his limitations. As late as 1939 he made his fictitious "Doppelgänger" Jean Citadin emphasize the gap between his ideals and practice: "No, I am not a poet yet [...]. I am still very much preoccupied with language; it rolls obstacles in my way; it is ill-disposed and stubborn. You can still feel that the poem was written by someone. It is still too much of a performance by a conjuror. I do not like shows. A poem is supposed to express feelings like a whistle or cry, or a hiccup after drinking wine. You are not supposed to be aware that it is constructed of some material. Are you aware of stone in Strassbourg cathedral?"[8]

2. From Eclecticism to Maturity

Pagan Salute (1930), despite of the qualifications formulated by some critics, is not an insignificant collection – whether we focus on the Surrealistic images, the references to Biblical prophecy, or the collective voice. Sometimes the pastoral mood, combined with a neoprimitive modality somewhat reminiscent of Francis Jammes, whose verse Radnóti translated, is in conflict with the interpretation of the story of Cain, full of autobiographical implications, but the overall impression is one of variety. Contrary to a wide-spread opinion, the weaknesses of the young poet's eclecticism were less apparent in his first volume than in its immediate successors. Both the tone of pastoral elegy and the Biblical allusions were continued without much improvement in *Song of Modern Shepherds* (1931). Occasionally social criticism made itself felt, thus anticipating the dominance of working-class ideology over poetry which became so conspicuous in *Convalescent Wind* (1933), published by the Szeged Youth Arts College. As for the political verse not included in this collection, George Gömöri called it "embarrasingly poor."[9] Whatever the intrinsic value of Brecht's ballads or chronicles, their influence on Radnóti's verse proved to be detrimental. Both the sequence *Male Diary*, incorporating newsclippings, and the *Song of the Black Man Who Went to Town* are mediocre. It is quite understandable that Babits used *Convalescent Wind* as an example in his attack on the revival of populism.[10]

Radnóti's interest in oral literature was one of the results of his close friendship with Gyula Ortutay, a left-wing folklorist who was a member of the illegal Communist party. Politics went together with a cult of non-European culture. Although the poet had no direct access to the folklore of black Africa, his reading of anthologies by Blaise Cendrars and Yvan Goll was undoubtedly related to the avant-garde cult of "primitive" art. In fact it was Kassák who drew Radnóti's attention to the activity of the two poets. The French translations of African songs were reshaped by the Hungarian poet; they were subjected to yet another stage of textual processing. Some of these adaptations were included in *New Moon* (1935), but their significance was historical rather than aesthetic. It would be difficult to find any great poem in Radnóti's fourth collection of verse.

In view of the ideologically conservative patriotism of his late poetry, it is safe to assume that after a relatively brief association with Communists he wished to become assimilated to non-Jewish Hungarians. As is well-known, in 1934 he applied for legal change of name to Radnóti and in 1943 he and his wife were baptized in Roman Catholic faith by Sándor Sík, one of his former professors, a Roman Catholic priest and poet of Jewish origin. These were symbolic gestures. The impact of Jewish visionary tradition was marginal on his work; that may have been the reason why no piece by him was included in what is probably the most comprehensive collection of Jewish poetry edited by Jerome Rotherberg, a vast anthology including texts by such avant-garde authors as Gertrude Stein, Max Jacob, Yvan Goll, Tristan Tzara, and Edmond Jabes.[11]

Having renounced Judaism, Radnóti turned to the cultural legacy of his country, Classical antiquity, and Christianity. His growing attachment to the Hungarian past can be seen in *While Writing* (17 March 1937), a poetic "hommage à Kazinczy," the organizer of Hungarian literary life and language reform in the early 19th century, in the essays, in the great joy he felt when Northern Transylvania was returned to Hungary,[12] and even in his dismissal of the readaptation of a 19th-century Transylvanian novel by Zsigmond Móricz. The past is to be preserved, and the most severe criticism is justifiable if someone tries to violate it by reinterpreting it from the perspective of the present. "He should be punished, his work has to be confiscated and banned," Radnóti wrote about Móricz in his diary on 4 January 1941.[13] In sharp conrast to the Expressionist Benn, who made a clear-cut distinction between culture and art, he viewed the former as an indispensable precondition of the latter. The late poem *Root* (8 August 1944) suggests that the creative process is incompatible with being uprooted. The speaker is an artist who is indifferent to the affairs of the world. For him culture is comparable to the root nourishing a plant from below; "there, I am building the poem," he says.

"Wozu Dichter in dürftiger Zeit?" The question asked in the seventh stanza of *Brot und Wein* made both Radnóti and Celan reassess the function of poetry. The Hungarian poet translated and his German colleague often cited Hölderlin. While the author of *"Wie wenn am Feiertage..."* seemed to suggest a critique of the highest traditional values of the Western world by emphasizing the ambivalence in the relationship between the Classical and Christian worlds, Celan reached a more radical conclusion. *Zürich, zum Storchen*, an imaginary dialogue with Nelly Sachs, is a violent attack on God:

"Vom Zuviel war die Rede, vom
Zuwenig. Von Du
und Aber-Du, von
der Trübung durch Helles, von
Jüdischem, von
deinem Gott."

The rage against the Creator is replaced by the interpretation of God as unnameable and unidentifiable in *Psalm*:

"Niemand knetet uns wieder aus Erde und Lehm,
niemand bespricht unsern Staub.
Niemand.

Gelobt seist du, Niemand."

This is a far cry from Radnóti's growing attachment to a Christian God. The survivor turned against religion, whereas the victim found relief in it. This paradox is the key to the understanding of the peculiar place of Radnóti's verse in the canon of Holocaust literature.

The first signs of a stylistic development can be seen in *Keep Walking, Condemned to Death* (1936). It is perfectly understandable that Radnóti was awarded the Baumgarten prize for his fifth volume by Babits, who was the most severe critic of his earlier work. This collection is marked by images of winter and death, as well as by an interesting discrepancy. While there is a growing emphasis on the preservation of poetic conventions, some of the imagery is highly innovative. The short lyric *Praise* (1936), consisting of two four-line stanzas, can serve as a characteristic example of this ambiguity. The title refers to songs contained in the official song-books of the Hungarian Reformed Church, but the closure is in conflict with the archaic style:

"Ha meghalsz, meghalok; porainkból
egyszerre sodor majd forgó tornyot a szél."

The verbal economy is new in Radnóti's verse and is dependent upon the grammar of a non-Indoeuropean language. Accordingly, the degree of translatability is very low. The first three words allow for two interpretations. "If you die, I shall die" and "If you and I perish." No less com-

223

pressed is the meaning of the next sentence: "our ashes are suddenly, simultaneously and violently transformed – literally 'twisted' – into a tower
or spire that is turned around by the wind."

Experimentation with imagery and intertextuality was continued in *Steep
Road* (1936). If the original poems are read side by side with the English
version, it is difficult not to observe that not all the complexity is preserved
in translation. Here is the crucial passage of the *First Eclogue* (1938) as
rendered by Emery George:

> "Still, I write, and I live in the midst of mad-dog world, as
> lives that oak: it knows they'll be cutting it down; that white cross
> on it signals: tomorrow the tree men will buzz-saw the region,
> waits for that fate; in the meantime it sprouts its new leaves regardless."

In some cases the English text is somewhat mannered: for the adjective
"kerge" – usually associated with "sheep" – the compound "mad-dog" is sub-
stituted. On other occasions the grammatic value of the English word is too
weak: the strength of the verb "fehérlik" is absent from the adjective "white".

However impressive Radnóti's last volume, in which the language of
the seeker gets a deeper significance, the continuity of his style is more
than apparent. Metonymy and simile are still frequently used. In *New Moon*
the first poem starts with a comparison and the second ends with one, and
Clouded Sky has a piece entitled *Similes*. Between 1933 and 1941 the poet
relied systematically upon such explicit metaphors. Gottfried Benn insisted
that the use of the word "as" is incompatible with modern poetry, for it is
"immer ein Einbruch des Erzählerischen, Feuilletonischen [...], ein
Nachlassen der sprachlichen Spannung, eine Schwäche der schöpferischen
Transformation."[14] In this sense Radnóti cannot be called a modern poet.
It is more accurate to regard him as one of the representatives of the Neoclassicism predominant in the interwar period.

In his voluminous monograph Emery George maintained that Radnóti's
work as translator was so closely related to his own verse writing that in
some cases the distinction became blurred. This was a logical consequence
of the poet's firm belief that poetry was an intertextual and perhaps even
interlingual activity. Accordingly, some of his best work can be seen in his
"Nachdichtungen." This is by no means exceptional in twentieth-century
poetry, as the achievement of such poets as Ezra Pound or Sándor Weöres
may testify. Miklós Szabolcsi has discovered allusions to poems by Petőfi,

Verhaeren, Ady, Kosztolányi, and Attila József in *Restless Turning of Fall* (10 October 1941), and traces of Tibullus, Vergil, Hölderlin, Babits, and Kosztolányi in *End-of-October Hexameters* (between 28 September and 14 November 1942).[15] *Only Skin and Bones and Pain*, (August – September 1941), the poem on the death of Babits, starts with the first word of the *Funeral Oration* composed around 1200 and continues with an explicit reference to *Supplication to Saint Blaise*, a poem on death by Babits himself. In *A la recherche...* (17 August 1944) the Proustian title is coupled with an "Auftakt" reminding the reader of the beginning of *The Flight of Zalán*, a long epic poem by Vörösmarty. The first stanza continues to imitate the Romantic work, so that the 19th-century text seems to be concealed behind Radnóti's work. The similarity of the metre may remind the reader of a palimpsest, and the speaker is making a point of remembering the epic about the Hungarians' conquest of the Carpathian basin in a forced labour camp in Serbia. Indirect generic or prosodic forms of intertextuality are no less obvious in Radnóti's poetry: *In a Restless Hour* (1939) is an Alcaic ode, and the versification of *Forced March* (15 September 1944), one of the poet's last and best poems, is heavily indebted to the form of Walther von der Vogelweide's elegy *Oweh, war sint verschwunden*.

The original meaning of the generic term eclogue has a deeper significance; it is related to Radnóti's idea that poetry is "selection" from existing texts rather than the creation of something entirely new. This conviction is in harmony with the poetics of Neoclassicism represented by the later Babits, author of *The Book of Jonah*, who viewed poetry as recreation. It is an open question whether the eclogues, these utterances of self-encounter and self-reflexivity, represent Radnóti's finest work. More innovative seem to be those short lyrics in which the tradition of German Romanticism and Expressionism is continued. In any case, they belong to a tradition represented by the late Kosztolányi, Attila József, and Pilinszky. *The Ragged Robin Opens* (26 August 1943), *Dream Landscape* (between 27 October 1943 and 16 May 1944), *May Picnic* (10 May 1944), and *Root* (9 August 1944) are characteristic examples of this generic type.

3. The Translatability of Radnóti's Poetry

"Is it possible to translate Radnóti's poetry? In my view Sylvia Plath could have been fit for the task."[16] Why did Pilinszky believe that the author of *Ariel* could have been an ideal interpreter of *Clouded Sky*? The only possible answer to this question is that except for Pilinszky, the American woman poet may have been the most imaginative non-Jewish artist to identify herself with the victims of the Holocaust. At least two pieces from her posthumous collection could be mentioned in this context. The following lines are from *Lady Lazarus*, a poem about suicide:

> "A sort of walking miracle, my skin
> Bright as a Nazi lampshade,
> My right foot
>
> A paperweight,
> My face a featureless, fine
> Jew linen."

The other poem, entitled *Daddy,* is addressed to a dead father who was German. The awareness of this ethnic origin gives a special emphasis to the speaker's assumed identity:

> "An engine, an engine
> Chuffing me off like a Jew.
> A Jew to Dachau, Auschwitz, Belsen.
> I began to talk like a Jew.
> I think I may well be a Jew."

How far have the translators succeeded in rendering what Pilinszky thought only Sylvia Plath could have recreated in the true sense? Understandably Emery George, who has translated and analysed all the texts of Radnóti, paid special attention to the intertextual aspects of the Hungarian poet's output. Sometimes he even did justice to the visionary and grotesque imagery of the late pieces, as in the following two lines of *Columbus* (1 June 1943):

> "Wind turns the pages. He leaves it, has other thoughts,
> above him there purrs a wild, taut sky with giant claws."

The same translator emphasized the limitations of his work, for example he admitted that "in 'A la recherche...' the polysyllabic internal rhymes are all but untranslatable."[17] In other words, much of what is remarkable in the late verse is lost in translation. The very title of the posthumous volume seems to have been mistranslated. "Clouded Sky" or "Sky with Clouds" is literal, whereas the Hungarian phrase "Tajtékos ég" is metaphorical. The adjective derives from the noun "tajték" meaning "foam" or "froth." The verb "tajtékzik" stands for the state of mind of someone who is very angry. Thus, the secondary meanings of the original title are lost in both translations. The menacing connotations are quite obvious if we remember the last stanza of the title poem, composed on 8 June 1940:

> "A holdra tajték zúdul, az égen
> sötétzöld sávot von a méreg."

These two lines are rendered by Emery George as follows:

> "Clouds slide down on the moon; on the sky
> poison draws a dark green shape."

Clouds are not even mentioned in the original, and the English verb is much weaker than its Hungarian equivalent, which is suggestive of violence.

Emery George did his best to find the equivalents of Radnóti's verse forms. In some cases, however, some stylistic devices may have escaped him. He argued that in his translation of *I cannot know...* (17 January 1944) he succeeded in rendering the phonic correspondences of "ők felelnek […] éji felleg" in English by way of sound repetition.[18] In fact not two but four words are linked together by alliteration:

> "a fojtott szavunkra majdnem friss szóval ők felelnek.
> Nagy szárnyadat borítsd ránk virrasztó éji felleg."

Not only the four alliterations but also the archaic connotations of "felleg" are lost in the English version, and the opposition between the two adjectives is weakened. All in all, the formal closure is hardly perceptible in the English version:

> "and they will answer our checked words in phrasing clear and loud.
> Spread over us your great wing, vigil nocturnal cloud."

Needless to say, it is easy for a native speaker of Hungarian to miss stylistic components in the English version of any piece of his own national literature. My last example is to show how translation may open a gap between the interpretations of the two texts. A highly original structure of an inner debate makes *Forced March* one of Radnóti's best poems. In the original the opening of the poem is a fragmented sentence:

"Bolond, ki földre rogyván fölkél és újra lépked,."

In English the first line reads as follows:

"The man who, having collapsed, rises, takes steps, is insane;."

This is less close to the Hungarian than Markus Bieler's German version:

"Narr, der, zu Boden sinkend, aufsteht sich neu entlangbringt."

The key-word is "insane." In Hungarian it is possible to have an adjectival predicate without using the copula, whereas in English no such ommission is acceptable. As a result, there is no way of making the violent contrast between the fragmented syntax of the first and the elaborate sentence structure of the second ten lines, so the reader of the English text cannot be made aware of the structural originality that gives an extra dimension to the antithesis between the surrealistic vision of a tragic form of existence in which death can be the only form of liberation and the deliberately artificial evocation of an idyllic return to man's archetypal unity with nature.

The first and last words are highly emphatic: "bolond" (crazy) is opposed to "fölkelek" (I will rise). This fundamental structural principle is respected by the German translator, who starts with "Narr" and ends with "ich stehe auf!" The fact that the English translator had to sacrifice this important correspondence makes me wonder whether it is easier to translate Radnóti's poetry into German than into English. The Classical metre is preserved by Emery George but the archaic verbal and adjectival forms in the opening and closing lines of the first part ("fölkél" and "honni") are absent from the English version. In the original these elements represent a stylistic domain which is in striking contradiction with the following images:

228

"[…] ott az otthonok
fölött régóta már csak a perzselt szél forog,
hanyattfeküdt a házfal, eltört a szilvafa,
és félelemtől bolyhos a honni éjszaka."

"[…] over the homes, that world,
long since nothing but singed winds have been known to whirl;
his house wall lies supine; your plum tree, broken clear,
and all the nights back home horripilate with fear."

The question is not how far the highly visual imagery is preserved in the translation. What is lacking is the stylistic tension betweeen archaism and innovation. Considering the fact that this tension may be the distinguishing feature of Radnóti's style, the loss cannot be called negligible.

Since Radnóti's works have a relevance beyond the boundaries of Hungarian literature, it is quite understandable that his works have been widely translated. The studies of his poetry published in the West are remarkable and should inspire Hungarian literary historians to reassess his achievement. Still, the interpretation of his verse depends largely on how the role it played in the evolution of Hungarian poetry is viewed. The reason for this is rather simple. Paradoxical as it may be, his artistic development was closely tied to his growing attachment to Hungarian culture. As one of the more recent interpreters of his work observed: "During his life he found himself in conflict with his ethnic origin, his education, and with several social forces including the working class. What he never found problematic was his sense of being Hungarian."[19]

Notes

[1] János Pilinszky, *Tanulmányok, esszék, cikkek.* Budapest: Századvég, 1993. Vol II, 265–266.

[2] István Sőtér, "Külföldieknek – Radnóti Miklósról," in *Gyűrűk.* Budapest: Szépirodalmi, 1980, 337.

[3] Lóránt Kabdebó and Ernő Kulcsár Szabó, ed., *"De nem felelnek, úgy felelnek": A magyar líra a húszas-harmincas évek fordulóján.* Pécs: Janus Pannonius Egyetemi Kiadó, 1992.

[4] Elie Wiesel, "For Some Measure of Humility," *Sh'ma* 5/100 (October 31, 1975), 314. Quoted in Alvin H. Rosenfeld, A Double Dying: Reflections on Holocaust Literature. Bloomington – Indianapolis: Indiana University Press, 1988, 14.

[5] Samuel Beckett, *Disjecta: Miscellaneous Writings and a Dramatic Fragment.* New York: Grove, 1984, 52.

[6] G. Béla Németh, "A halálhívás és az életremény vitája," in *Századelőről – századutóról: Irodalom- és művelődéstörténeti tanulmányok*. Budapest: Magvető, 1985, 383.

[7] Aladár Komlós, "Radnóti olvasása közben," in *Kritikus számadás*. Budapest: Szépirodalmi, 1977, 181.

[8] Miklós Radnóti, "Ikrek hava," in *Radnóti Miklós művei*. Budapest: Szépirodalmi, 1982, 520.

[9] George Gömöri, "Miklós Radnóti: The Complete Poetry," *World Literature Today* 55, no. 4 (Autumn 1981), 706.

[10] Mihály Babits, "Népiesség," in *Esszék, tanulmányok*. Budapest: Szépirodalmi, 1978. Vol. II, 382–384.

[11] Jerome Rotherberg, ed., *A Big Jewish Book: Poems and Other Visions of the Jews from Tribal Times to Present*. Garden City, NY: Anchor Press/Doubleday, 1978.

[12] Miklós Radnóti, *Napló*. Budapest: Magvető, 1989, 95.

[13] Miklós Radnóti, *Napló*, 1989, 129.

[14] Gottfried Benn, "Probleme der Lyrik," in *Gesammelte Werke*. München: Deutscher Taschenbuch Verlag, 1975, 1068.

[15] Miklós Szabolcsi, "Radnóti Miklós halálos tájai," in B. Csáky Edit, ed., *Radnóti tanulmányok*. Budapest: Magyar Irodalomtörténeti Társaság, 1985, 105–107.

[16] János Pilinszky, "Radnóti Miklós," in *Tanulmányok, esszék, cikkek*. Vol. II, 266.

[17] Emery George, *The Poetry of Miklós Radnóti: A Comparative Study*. New York: Karz-Cohl, 1986, 487.

[18] Emery George, *The Poetry of Miklós Radnóti*, 426.

[19] Tibor Melczer, Radnóti Miklós nemzeti klasszicizmusa," in *Radnóti tanulmányok*, 78.

The Rise and Fall of Bourgeois Literature in Hungary (1945–1949)

The origins of the literature of the Hungarian bourgeoisie can be traced back to the Freemasons of the late 18th century who tried to liberate themselves from the constraints of feudalism. Their initiative was continued by intellectuals of humble origin who could profit from the social mobility of the age of reforms that culminated in the 1848 revolution. Although the rise of bourgeois culture suffered setbacks in 1849 and at the end of World War I, such temporary declines were far less serious than the damage caused by the German occupation of 1944. At the end of that year chances for a continuity were so slim that it was an open question whether recovery was possible.

As is well-known, Hungary suffered serious military, material, civilian, and intellectual losses in World War II. Some 800–900 000 people were killed in the war and 40 per cent of the national wealth of 1938 was destroyed. About 450 000 Jews perished in the holocaust. Political and social changes were inseparable from a large-scale migration that affected approximately 450–550 000 people. 60–80 000 ethnic Hungarians fled to Hungary from the neighbouring countries, 170–180 000 ethnic Germans were forced to leave. Owing to a Czecho-Slovak-Hungarian exchange scheme, 90 000 ethnic Hungarians left Czecho-Slovakia for Hungary and 60 000 Slovaks left Hungary and settled in Slovakia. In 1949 the population of the country was 9 200 000. Of this number, 376 173 were born outside Hungary. Economic factors made it very difficult for the country to recover after the end of the war. In 1938 the per capita national income amounted to 120 US dollars, which was 60 per cent of the European average. World War II and its consequences led to a rapid decline, and the 1938 level was not reached until 1950.

In short, our period was marked by an increasingly backward economy and serious intellectual losses. The poets Miklós Radnóti and György Sárközi, the short-story writers Károly Pap and Andor Endre Gelléri, the essayists Antal Szerb and Gábor Halász died in forced labour camps. As many eminent writers were killed by the Communists in 1945. The philosophers Tibor Joó and József Révay and the short-story writer and critic István Örley were among them. Continuity was broken also by the arrival of a group of Communists from Moscow. The film critic and writer Béla Balázs, the philosopher György Lukács, the journalist Andor Gábor, and the critic József Révai belonged to a generation active since the early 20th century. Like the somewhat younger novelists Béla Illés and Sándor Gergely, they lived in the Soviet Union before and during the war. Largely ignorant of the conditions in Hungary, they made an immediate attempt to force the Soviet system on the country. What the American historian John Lukacs wrote about his namesake, recalling their meeting shortly after the philosopher's return to Budapest, may give some idea of the distance between a Communist leader who had spent long years in Moscow and the experience of someone who survived the holocaust and the siege of Budapest: 'His conversation, or what I remember of it, consisted mostly of tired *Kaffeehaus* witticisms with which he tried not only to lighten the customary Marxist platitudes but also to cover up the condition that he knew remarkably […] little of what Hungary had lived through and what Hungarians were thinking" (Lukacs 1990: 97–8).

In spite of the lack of material resources and the presence of the Soviet troops, the Muscovite Communists met with considerable resistance. The surviving representatives of the literature of the interwar period tried to restore the continuity broken by the German occupation which had started on 19 March 1944. In April 1945 the journal *Magyarok* was set up with the idea of preserving the tradition of *Nyugat*, the organ of the liberal bourgeoisie and the most important literary journal of the first half of the century. The next autumn *Válasz*, the periodical of the Populists, began appearing. Lajos Kassák (1887–967) also made an attempt to continue the activities of the literary and artistic avant-garde by publishing *Kortárs* (1947–48). In 1946 members of the younger generation, the poets Sándor Weöres (1913–89), János Pilinszky (1921–71), Ágnes Nemes Nagy (1922–91), and others also decided to start a monthly. By adopting the title of a collection of poems by Radnóti, published in 1935, *Újhold* openly referred to the tragic experience of the holocaust. The same year saw the publication of Radnóti's posthumous volume, containing the poems composed in a forced labour camp that are justly regarded as this poet's most significant contribution to Hungarian literature, texts which have an additional documentary value because they represent the unexpected legacy from the dead. Since my assessment of Radnóti's late works, together with a critique of their English translations, originally read at the University of Cambridge in December 1994, has been published with some other papers of the Radnóti Memorial Conference (Gömöri 1994: 3–12, Szegedy-Maszák 1996: 13–28, Ozsváth 1996: 29–44, K. Géfin 1996: 45–57), on this occasion I merely state that this posthumous publication served as a starting-point for Pilinszky, the most important Hungarian poet to emerge in the years following the end of World War II. *Trapeze and Parallel Bars* (1946) represented a new start: identifying himself with the fate of the victims of the holocaust, the young Catholic poet focused on a cosmic homelessness and created a language of great complexity in short and cryptic pieces. His influence was felt even in the work of Weöres, an outstanding poet of the previous generation, who in *The Colonnade of Teeth* (1947) published a series of one-line poems.

The movement represented by Pilinszky and others, sometimes characterized as a form of Central European 'catastrophism', was at odds with the propaganda literature written in the spirit dictated by the Muscovite Communists. Its first product was an anthology entitled *May Choir, 1945*, which contained poems by Tibor Méray, who is known in the West as the co-author of a book on the revolution of 1956. For György Lukács and József Révai, the chief architects of the culture controlled by the Hungarian Communist Party, the immediate purpose was to lay down the political grounds of the ideology of what Mátyás Rákosi was to call 'salami tactics'. The first step towards this goal was made by Révai, who in *Marxism and Populism*, a book published in Moscow in 1943, proposed a popular front.

There are two radically different interpretations of the years 1945–1949. Some argue that after the end of the war Hungary had a better chance for democracy than in previous times and the high hopes were lost only because of the Communist take-over. Others believe that the fate of the country was sealed from the beginning of 1945. It is difficult not to find the topic depressing and controversial. Some of the documents are still not accessible and may prove to have been lost. Popular beliefs notwithstanding, the post-war years cannot be called a closed chapter. Surprisingly little has been written on this period since 1989. There are some survivors with painful memories and the interpreter may hurt personal feelings.

As my field is limited to the sphere of literature, I cannot claim to make a general statement. All I can suggest is that the plan to have a full control over literature was made by a group of Communists in Moscow before the Soviet troops reached Hungarian territory.

In 1945 Révai and Lukács were given roles that suited them well. Révai's task was to take measures against 'the enemies of the people', while Lukács was expected to provide a theoretical framework for the campaign against bourgeois culture. One of the lessons the Hungarian Communists had learned after the failure of the 1919 Commune was that the one-party system could not be introduced without the support of some spokesmen of the rural population. In the 1930s Révai worked out an ideology of popular front. After his return to Hungary his chief objective became to strike a deal with some members of the bourgeoisie and some writers who claimed to represent the interests of the peasantry in the interwar period. There were underground Communists in both groups who were eager to help him. The others had to make a quick decision. Since we are talking about a period that calls for a drastic reinterpretation, it is still not easy to make generalizations.

In 1945 it was stated by the new political leaders of Hungary, the members of the coalition government that included Communists, that no one was immune from accountability for personal conduct. To avoid any misunderstanding, I wish to emphasize that it is not my intention to suggest that more people should have been punished. According to independent (Western) estimates over 250 000 persons were deported to forced labour camps in the Soviet Union after the end of the war, and between January 1945 and March 1948 there were almost 40 000 political prosecutions which resulted in over 20 000 people being sentenced (Hoensch 1988: 161, 178). All I am saying is that Hungarian intellectual life was badly manipulated from the very beginning, so that the chances for the development of a democratic system were very slim. Some urban intellectuals were tolerated although their totalitarian or opportunistic inclinations were apparent in the 1930s, and some Populists were accepted as representing a 'progressive', democratic movement, while the questionable elements in their ideology were ignored.

Révai decided to have the poet and prose writer Gyula Illyés (1902–83) as an ally. In March 1945 he compared Illyés to such progressive figures in history as Ferenc Rákóczi II, Lajos Kossuth, and Sándor Petőfi. Illyés responded by arguing at a meeting of the National Peasant Party that 'the Communists have gone much further in guaranteeing freedom for writers than we expected. We have to appreciate this' (Standeisky 1987: 29). It is far from easy to define the role played by Illyés in the period. On the one hand, he is still respected by many Hungarians, on the other hand, it is undeniable that his artistic and political reputation has declined since the 1980s. Older people maintain that he saved some intellectuals, in a literal or metaphorical sense, while the younger generations blame him for never opposing the political establishment. It is certainly true that he was awarded the Kossuth prize in 1948 and 1953, and never stopped publishing in the early 1950s, when almost all Hungarian writers of distinction lived in internal exile. It cannot be forgotten, however, that as a shrewd tactician he often outwitted the authorities. In 1950 he composed *One Sentence on Tyranny*, a poem that later became associated with the 1956 revolution.

In more general terms, there may be several open questions concerning the position of the Populists in intellectual history. The only book available on the subject was written in the West. While it is reliable in most respects, it fails to address the question of anti-Semitism. The following statement may be open to criticism: 'As for the Jewish question and the interpretation of anti-Semitism, the Populist writers were balanced, good-natured, and humane; they condemned the discriminative measures, the persecution and extermination of Jews, and they regarded anti-Semitism as useless and detrimental' (Borbándi 1983: 390).

At the present stage the only hypothesis I can formulate is that the leaders of the Hungarian Communists sometimes tolerated writers who had compromised themselves in the 1930s or during World War II. My example would be József Erdélyi (1896–1978), whose volume of poetry *Violet Leaf* (1922) may be regarded as representing a paradigm shift in Hungarian literature by heralding the Populist movement that was to play a decisive role in the political, social, and intellectual life of the interwar decades. Erdélyi was an unquestionably talented poet of half-Romanian origin whose ideology was strikingly similar to that of Octavian Goga and Lucian Blaga, or the young E.-M. Cioran and Mircea Eliade.

For an understanding of the anti-Semitic elements in the ideology of the Hungarian Populists, it is necessary to refer to an incident in 19th-century history. On 23 May 1882 an anti-Semitic member of the Hungarian parliament reported the disappearance of a peasant girl from Tisza-Eszlár, a vil-

235

lage in Eastern Hungary, just a week before the Jewish Passover (Istóczy 1904: 118–125). A ritual-murder allegation was made and another member of the Lower House, Győző Istóczy, who modeled his activities on those of Wilhelm Marr and made a speech in the Hungarian parliament on 25 June 1878 with the title 'Jews, the Iron Ring Around Our Necks', (Levy 1991: 100–3) appeared with a portrait of the alleged victim at an international anti-Semitic congress held in Dresden. The case resulted in a trial and the fifteen defendants were acquitted. The defence was represented by Károly Eötvös, a Liberal member of the parliament who was also well-known as a writer. His account *The Great Trial That Started a Thousand Years Ago and Is Still Not Over* (1904), published in three volumes, was widely considered a document about the triumph of Liberalism over superstition at the time when József Erdélyi composed a poem entitled *The Blood of Eszter Solymosi* (1937), suggesting that the verdict had to be reversed because the girl had been a victim of ritual murder. In post-war Hungary Erdélyi was brought to justice. After spending close to three years in prison, he could make a new start as a poet. His collection *A Return* (1954) contained poems written between 1945 and 1954.

My intention is not to find fault with Erdélyi or such other Populists as István Sinka, Péter Veres, or János Kodolányi, who expressed similar anti-Semitic views, but to suggest that such prominent Communists as Lukács or Révai were responsible for not only a large decrease in personal liberty in the years following 1945 but also for the survival of anti-Semitism.

Instead of passing a moral judgment on some Populists, it needs to be admitted that in their works anti-Semitism was not only closely tied but even subordinated to anti-capitalism. Historians are divided in their assessments of the role played by the industrial magnates who were largely responsible for the economic growth of Hungary around 1900. As in some other cases, the truth may be rather complex. On the one hand, Manfred Weiss, the owner of the factories of Csepel made a very important contribution to the rise of Budapest; on the other hand, his success was partly due to his significant involvement in the war industry in the years 1914–18.

Some Populist writers were uneducated and their anti-Semitism was largely emotional. The other side of the coin is that several Hungarian Communist leaders who had important functions in the years following 1945 came from families closely associated with capitalism. Because of their social background, they felt vulnerable to the criticism levelled at the capitalist exploitation of workers and agricultural labourers and tolerated

236

the anti-Semitism of some Populists. They may have been taken by surprise by the fact that the most sophisticated analysis of anti-Semitic feelings came from István Bibó, a political scientist associated with the Populists. His long essay *The Jewish Question in Hungary After 1944* was published in the Populist journal *Válasz*, in October and November 1948, shortly before he was silenced by the Communists.

It is almost certain that the reason the Populists were favoured by the Hungarian Communist Party was political. The first issue of *Újhold* came out in July 1946. Shortly afterwards, the Communist monthly *Forum* appeared, edited by György Vértes, György Lukács, and two intellectuals who were called fellow-travellers by some historians. The term is somewhat misleading, since both had joined the Communists in the 1930s and had been given the task of undermining other political parties. Officially the folklorist Gyula Ortutay was a member of the Smallholders' Party, while the prose writer József Darvas belonged to the National Peasant Party. The first issue of *Forum* contained an article by Lukács attacking *Újhold*. A few months later *Válasz* appeared almost simultaneously with an essay by Lukács in *Forum* that praised the Populists' journal edited by Illyés.

The discrimination was obvious. In his opening statement Illyés claimed that in politics the working-class was destined to lead, whereas in literature the peasantry would lead. This division of labour was tacitly accepted by Lukács. Of course, there is every reason to believe that the philosopher regarded the pact with some Populists as temporary. After twenty-five years spent abroad, Lukács badly needed followers. Among his first disciples were the philosopher József Szigeti and the literary critic István Király. Szigeti's attack on the bourgeois decadence and irrationalism of the poetry of Weöres, in his essay *Hungarian Lyrics in 1947*, published in the October issue of *Forum*, was followed by the banning of *Újhold*. Király was rumoured to have been affected by right-wing ideas, so his sudden conversion to Marxism may have been influenced by a desire to make people forget his earlier activity. In October 1946 he published a long article on László Németh, in which he downgraded this author's essays and insisted on the significance of his narrative fiction (Király 1976: 339–52). This text signaled the intention of the Communists to put a political pressure on the representatives of what they viewed as the most important intellectual movement of the interwar years. Németh was known to have a strongly anti-Communist ideology. Before the war he published a lucid analysis of Stalinism and insisted that Hungary was part of the Western world. At the same time, he had one important advantage over the urban intellectuals: he paid a serious attention to the other nations of Central Europe. Although what he called "the revolution of quality" was conceptually unclear, it implied a rejection not only of Western capitalism but also of Eastern Bolshevism. By defending Németh, Király set himself the task of manipulating him. Although in our period Németh refused to make concessions and his novel *Revulsion* (1947) is free of any Communist influence, other Populists proved to be less independent. They paid a heavy price for their survival: they became compromised in the eyes of the later generations.

It has to be added that social democrats and bourgeois radicals expressed discontent with the compromise between the Communist leaders and the Populists. Moreover, by 1947 even some Communists thought it was time to end the alliance with the spokesmen of the rural population. On 16 February Géza Losonczy – who after 1956 was executed with Imre Nagy – condemned the pessimism of Illyés in an article published in the daily of the Communist Party, and in June László (B.) Nagy – a young Communist born in 1927 who committed suicide in 1973 – harshly criticized the Populists and attacked Bibó as the architect of their reactionary ideology (Nagy 1947: 446–470).

By this time the goals of the campaign against bourgeois values were largely accomplished. After the publishing of a considerable number of articles and books attacking contemporary writers associated with these values, the next task was rewriting the past. A new canon had to be established and institutionalized. During their years spent in Moscow Lukács and Révai interpreted works on the basis of a dichotomy: progressive traditions were opposed to reactionary trends. Sándor Petőfi and Endre Ady were regarded as representing the main stream of Hungarian literature. After 1945 a third name was added, mainly because of an initiative taken by Márton Horváth. A drastic selection of the texts by these three poets was made with official interpretations attached to them. Later the most trustworthy literary historians were commissioned to write books on the three poets. The task of Pál Kardos (Pándi) was to develop Marxist interpretations of the poetry of Petőfi that could replace the highly influential book published in 1922 by János Horváth, who was to be forced to give up his position at the university together with other bourgeois scholars. István Király, the son of a Presbyterian priest, was asked to find an explanation for Ady's attachment to socialism and Calvinism, and Miklós Szabolcsi, a well-educated critic with a special interest in 20th-century French literature, was destined to discuss the poetry of Attila József, which had obvious links with the international and Hungarian avant-garde.

The consequences of this canon formation were far-reaching and sometimes damaging. At a conference celebrating the 175th anniversary of the birth of Petőfi, held at the beginning of April 1998, several participants spoke of a general lack of interest in the works of this 19th-century author, and in February 1998, at a colloquium devoted to the activity of Ady, most of the papers addressed the issue of the decline of this poet's reputation. As for József, in recent years documents concerning his conflict with the Communists were published, and the interpretation of his works had changed radically since the post-war years.

Some poems by Petőfi, Ady, and even József seem unreadable today. Teachers do not know how to handle them, and they are usually avoided by the authors of dissertations. By contrast, the young critics of the 1990s are avid readers of works by the authors who were dismissed by the Marxists in the late 1940s. In June 1998 a collection of essays, mainly by scholars in their twenties, appeared, testifying to the high reputation of Dezső Kosztolányi (1885–1936). In the years following 1945 this writer of the middle class was the main target of the Communists. In March 1947 Árpád Szabó – today emeritus professor of classical philology and a prominent member of the Presbyterian Church – published an essay in which he condemned Kosztolányi as a Fascist. 'I belong to that part of the Hungarian intelligentsia', he wrote, 'which needs Kosztolányi to be aware of what we wish to eliminate for the sake of the future' (Szabó 1947: 220). The essay appeared in *Valóság*, a monthly edited by Sándor Lukácsy, who later was at least partly responsible for the abolition of the Eötvös College, the equivalent of the École Normale Supérieure founded in 1895, and for making a long list of books that the Communists wished to destroy (Lukácsy 1985: 10–18).

Szabó's article was part of a large-scale campaign led by Lukács and Révai with the purpose of restructuring the canon of Hungarian literature. Lukács was consistent in the condemnation of certain representatives of the bourgeois tradition and expected his disciples to support him. In 1957, when he was afraid of a revival of the legacy that has been virtually eliminated in the late 1940s, he urged a former student of his to repeat the attack on Kosztolányi. The main thesis of the book entitled *The Disintegration of Ethical Norms* by Ágnes Heller (b. 1929) – currently professor of the New School for Social Research and a member of the Hungarian Academy – is but a variation on the line of argument followed by Szabó ten years earlier.

Both works are indebted to the articles Lukács published between 1939 and 1941 in *Új Hang*, the organ of the Hungarian Communists who lived in Moscow. In 1945 these pieces appeared in Budapest with a twenty-page-long preface, also written in Moscow in March 1945, with the aim of heralding a new era marked by 'the annihilation of the relics of feudalism, the creation of Hungarian democracy, and the defence of the independence of the Hungarian people' (Lukács 1945: 4). Since Lukács was convinced that greatness in literature could be achieved only by serving social progress, writers who did not seem to have an unqualified belief in progress were dismissed as inferior. Lajos Kassák, a free-verse writer and constructivist painter who in 1919 refused to subordinate his creative activity to the principles laid down by the Communist Party, was rejected for 'having obscured the real interests of the workers', and Kosztolányi was called 'a conscious and malicious reactionary' (Lukács 1945: 11).

On 20–21 May 1945 the Hungarian Communist Party held a conference. There were long and passionate debates over the tactics to be followed. On 31 May, Márton Horváth (1906–87), the editor of the Communist daily *Szabad Nép*, launched a campaign against bourgeois culture in a summary of the conclusions of the conference entitled *The Death Mask of Babits*. His main target was Sándor Márai (1900–89), who was widely regarded as the most celebrated representative of the bourgeois liberal tradition of Mihály Babits and Dezső Kosztolányi.

One of the most important books published in Hungary in 1945 was the diary Márai kept during the German occupation. This work was characterized as reactionary by Lukács in a lecture he gave in December 1945 under a title that is hardly translatable. 'The Hungarian middle class is so rotten that it still does not want and has no courage to face reality', Márai wrote in 1943 about those who believed in a German victory (Márai 1945: 149). After 19 March 1944 he lived in internal exile, and when the persecution of the Jews started, he identified himself with the victims. 'I cannot expect anyone to forgive me that I was alive, writing novels while (s)he was in a labour camp' (Márai 1945: 231). To my knowledge no one formulated a conclusion comparable to the following: 'Although we all suffered much, we are all guilty' (Márai 1945: 462).

Lukács made his unfavourable interpretation from the perspective of 'pártköltészet', a term denoting a strong political commitment defined in the following manner: 'to give a wide, profound, and all-embracing picture of the development of social life. To fight for the progress of mankind,

240

for a higher development by revealing the direction of such a progress, the driving forces behind it, and the interior and exterior powers that try to block it. The true and faithful reflection of social life is the main instrument that can be used to exert an influence on the people' (Lukács 1948: 119).

Since Márai was the most important writer forced to leave Hungary by the Communists, his case might help us understand their cultural policy. Born in Kassa (today Košice) in 1900, he came from the Saxon bourgeoisie of what was Upper Hungary until 1920. His original name was Grosschmid, but he adopted the name of one of his Hungarian ancestors at the very beginning of his career. His first book, a collection of verse, was published in 1918. Although he was a non-Communist, after the fall of the first Hungarian Commune of 1919, he left Hungary because he disapproved of the right-wing regime. In the Weimar Republic he became a respected journalist and published fiction, drama, and essays in German. In 1923 he married the daughter of a Jewish merchant. Having spent the years 1923–28 in Paris, where he was associated with the movements of the international avant-garde, he returned to Hungary. The motive behind this move was quite simple: he loved the Hungarian language and wished to continue the tradition of Dezső Kosztolányi and Gyula Krúdy, the outstanding prose writers of the early decades of the century.

In Search of Gods: The Novel of a Journey (1927), written at the end of the author's first period of exile, gave a shrewd analysis of the ethnic and religious conflicts in the Near East. As a publicist he wrote a series of articles from 1933 onwards attacking Hitler. His two-volume autobiography, *The Confessions of a Citoyen* (1934–5) was received by many as an imaginative characterization of the life style of the Hungarian liberal bourgeoisie. By the end of the 1930s he developed a high reputation as novelist, short-story writer, essayist, playwright, and poet. Because of his violent opposition to the Nazis, after 19 March 1944 he had to seek refuge in a village north of Budapest and could not return to the capital before the Soviet occupation.

Márai was described by Lukács in the above-mentioned lecture as representing 'vulgar bourgeois individualism' (Lukács 1948: 126), the opposite of a progressive writer who 'never stops singing of the great, national, humanistic mission of the party that plays a role in world history' (Lukács 1948: 128). As for world history, it was said to be dominated by such great individuals as Cromwell, Marat, Lenin, and Stalin, 'who could unite their individual strengths with the task given them by the party in a higher synthesis that is new, exemplary, and had the status of the Classics (Lukács 1948: 127).

In April 1947 the text of this long lecture was placed in a larger context in a book called *Literature and Democracy*. To promote Realism, the author asked for the introduction of tighter controls and outlined a program with the aim of 'destroying the reactionary thought of imperialism' (Lukács 1948: 7). In the introduction Lukács specified the following features of the culture that was to be rejected: 'aristocratism, the rejection of equality, a contempt for the masses, the underestimation of economic, political, and social motives, the cult of irrationalism and myth, an emphasis on the vanity of life, a distance from life, and a focus on the psyche' (Lukács 1948: 10). Assuming that after the 1848 revolutions the bourgeoisie ceased to be a progressive force in European history, Lukács argued that in the 20th century bourgeois writers could produce either so-called pure literature, dominated by the cult of the ivory tower, or works of kitsch. Both weaknesses were detected in the works of Márai. According to the deal struck with the Populists, great art was defined as inspired by peasant or working-class culture. In conclusion, Márai had no place in the literature of post-war Hungary.

In May 1947 the younger Communists started new journals. *Emberség* was edited by Imre Keszi, Tamás Aczél, and Tibor Méray, while one of the two editors of *Tovább* was Géza Losonczy. Supported by the daily *Szabad Nép* and the periodical *Forum*, they urged writers to follow the instructions of Zhdanov and the example of Fadeev, the main representative of Socialist Realism. Márai's comment on one of these journals was not published until 1993. He called *Tovább* 'a perfect copy of the Fascist *Egyedül vagyunk* in typography, setting, spirit, and tone', and gave the following characterization of the anti-Semitic articles that appeared in the Communist weekly: 'The photographs of Jewish bankers appear with a text entitled "We have worked for such people." This is what the Fascist newspaper did three years ago. The only difference is that in the past the attacks on Jewish capitalists were made by blackmailing Christian journalists, whereas now the authors of similar articles are blackmailing Jewish journalists' (Márai 1993: 209–10).

In the September-October issue of *Emberség* Imre Keszi asked for 'the art of the rising workers' and condemned 'the trends serving the taste of the old ruling classes' (Keszi 1947: 298). By that time Rákosi, whose desire was to be called 'the Wise Leader of the Hungarian Nation', could boast that he had 'sliced off like salami' most of the parties and factions other than his own. After the expulsion of those from the Smallholders' Party who spoke about Communist malpractices, the revelation of an alleged 'counter-revolutionary conspiracy' led to the arrest and deportation of Béla Kovács, Secretary of the Smallholders' Party, by the Soviet military police. A great flow of refugees began. After Ferenc Nagy, the Smallholder prime minister, Béla Varga, the Roman Catholic priest and speaker of Parliament, and Imre Kovács, one of the leaders of the National Peasant Party, had left, it was time for Social Democracy to be liquidated. In October 1947 *Kortárs* was started. Edited by Kassák, it was a last attempt to preserve the tradition of the socialist avant-garde. On 16 December Géza Losonczy dismissed Kassák's movement as representing 'anti-Realism' and the contributors to his periodical as the most consistent enemies of Marxist-Leninist aesthetics. At the same time, the first issue of *Csillag* appeared. Until 1956 this monthly would determine the ideological principles for Hungarian culture.

One of the functions of *Csillag* was to strengthen the links with Soviet culture. In this respect the activity of Béla Illés (1895–974), a Soviet major and editor of the Red Army's Hungarian journal *Új Szó*, has to be mentioned. In 1947 he published a story *The Gusev Affair* with the purpose of setting the tone for the centenary of the 1848 revolution. To play down the Russian invasion that quelled the Hungarian uprising, Illés decided to give publicity to the merits of a previously unknown lieutenant. Gusev was said to have revolted against the Tsar in support of the Hungarian revolution. A street in the centre of Pest was named after him, and an abridged version of the story was included in the textbooks published for primary schools. In recent years the street got back its original name, since Gusev proved to have been invented by Illés, an author whose works are entirely forgotten today.

In Communist historiography 1948 was called the 'year of the turning-point', which transformed the country into a people's democracy. On 12 February the Politburo of the Communist Party made a decision to establish ideological unity. In his speech *The Analysis of Literary Life in Hungarian Democracy*, published in the March issue of *Csillag*, Márton Horváth condemned writers as different as Kassák and Márai, Németh and Weöres, and associated even Illyés with 'anti-democratic' forces. On 7 March the leader of *Szabad Nép* was by Rákosi himself. He called for an improvement of the theoretical activity of the Communist Party. A Committee of

Cultural Policy was set up with the aim of defining the norms that artists and writers should respect. All cultural institutions were to be subordinated to the Committee that had four members, including its chairman Márton Horváth. Otto Klemperer, the artistic director of the Budapest Opera, was sacked on the grounds that he was an American citizen of German birth and conducted works by Wagner. Painters were commissioned to work for a project called 'The Portrait Gallery of the Heroes of Labour'.

The first draft of the declaration of the Hungarian Workers' Party was published in *Szabad Nép* on 9 May. At the first congress of the 'new' party, held in June, Lukács spoke of the liberation of creative activity from the pressure of capitalism, the end of reification and alienation, the triumph of Realism, and the supreme value of the Soviet experience. What followed was the darkest period in the history of Hungarian culture, dominated by an extreme form of censorship.

After the Hungarian Communist Party merged with the Social Democratic Party, several books were banned. One of these was the fifth volume of Márai's 'roman-fleuve' *The Work of the Garrens*, containing a visionary presentation of a 'Leader' addressing a public demonstration and the narrative of a meeting of the autobiographical hero Péter Garren with the famous writer Berten, who has been placed under house-arrest. Although these parts were based on Márai's article about Hitler's 1933 speech in the Berlin Sport Palace and on his interview with Gerhart Hauptmann, retrospectively it is possible to assume that the Communist authorities saw a general criticism of totalitarian systems in the book. The scene in which the 'Leader' succeeds in manipulating his audience is about fanatics who lose their personalities and are controlled by the 'centre', a small group which has power and is alienated from the community. The general import of the meeting of the two writers, the young Péter Garren and the old Berten is no less obvious. Berten's hypothesis is that only communities with discontinuous memory can be manipulated from above. In other words, despotism is made possible by the destruction of historical consciousness, the distortion of collective memory.

Other works by Hungarian writers had a similar fate in 1948. A volume of poetry entitled *A Dream*, by the Transylvanian-born Zoltán Jékely, was printed but not published. From 1949 many writers were silenced, including the avant-garde poet Kassák, the Roman Catholic Pilinszky, and the Populist Németh. In 1948 the Geistesgeschichte philosopher Lajos Prohászka was expelled from the university, and during the next two years a great number of scholars lost their positions at the universities or at the Hungarian Academy of Sciences.

To my knowledge Márai's diary and his memoirs *Land, ahoy!* (1972) represent the only account of the years 1945–48 that can claim credibility. Ironically, his diary was not made accessible in its entirety until the 1990s. István Csicsery-Rónay (b. 1917), a Smallholder, made a drastic selection when he published the diary covering the years 1945–57 in Washington in 1968. As he told me some years ago, he refused to include those passages in which Márai called the Populist writer Gyula Illyés an opportunist. Other parts were excluded because of the strong opinions the author had on sensitive issues. Here is one example, an entry from 1946: 'The problem with Jews is not that they failed to learn anything from suffering and misery. Who would have been different from them in this respect? The problem is that they have learned to continue Fascism in their own style' (Márai 1992: 131–2).

It is not easy to generalize about why so many writers renounced their past in the years following the end of World War II. Except for Márai, no one is known for having expressed strong reservations about the behaviour of the Soviet soldiers, and no other writer questioned the lawfulness of the expulsion of ethnic Germans. By 1948 he became increasingly isolated for two reasons: he was unwilling to paint in black and white and refused to accept any political function. He asked for a discrimination between Germans who had supported and those who had opposed Nazi Germany. 'It is hard to win and hard to be defeated. It is hard to be Russian and to be human', he wrote in the summer of 1945 (Márai 1968: 15), and later made the following observation about the Soviet soldiers he met: 'Their aim was to give up their personality […]. I as a Western man cannot accept this argument. Giving up my personality – this crazy ideal – would mean giving up my attachment to life' (Márai 1972: 78).

In a period when many of his colleagues modified their views under political pressure, Márai was consistent: throughout his life he approved of socialism but he never renounced his individual freedom. 'My experience is that writers lose as much of their artistic and moral integrity as they gain in political significance', he remarked in 1945 (Márai 1968: 17), and two years later he expressed his disgust when he witnessed manipulation and corruption: 'Elections. […] It is no solution to keep silent in the midst of idle talk. *Not to respond from the inside,* not to listen – that is the real task' (Márai 1993: 152). He regarded radical land reform as 'the greatest event in the life of the Hungarian people' (Márai 1968: 46) and held the whole nation responsible for the massacre of Jews but described the Soviet soldiers' idea of the bourgeois as ridiculous and felt contempt for those who enjoyed the executions. 'It is not enough to like what they like; they expect you to hate what they hate. There we drift apart' he declared about the Communists (Márai 1968: 57).

In the summer of 1947 Aragon and Elsa Triolet visited Budapest. In his public lecture Aragon attacked those who lived in an ivory tower and called Paul Valéry a Nazi sympathizer who admired Pétain and Salazar. Márai wrote about Aragon's visit with contempt. For him continuity was unbroken between the German and Soviet occupations. He refused to distinguish between class-hatred and racism. No one had the inclination or the courage to share this view. The first sign of his alienation from a country living in fear was that on the Day of Hungarian Books, in the summer of 1946, Ferenc Nagy, the Smallholder prime minister avoided him. 'I cannot side with the left,' he confessed one year later, 'because it would be moral suicide to leave my class. I can criticize it from the inside, but do not wish to be treacherous. Nor can I make a single step towards the right, because I am not willing to support the Fascism which may be hiding behind honest right-wing people' (Márai 1993: 147).

Although feudalism had been abolished in Hungary in 1848, the rise of bourgeois culture was aborted by Communism. This was the conclusion Márai reached in 1948, shortly before he left his country: 'In Hungary two types of man could play a full role: the aristocrat and the peasant. What stood between them had to step down before it could fulfill its function in history' (Márai 1968: 64).

One of the clichés of Marxist historiography is that Hungary never had a bourgeoisie. One of the worst consequences of the impact of the works of György Lukács and József Révai was the transformation of Hungary into a country with a history of backwardness. In 1948 Márai was forced to emigrate. A sense of foreboding haunted him, and his predictions proved to be correct: the persecution of kulaks, the nationalization of the Hungarian industry, the banking system, and education were followed by the trials of Cardinal Mindszenty and the Communist Rajk in 1949 and by the large-scale deportations of 'class-aliens'. György Lukács himself came under criticism. On 29 April 1949 Rákosi received a long essay from László Rudas, an arch-enemy of the philosopher, in which Lukács was attacked for viewing Hitler as a tragic figure in history. Although the essay was not printed without significant changes in *Társadalmi Szemle*, the theoretical journal of the Hungarian Workers's Party, others joined in the debate. On 25 December *Szabad Nép* contained an article in which Márton Horváth blamed Lukács for downgrading Socialist Realism to 'an obscure generalization that can be approached with the help of abstractions rather than with that of the living reality of Soviet literature' (Urbán 1985: 174). The philosopher had to exercise self-criticism. Ironically, the main target of his opponents was *Literature and Democracy*, the book which was largely responsible for the fall of bourgeois literature.

By this time most of those he attacked between 1945 and 1948 were involved in writing fairy-tales for children or translating from Russian. The only major exception was Márai, who was facing poverty in exile. The rest of his life proves how difficult it had been for him to leave his country and can be interpreted as a sad epilogue to the history of bourgeois literature in post-war Hungary. For forty years he continued to write and publish in Hungarian, but his works were inaccessible in his native country. The reason for this distortion of the past was quite obvious: those historians and critics who identified Hungarian culture with the traditions of the gentry could not find a place for a writer whose works contradicted their ideological assumptions.

'Darkness surrounds me and I can see only one goal: I have to write in Hungarian as long as I can. This is the only task that is still meaningful. I have signed a contract with this language; this is the destiny I can never forget' (Márai 1993: 107). These words were written in 1947, at a time when many Hungarian writers denied their attachment to the bourgeoisie. Márai had expressed many reservations about his class throughout his career, but remained committed to its values to the very end. One of the reasons for his decision to commit suicide in San Diego (California) on 21 February 1989 was that he saw no chances for the recovery of bourgeois literature in Hungary. After forty years of Communism those chances still remain very much in doubt.

References

Borbándi, Gy. 1983. *A magyar népi mozgalom: A harmadik reformnemzedék.* New York.
Gömöri, G. 1996. Miklós Radnóti and the Bible. *Hungarian Studies* 11.
Hoensch, J. K. 1988. *A History of Modern Hungary 1867–1986.* London – New York.

Istóczy, Gy. 1904. *Országgyűlési beszédei, indítványai és törvényjavaslatai 1872–1896.* Budapest.

Keszi, I. 1947. Buta, de tehetséges. *Emberség* 1.

Király, I. 1976. *Irodalom és társadalom: Tanulmányok, cikkek, interjúk, kritikák 1945–1975.* Budapest.

Levy, R. S. (ed.). 1991. *Antisemitism in the Modern World: An Anthology of Texts.* Lexington, MA.

Lukács, Gy. 1945. *Írástudók felelőssége.* Budapest.

Lukács, Gy. 1948. *Irodalom és demokrácia.* 2nd ed. Budapest.

Lukacs, J. 1990. *Confessions of an Original Sinner.* New York.

Lukácsy, S. 1984. Boldogult funkcikoromban. *Négy évszak* 9/9.

Márai, S. 1945. *Napló (1943–1944).* Budapest.

Márai, S. 1968. *Napló (1945–1957).* Washington, D. C.

Márai, S. *Föld, föld!... Emlékezések.* Toronto.

Márai, S. 1992. *Ami a Naplóból kimaradt 1945–1946.* Budapest.

Márai, S. 1993. *Ami a Naplóból kimaradt 1947.* Budapest.

Nagy, L. 1947. A Válasz útja. *Valóság* 3.

Ozsváth, Zs. 1996. From Cain to Nahum. *Hungarian Studies* 11.

Standeisky, É. 1987. *A Magyar Kommunista Párt irodalompolitikája 1944–1948.* Budapest.

Szabó, Á. 1947. Írástudóknak való. *Valóság* 3.

Szegedy-Maszák, M. 1996. National and International Implications in Radnóti's Poetry. *Hungarian Studies* 11.

Urbán, K. A Lukács-vita. Újabb adalékok az 1949–1950-es vita hátteréhez. In *Tanulmányok a magyar népi demokrácia negyven évéről.* Budapest.

A Conservative Reading of Jacques Derrida

Il faut pousser les questions aussi loin qu'il est possible. Such could be
the starting point for *une lecture déconstructrice* of a text by Jacques Derrida.
The task is difficult if not impossible, because it is not easy to start a dialogue with "L'avenir de la profession." As Derrida himself argued some
fifteen years ago, "un texte ne saurait *appartenir* à aucun genre" (*Parages*.
Paris: Galilée, 1986, 264.). His admission towards the end of the text he
has kindly sent us for discussion is in perfect harmony with his earlier
statement: "Je ne sais surtout pas quel est le statut, le genre ou la légitimité
du discours que je viens de vous adresser" (41.). Our difficulties may be
related to Derrida's deconstruction of the dichotomy of speech and writing. "On m'associe souvent à la théorie de l'écriture," he warns us in an
interview, "mais je suis un homme de parole" (*Points de suspension:
Entretiens*. Paris: Galilée, 1992, 9.). *L'attention portée à la langue* is so
conspicuous that the reader can hear a *ton* while reading this text. Needless
to say, this is not an authorial but an intertextual voice. That is why the text
is hardly decipherable (*déchiffrable*). *On sent un plaisir de parler une langue
qu'on peut interpréter comme littéraire et philosophique. En tous cas je lis
Derrida comme je lis Montaigne ou Rousseau. Chaque texte de Derrida
appelle, si on peut dire, une autre 'oreille'.* Before making any comments, let me stress the strict limitations of my reading. I am not a systematic reader of Derrida's works. He has published a great number of works
– *qui prétend les avoir déjà lu?* – on a wide range of topics which are
beyond my competence. Some of the issues tackled in "L'avenir de la profession" have to be addressed by professional philosophers. As for myself,
all I can say is that as a literary scholar I have found Derrida's works a
constant source of inspiration. The strong reservations he expressed about

249

Comparative Literature many years ago have become a point of reference for me in my criticism of the discipline I am supposed to represent. In an address to the Hungarian Academy in the early 1990s I compared Derrida to Glenn Gould (*"Minta a szőnyegen": A műértelmezés esélyei.* Budapest: Balassi, 1995, 19–20). Some blamed me for being too sympathetic to what they regarded as Derrida's anarchism. My impression is that the comparison reveals my conservatism. I feel more at home with Edwin Fischer's traditional than with Gould's postmodern reading of the *Appassionata Sonata.* Heidegger used a pencil; Derrida is a public figure in a jet age. A couple of decades ago Derrida represented opposition vis-à-vis cultural institutions. By now he himself has become institutionalized. Subversiveness or conservatism is a matter of perspective. The composer of *Elektra* was an avant-garde musician; that of *Vier letzte Lieder* was a conservative artist. I would apply Derrida's own thesis to his work: "Nous avons reçu plus que nous ne croyons savoir de la 'tradition', mais la scène du don oblige aussi à une sorte d'impiété filiale, grave et légère à l'égard des pensées auxquelles on doit le plus" (*Points de suspension,* 139.).

Thanks to Derrida, logocentric oppositions are now in thorough disrepute. One of the most thought-provoking parts in his lecture is the ambiguous characterization of "Geisteswissenschaften": he desires to deconstruct the concept and to cultivate the tradition behind it. He seems to adopt a position that I find even a shade conservative when he refers to the established canons "dont je crois néanmoins qu'ils doivent être protégés à tout prix" (7). Since canons are linked to power, I sense a slight contradiction between the desire to deconstruct the concept of humanities and the preservation of "leurs anciens canons" (7).

I any case, I would place a high priority on the transformation of "Geisteswissenschaften." Here Derrida's own activity can give us invaluable support. He has done more than anybody else to undermine the institutionalized distinctions (oppositions reçues) between philosophy and literature, essay and imaginative (or creative) writing, text and metatext (commentary), concept and metaphor, logic and rhetoric, nature and culture/artifice/convention/technique, experience and experimentation, emancipation and alienation, public and private, etc. It needs to be remembered that his intention was never reduction but the reintepretation of the relations (une autre "logique" des rapports) between these terms.

I hope it is not impolite to ask a question at this point. The word "tradition" occurs several times in the text. Could it be that today Derrida is slightly more sympathetic to Gadamer's emphasis on tradition than he was at the time of their debate? Or should the expression "la tradition classique-moderne" be taken as another example of deconstructing binary opposi-tions? The word "classique" may suggest permanence of values, whereas modernity involves teleology, even progress and the mutability of values. One of the features common to Paul de Man and Derrida may be the incli-nation to focus on canonized texts. As Derrida remarked in an interview published in *Le Monde* in 1982, "j'ai toujours le sentiment que, malgré des siècles de lecture, ces textes restent vierges [...]. D'où la nécessité d'une inteprétation interminable" (*Points de suspension*, 88). While finding his readings of Plato, Descartes, Rousseau, Kant, Shelley, Nietzsche, Joyce, Heidegger, Celan, Blanchot, Genet, and others both refreshing and illumi-nating and the insistence on interpretation as an infinite process absolutely legitimate, I miss the analysis of less well-known, if not marginal texts. I may be wrong, but I have to admit that while I find the distinction between "clôture" and "fin" admirable and the claim that "la tradition n'était pas homogène" absolutely justifiable, I look forward to seeing more evidence of the "intérêt pour les textes non canoniques" (*Points de suspension*, 237).

Derrida's works have strengthened my belief that all texts are not only intertextual but also multilingual. "On n'écrit jamais ni dans sa propre langue ni dans une langue étrangère" (*Parages*, 147). Of course, what are called multiculturalism and globalization – I tend to view such fashionable clichés with suspicion – are mutually interdependent. "Nationalisme et universa-lisme indissociables," (*Parages*, 140) Derrida says and I can accept this as a starting point. What I regret is that Derrida seems unwilling to elaborate on this thesis. Since "la mondialisation" is taking place irrespective of our desires, it seems a bit pointless to insist on a "résistance inconditionnelle au pouvoir de l'état-nation." I agree that a nation state is tied to a "fantasme de souveraineté indivisible." My impression is that in 2000 it is too obvi-ous that this "fantasme" belongs to the legacy of the past. By now many nations have disintegrated in the sense that each consists of several inter-pretive communities with radically different value systems. No less obvi-ous is that the word "university" suggests cosmopolitanism. My only com-plaint – the word may be too strong – would be that Derrida lumps to-gether different kinds of power. Of course, nationalism is far from being extinct, but the nations which I would call tentatively and with much hesi-tation more civilized seem to move towards diversity on the one hand and "mondialisation" or "Americanization" on the other. To take Hungary as an example, the people living in this country are so divided that it would be misleading to attribute any national identity to them. At the same time, they are on the way to being assimilated to an international community dominated by the United States.

What Derrida calls "pouvoirs économiques" and "médiatiques" are different from the power of the nation state, since they are far from being incompatible with "mondialisation." I would even risk the hypothesis that while in the 19th century it may have been difficult for a Western university to resist the power of the nation state, today it is virtually an illusion to believe that the institutions of higher education can oppose economic power and the power exercised by those who control the media. Needless to say, I would love to teach at a university that can assert "le droit principiel de tout dire, fût-ce au titre de la fiction et de l'expérimentation du savoir, et le droit de le dire publiquement, de le publier" (4). For more than fifteen years I have been teaching at a large state university in the U. S. and at a major university in the Hungarian capital. During these years my North American university has moved further and further away from the ideal of "l'université sans condition," "la liberté prise de tout dire dans l'espace public" (6). My American students, even the most brilliant among them, are forced to think in terms of vocationalism and the rules of the job market. As for Hungary, it is true that today I can teach Nabokov, praise Beckett, and neglect Marx without running the risk of punishment from the Politburo. Still, I would be reluctant to argue that Hungarian universities are moving in the direction of "cette liberté prise de tout dire dans l'espace public" (6). I have two reasons for skepticism. On the one hand, totalitarianism has had such a deep impact on mentality that it will take a longer period to improve public spirit. On the other hand, Hungarian universities are being transformed in harmony with the American model. "L'université sans condition et sans pouvoir propre" – our distinguished visitor will correct me if I am wrong – conforms to the ideals of Wilhelm von Humboldt rather than to the living reality of the American university.

The idea that a university should be "le lieu dans lequel rien n'est à l'abri du questionnement" (4) is very attractive, but it is easier to declare such openness than to remain faithful to it in an institution that has teaching as one of its activities.

Deconstruction has been associated with the distrust of certain logocentric oppositions. This time Derrida returns and makes much of Austin's distinction between constative and performative. In what sense is this distinc-

252

tion more legitimate than the one, say, between literal and metaphoric? Of course, it is true that at the end of the text Austin's distinction is mentioned as one "à laquelle nous avons jusqu'ici feint de faire confiance" (34). These words may express some reservations. I detect a similar ambiguity in the approach to tradition, *le rapport que vous indiquez à la tradition*. Undoubtedly, *une certaine position double* was never absent from Derrida's works. Let me quote an earlier statement on tradition: "la volonté de ne renoncer [...] ni à la fidélité, ni à une certaine infidélité [...]. Il n'y a pas d'équilibre [...]; chacune séparément est une espèce de folie, de mort" (*Points de suspension*, 161).

Is it possible that Derrida's dream of "une université sans condition" is the reincarnation of an ideal inherited from the past? If this is true, his thought is much closer to a conservative tradition than some may believe. Conservatism is inseparable from a desire to preserve, and Derrida frequently requests his Hungarian translator to preserve French words or expressions. Has he looked at the English versions of his works? For me Jacques Derrida is a French writer. I would like to know what he thinks of the English translations of his works. Is it not true that more people have read him in English than in French, and if so, cannot it be argued that there is a gap between the fashionable theoretician and the fine artist in the French language? I would like to raise this question in the belief that Jacques Derrida postulates a close link between philosophy *et la langue dite naturelle*.

Nonteleological Narration

If postmodernism is to be accepted as a period term; its continuity with some phenomena of the early twentieth century should also be accepted. It is not very easy to draw a line between postmodernism and its antecedents because it does not seem to imply more than a reorganization – in terms of priority – of older strategies. Such characteristics of postmodernism as the aesthetic and epistemological break with the past or the crisis of cultural authority and the destruction of canons should not be overemphasized. For one thing, it cannot be denied that the weakening of historicity and the collapse of the semi-autonomy of the cultural sphere began earlier, with the eclecticism of the nineteenth century, with the Biedermeier and the "Sezession." Furthermore, it is by no means true that all the innovations of the early twentieth century have become commercialized and no longer provoke resistance. It cannot be taken for granted that the art of the avant-garde has become familiar and that the contemporary artist lives in submission to the rules of the market. Most readers find *Finnegans Wake* still unreadable, the compositions of Webern are rarely performed by the major orchestras of the world, and such works written in the last decades as, for instance, *Abend mit Goldrand* (1975) by Arno Schmidt or *Rituel in memoriam Maderna* (1975) by Pierre Boulez are accessible only to very few people.

It is not surprising that once a literary critic tries to put his or her finger on a specific structural device which supposedly characterizes postmodernism, such as the discontinuity and fragmentation of character – the denial of an essentialist view of human nature –, he or she must go back to the last work of Joyce or to *Between the Acts* (Caramello 1983: 36; Wilde 1981: 48, 87). Or, to take another criterion proposed by some critics, I

254

cannot accept the thesis that pastiche – and not parody – is characteristic of postmodern cultural production (Jameson 1984: 64), because it depends not only on the artistic intention but also on the consumer's attitude whether an imitation is ironic or not. "Le comique, la puissance du rire est dans le rieur et nullement dans l'objet du rire" ("the comical, the ability to laugh is in the one who laughs, not in the object one laughs about") (Baudelaire 1971: I 308). It would not be easy to show that Stravinsky's *Pulcinella* (1919) is closer to parody than some of the stories of Donald Barthelme or the treatment of Sadean conventions in *Virginie, Her Two Lives* (1982) by John Hawkes.

1. Causality and Teleology

To show that the existing definitions of postmodernism overemphasize the novelty of contemporary culture, I shall focus on one of the most widely held assumptions, the thesis that "causality is lost" in postmodernism (Foster 1985: xiv). I shall confine my analysis to narrative fiction, which suggests that causality is bound up with a sense of teleology, or, as Nietzsche (1980: 424) said: "Der Glaube an *causae* fällt mit dem Glauben an τέλη" ("The belief in causes collapses if the belief in ends is lost.")

Causality and teleology are regulating principles: "we construct these from the text and then read the text as formed by them" (Harshaw 1984: 229). As such, they seem to be essential in narrative structures. Story development, implying continuity, is almost inconceivable without these interdependent fictional constructs; they determine the perspective from which events are evaluated. Causality often goes together with a sense of purpose, which, in turn, implies the preservation of an individual, a community, an institution, a faith, or a culture (Nietzsche 1980: 186). A loss of causality may be the consequence of a loss of belief in such end-values. The thesis of the death of Christianity comes close to such a skepticism, but it seems probable that the interpretive habits of most people in the Western world are still under the influence of some more or less secularized form of the two-thousand-year-old tradition.

It is easy to assert that before the twentieth century the structure of most works of narrative fiction was based on some kind of teleology, whereas from the early decades of this century onwards post-Nietzschean doubt began to undermine belief in linear succession, and that this reaction transformed the textual composition of fiction. The desire to give a random ordering of bits of plot became especially strong then in recent years, changing our reading habits and generic expectations.

The truth may be more complex. Postmodernism has had its great precursors, and Sukenick may be right to assert that "the new tradition coexisted with the old tradition from the beginning, not as the exception that proves the rule but as an alternative rule" (Sukenick 1981: 37). There may be different modes of teleology, and with respect to some of these *The Life and Opinions of Tristram Shandy* or *Jacques le fataliste* may be more subversive than Sukenick's *98.6* (1975).

The other factor complicating matters is the teleology of reading. I have the impression that literary scholars have not considered seriously enough the question how far the reader's expectations are responsible for interpreting a piece of narrative as a goal-directed process. Lucien Goldmann's interpretation of *La Jalousie* (1957) has been written off by Robbe-Grillet, and with good reason, for to read that novel as an illustration of reification (Ricardou and van Rossum-Guyon 1972: I, 179) is to jump to a grossly simplifying conclusion. Important as it may be to refute such reductionist distortions, it would be even more important to know whether readers brought up in a Western culture with a heritage marked by Christianity and historicism can resist the temptation of reading some kind of teleology into narrative texts. If literature is an exchange, the recuperation of sense is irresistible. The point to make is not so much that postmodern art is derivative, it is rather that its consumers cannot help viewing it in relation to the past.

A good example is the history of the reception of *Naked Lunch* (1959), which some critics believe to be the work that "marks the beginning of the Postmodern era" (Federman 1984: 5). Thirty years ago this book seemed to be chaotic to many readers. Their impression may have been influenced by the narrator's own words: "There is only one thing a writer can write about: *what is in front of his senses at the moment of writing*. ... I am a recording instrument. ... I do not presume to impose 'story', 'plot', 'continuity'." Today *Naked Lunch* may seem to be far more teleological, a negative parable about the destruction of the soul, an attack upon addiction, the loss of personality, and brainwashing.

Sometimes it is argued that any metaphysical interpretation of a postmodern text is invalid, because postmodernism is bound up with a total disbelief in ultimate goals. For Proust or Joyce, God had been replaced by art, whereas for Beckett even art has lost its supreme value. Undoubtedly, numerous postmodern novels published in the United States deny any form of transcendence, from Donald Barthelme's *The Dead Father* (1975) to *The Living End* (1980) by Stanley Elkin, and a similar refusal characterizes the *nouveau roman*, but once again I should like to caution against sweeping generalizations. The work of William H. Gass embodies a devotion to cultural traditions in general and to art in particular which is as religious as that of Henry James, such works of short fiction as *Spanking the Maid* (1982) by Robert Coover testify to a devotion to craftsmanship which characterized such modernists as Gide or Virginia Woolf, and the first section of Pynchon's *Gravity's Rainbow* (1973) has an inscription from Wernher von Braun about his "belief in the continuity of our spiritual existence after death."

The assumption that postmodern literature is anti-religious becomes even more questionable if we turn to the literatures of Central Europe. Péter Esterházy, who has been recognized as the most important postmodern novelist in Hungary, is a Roman Catholic writer. The last section of his *Bevezetés a szépirodalomba* (1986, An Introduction to Literature) – a huge work that is meant to explore different possibilities of prose writing – is written in the form of a prayer.

With all these reservations made, it may be understandable why I am rather unwilling to accept the assumption that the loss of teleology is a distinguishing feature of postmodern fiction. Instead of subscribing to such a generalization, my aim is rather a modest analysis of some narrative strategies used by postmodern writers to undermine traditional forms of teleology and to suspend meaning by frustrating our reading habits and assumptions about intelligibility, thus blocking our regular interpretive moves. To be sure, it is a truism that the postmodern devices for disrupting narrative make it difficult to piece together a story, to decide what "actually" happens and what is memory, dream, hallucination, or simply part of the narrative act, but it is probably less often realized that all these strategies are successful only if they both activate and disrupt the reader's sense of teleology.

Far from pretending to give a full classification, my intention is to focus on three types of narrative strategy: circularity, open ending, and aleatory arrangement.

2. Circularity

The first seems to be the simplest, but also the most radical of these methods. Some believe that *Finnegans Wake* has still not been surpassed in certain respects by later experimentation, and this claim is supported by the fact that Joyce aimed to invalidate one of the most universal laws, the teleology of reading. A less well-known precursor is *Le Chiendent* (1933, The Trouble), the first novel of Queneau. Without exaggeration, it could be safely maintained that this book is a *nouveau roman avant la lettre*. *Le père* Taupe, a poor dealer in second-hand goods, is unwilling to sell a door. Madame Cloche, *la sage femme*, has the idea that *le père* Taupe is an avaricious millionaire whose treasure is hidden behind the door. She makes a young and pretty waitress marry the old beggar to get hold of his money. Several people are told about the secret and they all want to have the treasure. A war starts. After the death of *le père* it becomes evident that nothing is hidden behind the door, but the war lasts several decades. One of the very few survivors suggests that everybody should go home and start a normal life again, but another reminds him that this would be impossible, because the survivors are no more than characters in a novel which is almost finished. The last two sentences correspond to the beginning of the book.

The analogy with a novel like *Dans le labyrinthe* (1959; *In the Labyrinth*, 1960), written some twenty-five years later, is quite obvious. In Robbe-Grillet's work the soldier has a box which seems to have some hidden meaning, in the same way that the door of *le père* Taupe takes on an almost mysterious significance in the war fought by the characters in *Le Chiendent*. The meaning – the goal towards which the whole sequence of events is directed – becomes invalidated at the end of both novels.

There is no progress, development, overcoming, or *novum*, only repetition. Accordingly, narrative is not teleological, but circular. Works suggesting such a conception are numerous in the last decades – from Nabokov's *Pnin* (1957), at the end of which a character begins to tell a story related in the first chapter, to *L'Immortelle* (1963), a *ciné-roman* by Robbe-Grillet, which ends with the smiling face of the woman whose death seemed to give a tragic turn to the story, or to "Menelaiad," a story by Barth included in *Lost in the Funhouse* (1968), consisting of fourteen sections half of which are variations upon the other half (and these rewritten versions are printed in reverse order).

Circularity is at odds both with our sense of history and with the idea of the development of the personality. That is why the traditional concepts of the historical novel and the *Bildungsroman* are incompatible with postmodern writing. Noah's story and the incident which inspired Géricault to paint *The Raft of Medusa* are presented as variations on a theme by Julian Barnes in *A History of the World in 10 1/2 Chapters* (1989), and travelling is presented as having no direction in *Átkelés az üvegen* (1992, Passing through the Glass), a parody of the novel of education by László Márton.

In many postmodern narratives circularity is based on repetition, which is also a favorite regulating principle in recent music. As in the compositions of Steve Reich and others, in stories by Coover or Barth repetition makes dialectical development impossible. What we have here is not a brand-new discovery, but rather a greater emphasis on a way of organizing one's material which has been somewhat neglected in the last centuries. Once it has been pushed into the foreground, more and more antecedents can be discovered. Like earlier movements, postmodernism has reinterpreted the past. Flann O'Brien's *The Third Policeman*, written in 1940, is about a circular and interminably repetitive private hell. Nabokov's *Zashchita Luzina* (1931; *The Defense*, 1964) has a hero for whom everything seems to have happened before. One could go even further back to Borges, Gertrude Stein, and Raymond Roussel, and point out circularity and repetitive structures in Proust. The question is not so much whether Nietzsche's idea of eternal recurrence had any influence on writers; it is more important to observe that by the end of the twentieth century there may exist readers who do not look for teleology. Postmodernism is also a matter of reading habits and of a conception of time, although it depends on certain structural elements whether a "postmodern reading" is possible or not.

3. Open ending

The teleology of narrative can be conspicuously manifest in the ending of a text and thus an open ending seems to be an effective way of undermining teleology. Barbara Herrnstein Smith (1968) distinguishes two basic types of closure, formal and thematic, and a similar distinction can be made between anti-closures. Formal anti-closure is exemplified by texts

259

which break off in the middle of a sentence, such as "Title" in *Lost in the Funhouse* by Barth, "Sentence" in *City Life* (1970) by Barthelme, or "An Encounter" in the collection *In Bed One Night and Other Brief Encounters* (1983) by Coover. One could also cite "Views of My Father Weeping," another story collected in *City Life* but this is a slightly different case: the last word is "Etc.," suggesting the impossibility not only of formal but also of thematic closure.

Before going on to the second type, I wish to underline the limitations of formal endings. Syntactic fragmentation in itself does not necessarily indicate the absence of teleology in the world constructed by the narrative work, especially not if the text is of some length. Several sections, including the finale, break off in the middle of a sentence in *Gravity's Rainbow*, but this surface fragmentation merely conceals, and does not contradict the antisocial message formulated by Enzian near the end of the novel.

We must be very cautious when speaking of anti-closures, because to a great extent it is the addressee who decides whether the last words or pages of a narrative text mark the end or the beginning of a process. To mention but one example, *Robbe-Grillet's L'Année dernière à Marienbad* (1961; *Last Year at Marienbad*, 1962) can be interpreted in two different ways: as a story about two lovers who escape from the labyrinthine castle of M (*mari/maître?*), or as an endless repetition of the same scene, depending upon the elements you wish to highlight in the closure.

There are, of course, more obvious cases. The text may end just before a climax is reached or an enigma solved. The point of Pynchon's *The Crying of Lot 49* (1966) seems to be an auction to which the title refers, but the last words do not fulfill that expectation: "The auctioneer cleared his throat. Oedipa settled back, to await the crying of lot 49."

A more ambiguous case seems to be *Egy családregény vége* (1977, The End of a Genealogical Novel) by Péter Nádas. The ready-made pattern of a well-known subgenre is invoked. The main character is called Péter Simon, a name which not only refers to a disciple of Jesus but is also identical with the name of one of the hero's ancestors. To what extent will the fate of a young Jew living in Central Europe in the second half of the twentieth century conform to the prophecy of his ancestor? That is the question raised by the novel. The ending may admit of different interpretations. The life of the earlier generations seems to have confirmed the relevance of tradition, and there are signs indicating that the hero may be one of the elect. In the last chapter, however, Péter Simon enters a chaotic world full of uncertainty. He may have lost his belief in the values inherited from the past, and this may lead to an alienation from tradition. If this is so, the novel will be read as an anti-parable suggesting the impossibility of continuing to write genealogical novels. I would even risk a more general hypothesis and assume that the reader allegorizes a tale when reading some teleology into it; thus the parable may be an archetype of narrative teleology.

The polysemy of the open ending can also be felt in a genre that is known as the "pop-up book." *Griffin and Sabine* (1991) by the British-born Nick Bantock represents a return to the old tradition of the imaginary correspondence. Its hero is an artist who creates a fictional character to soothe his loneliness. He and his imaginary correspondent live far from each other and communicate only by mail. Their story is told in nice picture postcards and decorated letters that must be removed from their envelopes by the reader. At the end of the book Sabine, the imaginary lover, decides to visit Griffin. Suspense is postponed by the sequel *Sabine's Notebook* (1992), containing material which informs the reader that Griffin has escaped from his home in London before Sabine's arrival. His journey through Europe and the Mediterranean is a travelling backward in time and in a psychological sense. The second volume of the series ends on the same note of uncertainty as the first; the reader cannot tell whether the two characters will ever meet.

Besides open closures, variant endings may also undermine teleology. An obvious example would be Fowles' *The French Lieutenant's Woman* (1969), but the overall structure of this novel is too conventional to make it more than symptomatic of the dependence of the teleology of action on the paradigmatic expectations of the reading public – symptomatic also of the aversion of the present age for Victorian endings, the "distribution at the last of prizes, pensions, husbands, wives, babies, millions, appended paragraphs, and cheerful remarks," to cite the previously mentioned passage by Henry James (James 1963: 52–53). More radical is Robbe-Grillet's *La Maison de rendez-vous* (1965; English translation with the same title, 1966), which relates thirteen versions of a murder. In this case the reader's expectations are frustrated because the novel gives no clues as to the identity of the murderer and the victim. Nor does it disclose what instrument has been used in the killing.

An ending can be called open if it does not gratify the reader's desire. *Kairos*, "a point in time filled with significance, charged with meaning derived from its relation to the end," as opposed to chronos, "passing," "waiting time" (Kermode 1967: 46), is also a matter of convention. Gombrowicz has become a model for postmodern writers in Central Europe, partly because he reversed the accepted order of *chronos* and *kairos*. In the middle of his early novel *Ferdydurke* (1937) there are two prefaces, and the book ends with the hero's marriage to the girl he does not want to have for a wife. The conventional value attached to *kairos* has been lost, as in Queneau's *Zazie dans le métro* (1969), where the heroine's lack of fulfillment is emphasized in the final words:

– Alors tu t'es bien amusée?
– Comme ça.
– T'as vu le métro?
– Non.
– Alors, qu'est-ce que t'as fait?
– J'ai vielli.
(– Well, did you amuse yourself?
– So so.
– Did you see the metro?
– No.
– But what did you do?
– I have grown older.)

Many of the more recent postmodern novels stress the irrelevance of the genealogical novel or the *Bildungsroman*. Both anticipations and closures have lost their distinctive features. "It is important to begin when everything is over," because "in eternity, beginning is consummating," as Coover writes in his metafictional story "Beginnings," published in *In Bed One Night and Other Brief Encounters.*

4. Aleatory arrangement

Open endings mark a departure from the principles of Aristotelian poetics. An open ending resembles an anticipation, an *Auftakt*. Teleology is related to proportion and to the order of structural elements. An unexpected order may weaken teleology. Thus, teleology has questionable relevance if the narrative space is composed of parallel planes, so that different parts of the text may be read in different order. Readers of Nabokov's *Pale Fire* (1962) can either read the verse novel first and commentary next or they can turn to the latter whenever they wish to consult it. Similar alternatives are proposed in *Termelési-regény* (1979, A Novel of Production), Esterházy's third book. This work was published with two bookmarks, one red and the other black, to encourage the public to read the first part, a parody of a genre of socialist Realism, simultaneously with the second part, a spiritual autobiography of the author. A superficial reading will disclose no connection whatsoever between the main text and the endnotes. On closer consideration, however, the latter create an alternative teleology which contradicts that of the generic parody.

Esterházy's works show the postmodern writer's ambivalent attitude toward teleology. He has a double allegiance, taking a passionate interest both in writing practices for their own sakes and in the achieved forms. A careful reader of his books cannot help arriving at the conclusion that form and teleology are inextricably linked. On the one hand, he shows a preference for the open, intertextual work of art, which implies an abolition of the Romantic distinctions between artist and non-artist, art and life, fiction and nonfiction, novel and autobiography, and a dismissal of the teleological view of artistic creation. The logical consequence of this attitude would be the conviction that art is on a level with life in being non-intentional.

It is quite possible that Cage's idea of aggregates has inspired the Hungarian writer to juxtapose disparate linguistic utterances and let unexpected relationships between incompatible texts emerge. Esterházy seems to have endorsed the American composer's ideal of open form, which implies a refusal of hierarchy – possibly the basis of all teleology. Yet the ideal of the "open work," which plays a crucial role in the partly metafictional second half of *Termelési-regény*, seems to be at variance with Esterházy's concern for craftsmanship, for a total control over the material, for the finely wrought work, the well-made form of the finished product. The first of these two attitudes implies a rejection of the hold of any élite, whereas the second is a manifestation of a highly elitist view of art: the writer works for a relatively small circle of connoisseurs who can identify the texts he quotes from and will understand what is written between the lines.

These tendencies are even more apparent in Esterházy's more recent work. The idea of *Bevezetés a szépirodalomba* is at variance with any possible interpretation of teleology. The different sections of this monumental work have very little in common; they are not governed by comparable regularities. The incessant flow of words characterizing "Függő" (Dependent) does not seem to be related to the extremely economical, decidedly artificial, "précieux" style of "Fuharosok" (published in English as *Trans-*

porters, 1985), and even the two parts of "Ki szavatol a lady biztonságáért?" (Who Would Guarantee the Lady's Safety?) are poles apart: the metafictional strategies used in "Ágnes" are prosaic if compared to the visionary style of "Daisy." "Kis magyar pornográfia" (A Handbook of Hungarian Pornography) comes very close to representing exclusively the anarchistic side of his art, being a collection of fragments, some of them dirty or political jokes, whereas "A szív segédigéi" (published in English as *The Helping Verbs of the Heart*, 1990) is a sublime and even religious testimony to the memory of the author's mother. In sum, ontologically different possible worlds are joined together with the apparent aim of making the reader responsible for discovering links between apparently disjointed parts. To make the recuperation of meaning difficult, the hermeneutic code – another of the preconditions of teleology – is neglected. The almost total absence of narrative suspense suggests that Esterházy is not fascinated by the technique of detective stories, and does not count on the reader's ignorance of a given move. Pushing psychological motivation into the background, he generates a polysemy which admits of a wide range of interpretations. In order to change reading habits, he rejects a number of narrative conventions, among them that of the narrator as a generalizing observer – which is another means of creating the impression of teleology.

Esterházy's activity shows important analogies with that of other postmodern writers. The title of "Függő," for example, referring both to a grammatical category and to the uncertainty of man's position in the universe, implies a treatment of relatedness which Barthes detected in the novels of Sollers: "Les 'routes' suivies par le discours ne sont [...] ni celles de la chronologie (*avant/après*), ni celles de la logique narrative (implication d'un événement par un autre): le seul régime ici est celui de la constellation" ("The 'routes' followed by the discourse are [...] neither those of chronology [*before/after*], nor those of narrative logique [the implication of one event by another]: here the only regime is that of the configuration") (Barthes 1979: 40). Like Sollers' *Paradis* (1981), "Függő" seems to be an endless flow without a real beginning or end, lacking points of expectation and fulfillment. The a-causal structuring of the narrative prevents any closure of the text or resolution of the plot.

The same idea of aggregates underlies lexicon novels ranging from *Splendide-Hôtel* (1973), a short book by Gilbert Sorrentino, to *Por* (1987, Dust), a two-volume presentation of a city by Ferenc Temesi, as well as such computer-generated novels as *Az ibolya illata* (1992, The Scent of a Violet) by Gábor Farnbauer and works which sometimes are called shuffle novels. Once more, I wish to emphasize how relative the originality of postmodern innovations is in a historical perspective. Some of these works follow the pattern of the picaresque, in which certain episodes are interchangeable. A characteristic example is Raymond Federman's *Take It or Leave It* (1976), an unpaged autobiographical novel about someone born in France who escaped from a train transporting Jews to a concentration camp and later settled down in the United States. Even *The Unfortunates* (1969), a seemingly randomly assembled "novel in a box" by Brian Stanley Johnson, probably the most imaginative work in the genre, does not surpass the limits of the controlled aleatory. This *Ich Erzählung* relates the story of a football reporter sent to a city where he remembers a close friend who had studied there and had become a scientist of genius but died as a young man, pointlessly, horribly, of cancer. It consists of twenty-seven sections, "Temporarily held together by a removable wrapper." Memory is achronological; therefore, most of the sections can be read in any order. There are two exceptions: the first and the last sections are marked as such, indicating that even this original writer, whose ambition was to strip narrative almost completely of the traditional means of story development, could not accept a wholly uncontrolled aleatory arrangement, although he considered any form of teleology arbitrary, arguing that "one should act on one's own interests AS IF it were all chaos – that is, one will come to less harm, suffer less disappointment, if nothing is to be EXPECTED from such a chaotic state" (Johnson 1970).

Like circularity and the open ending, the shuffle novel can also be seen as a product of historical evolution. In this case montage is the obvious antecedent, and *Collages* (1964) by Anais Nin marks the transition between earlier types of discontinuity and postmodern assemblage. Since the unnumbered sections of this book do not constitute a plot, they suggest alternative orders of reading, reminding us that no one can be forced to read the different parts of a text in the order in which they have been printed. As always, the present reinterprets the past; postmodern works may encourage us to change our reading habits.

Postmodernism tends to relegate teleology to a lower rank than most literary trends of the past. A final question remains to be asked about the cause of this tendency.

I can think of two main reasons. One is the revaluation of personality, leading to a reinterpretation of human motives and of causality. No less fundamental seems to be the reaction against evolutionism started by Nietzsche. *Weltgeschichte* is but theodicy disguised, enlightenment is the secularized version of salvation, so the loss of religious faith may imply a loss of belief in progress. Still, it remains to be seen how far man can do without some form of teleology. That seems to be the fundamental dilemma of writers of postmodern fiction.

References

Barthes, Roland 1979. *Sollers écrivain*. Paris: Seuil.

Baudelaire, Charles 1971. *Écrits sur l'art*. Paris: Livre de poche.

Caramello, Charles 1983. *Silverless Mirrors: Book, Self and Postmodern American Fiction*. Tallahassee: University Presses of Florida.

Federman, Raymond 1984. "Fiction in America Today, or The Unreality of Reality." *Indian Journal of American Studies* 14: 5–16.

Foster, Hal, ed. 1985. *Postmodern Culture*. London and Sydney: Pluto.

Harshaw (Hrushovski), Benjamin. 1984. "Fictionality and Fields of Reference: Remarks on a Theoretical Framework." *Poetics Today* 5: 227–51.

James, Henry 1963. *Selected Literary Criticism*. London: Heinemann.

Jameson, Fredric 1984. "Postmodernism, or, the Cultural Logic of Late Capitalism." *New Left Review* 146: 53–92.

Johnson, B.S. 1970. Letter to the author, 2 February 1970 (unpublished).

Kermode, Frank 1967. *The Sense of an Ending: Studies in the Theory of Fiction*. New York: Oxford UP.

Nietzsche, Friedrich 1980. *Der Wille zur Macht: Versuch einer Umwertung aller Werte*. Stuttgart: Alfred Kröner.

Ricardou, Jean, and Françoise van Rossum-Guyon, eds. 1972. *Nouveau roman: hier, aujourd'hui*. Paris: Union Générale d'Éditions.

Smith, Barbara Herrnstein 1968. *Poetic Closure: A Study of How Poems End*. Chicago and London: University of Chicago Press.

Sukenick, Ronald 1981. "The New Tradition in Fiction." *Surfiction: Fiction Now... and Tomorrow*. Ed. Ray Federman. 2nd ed. Chicago: Swallow Press. 35–45. First edition 1975.

Wilde, Alan 1981. *Horizons of Assent: Modernism, Postmodernism and the Ironic Imagination*. Baltimore and London: Johns Hopkins UP.

Postmodernity and Postcommunism

1989 marks a turning-point in the history of Eastern Europe. In that year communism collapsed in Hungary. The reinterpretation of 1956 played a major role in the political change. On January 28 Imre Pozsgay, the "enfant terrible" of the Central Bureau of the Hungarian Socialist Workers' Party called 1956 a popular uprising, and the next meeting of that Bureau, held on 10–11 February, accepted his approach to what was condemned as a counter-revolution throughout the period 1956–1989 and decided to abolish the one-party system. On June 16 Imre Nagy and other politicians executed in 1958 because of their involvement in the uprising of 1956 were given a state funeral. On July 16 János Kádár, the leader of the Communist party died. The last congress of the Hungarian Socialist Workers' Party, held on October 5–9, led to the dissolution of that party. The cult of "Glasnost'" and "Perestroika" were replaced by the concept of postcommunism. Among the consequences of the peaceful revolution of 1989 were a change in the role of art and literature and a reinterpretation of Western postmodernism.

1. The Role of the Artist in Postcommunism

On 4 December 1993, following an annual exhibition, an international symposium was organized by the Institut Français en Hongrie and the Soros Center for Contemporary Arts. The participants of the second panel, art historians, artists, curators, and dealers, were asked to discuss the role of the artist in contemporary Hungary. Some of the artists associated with the project called "42nd Street" maintained that it was the duty of the artist to

267

be involved in social activity and stand for some community, some "alterity" or "otherness" – a term that (together with "open society") has become a cliché in most parts of the postcommunist world.

To what extent is contemporary Hungarian art tied to politics? In most cases the answer is not at all simple. After the official collapse of communism the sculptor György Jovánovics (b. 1939) was commissioned to design a monument for the site where the martyrs of the 1956 revolution were buried. The artist himself characterized this work as follows: "It is a misunderstanding to say that the Burial Place No. 301 is a political work. During the previous régime my work was inseparable from politics. […] This time, however, I designed a work that has no political character for a site full of political implications."[1] Although the monument has become a symbol of the postcolonial state of Eastern Europe, it represents continuity with the earlier avant-garde, especially if compared with the eclecticism of such works as *Rembrandt Studies* (1966) by László Lakner, *In Memory of Malevich* (1980), by István Nádler, *Untitled* (1981) by Tibor Csernus, *The Table* (1995) by Ilona Lovas, or *The Last Supper* (1995) by SI-LA-GY. These five works have two characteristics in common: a) none of them could be described as having any political message, b) all of them refer to earlier works of art. What they seem to suggest is that the pictorial equivalent of intertextuality is characteristic of the visual arts of Hungary since the second half of the 1960s. A recent example is *Cryptogram*, a project started in the form of an interactive installation at the exhibition called "The Butterfly Effect," in the Kunsthalle of Budapest, in February 1996. Using some sketches of Leonardo, Zoltán Szegedy-Maszák (b. 1969) constructed a draft model of a horse. He linked the points of the surface of the virtual horse to the characters that can be typed into a computer. The resulting image can be viewed in virtual reality. It is possible to fly around or even into the virtual horse with the help of a browser.[2] This work would suggest that the following characterizarion of some cultural phenomena of the First World also applies to the activity of some younger artists living in what was called the Second World until its collapse in the late 1980s: "We are left with that pure and random play of signifiers that we call postmodernism, which no longer produces monumental works of the modernist type but ceaselessly reshuffles the fragments of preexistent texts, the building blocks of older cultural and social production, in some new and heightened bricolage: metabooks which cannibalize other books, metatexts which collate bits of other texts – such is the logic of postmodernism in general, which finds one of its strongest and most original, authentic forms in the new art of experimental video."[3]

Most of the works of video art produced in Eastern Europe in recent years would confirm the view expressed by Katalin Keserü, who was the Director of the Kunsthalle in Budapest in 1993. She insisted that in the postcommunist world artists should liberate themselves from the political and social obligations forced upon them by totalitarianism. According to her assumption that art was dependent on an immanent system of values, she asked Joseph Kosuth, an artist born in Ohio, to represent Hungary at the 1993 Venice Biennale. Kosuth, a conceptualist who rejects the ideal of masterpiece and the distinctions between literature and the visual arts, text and context, text and metatext, has become very influential in such cultural centres of "Mitteleuropa" as Vienna, Prague, and Budapest. His attitude to modernism can be called somewhat ambiguous. On the one hand, he is inclined to dismiss modernism as "the culture of Scientism" and "the ideology of industrial capitalism;" on the other hand, he seems to rely on the opposition between art and culture introduced by the avant-garde: "Art is what we do. Culture is what is done to us."[4] Before the Biennale, on 24 February 1993, I asked Kosuth if he thought that his activity was part of "la condition postmoderne." He gave the following answer: "It is a problematic term. I used the term first in 1970. I had an exhibition at the Leo Castelli Gallery where I put up a statement in which I referred to the work as 'post-Modern'. I used it again in writing, I think, in the late 70s when it still was not widely in use as a term. I was then referring to *my* meaning of 1970, which had to do with a feeling that I had nothing to do with the École de Paris or with Jackson Pollock. They were no closer to me than Velázquez."[5] Instead of using some text by a Hungarian writer, Kosuth decided to rely on a passage from *La coscienza di Zeno* by Italo Svevo for his work in Venice. This served as a pretext for some Hungarian artists to attack Katalin Keserü for having asked Kosuth to represent Hungary in Venice.

At the beginning of 1995 Katalin Keserü was asked by the Hungarian minister of culture to resign from her post in part, I believe, because of her objections to the political engagement of Hungarian artists. It may be symptomatic that Róza El-Hassan, a talented artist born in Budapest in 1965, made the following statement: "artists are being manipulated by political groups that are committed to specific interests. Let me add that I am saying this not pejoratively at all."[6] I wonder if there is not a touch of cynicism in this statement. In any case, Róza El-Hassan, the daughter of an Arabic businessman, was one of the three artists who represented Hungary at the Biennale of 1997. In contemporary Hungary it happens sometimes that an artist is sponsored on the basis of her/his political attitude. The current identification between the market and the media seems to confirm Fredric Jameson's hypothesis that market ideology "has less to do with consumption than it has to do with government intervention. [...] The market is thus Leviathan in sheep's clothing: its function is not to encourage and perpetuate freedom (let alone freedom of a political variety) but rather to repress it."[7]

2. Western Interpretations of Postcommunism

In other respects, however, Jameson's analysis may prove to be misleading in view of postcommunism. In general, most theoreticians who attempt to politicize the postmodern seem to ignore the historical experience of the former communist countries. From the perspective of someone who spent several decades in a country controlled by the communists, much of the recent issue of *New Literary History* entitled "Cultural Studies: China and the West" (Winter 1997) reads like fairly old-fashioned, rather dogmatic Marxism.[8] What Jameson and Eagleton have to say about late capitalism may seem a re-hash of the ideas of György Lukács. Although they have explicitly called into question the simplistic idea that culture is a superstructure determined by underlying forces of production, their thought continues to be implicitly determined by it. In fact, contemporary Marxists often repeat the distorted interpretations of Lukács. One recent example is Jameson's remark in his book on postmodernism that Rilke's archaic Greek torso warns "the bourgeois subject to change his life."[9] This statement echoes the claim made by Lukács in *Die Eigenart des Aesthetischen* (1963) that the message of the poem *Archaischer Torso Apollos* for the reader is "daß seine im Leben sich betätigenden Leidenschaften neue Inhalte, eine neure Richtung erhalten, daß sie, derart gereinigt, zu einer seelischen Grundlage von 'tugendhaften Fertigkeit' werden."[10]

My suspicion is that some Western interpreters of the political implications of postmodernism know relatively little about the relations between politics and art in the former Soviet bloc. A characteristic example is the essay entitled "The Politics of Postmodernism after the Wall" by Susan Rubin Suleiman, a Harvard professor who was born in Hungary. The essay is a kind of confession based on information gathered by the author during her recent trips to Budapest. The honesty of the interpretation is beyond any doubt. "Things are not so simple," she admits. "The idea of a post-modern paradise in which one can try on new identities like costumes in a shopping mall [...] appears to me now as not only naive, but intolerably thoughtless in a world where – again – whole populations are murdered in the name of ethnic identity."[11]

The problem with such interpretations is that it is rather difficult to characterize postcommunism without some first-hand experience of communism. Although nationalism is a menace not to be neglected, it is by no means the only weakness of the societies of such countries as the Czech Republic, Poland, Slovakia, Hungary, Croatia, or Romania. At the outset of her essay Susan Suleiman refers to what she describes as "the current joke in Budapest": "'What is the worst thing about communism?' 'What comes after it.'"[12] What she fails to specify is the context in which she may have heard the joke. Who was the speaker? Is it possible that it was someone who had a highly privileged life as a member of the political establishment led by János Kádár? In any case, the society in the former East-bloc countries is so divided that it is quite risky to generalize. While it is justifiable to speak about political and ethical postmodernism, it is not certain that the highly politicized art and culture of former communist countries can be characterized in terms of postmodernism. The master narrative of Marx and Engels's manifesto may have lost its attractiveness but the legacy of totalitarianism is by no means extinct. Former communists often claim that they have forgotten their past. Would it not be somewhat risky to describe their transformation in terms of the dissolution of the subject characteristic of postmodernity? The interpretations of postmodernity made by Jameson and Eagleton seem rather vulnerable since they are based on a less than profound understanding of the Soviet or Chinese systems. Eagleton's argument that "Mao was about as far from socialism as Newt Gingrich"[13] may reflect a somewhat naive opposition between theory and practice. Only a limited or one-sided acquaintance with Marxism could suggest that Stalinism represented a complete rejection of its entire historical legacy.

To shift our focus to the literature of the former communist world, it is certainly true that even the most lucid theoreticians of postmodernity give little thought to Eastern Europe. Hans Bertens, for instance, speaks of "the relative marginality of the postmodern impulse within contemporary poetry."[14] This is probably true if we limit ourselves to Western literatures. In some East-European literatures, however, postmodern verse preceded postmodern fiction. Throughout his long career Sándor Weöres (1913-1989) rejected any claims to originality, advocated radical eclecticism, and confined himself to rewriting and pastiche. In 1972 he published a volume entitled *Psyché* ("Psyche"), a collection that claimed to be by a poetess who lived in the early 19th century. This work, written in a hybrid style, combining elements borrowed from diverse periods, served as a model for Péter Esterházy (b. 1950), who in 1987 published a book entitled *Tizenhét Hattyúk* ("Seventeen Swans"), a prose confession by a woman who lived roughly in the same period as the alleged author of *Psyche*. In other works by Weöres several levels of citation are superimposed in a way that contradicts historical teleology. This technique clearly foreshadows the structure of Esterházy's chef-d'oeuvre *Bevezetés a szépirodalomba* ("An Introduction to Belles-lettres,"1986). Moreover, Weöres also published texts comparable to "objets trouvés," doggerels allegedly "composed" by young children or mentally handicapped people, thereby undermining the privileged status of poetry. Since his death a remarkable amount of verse has been written incorporating nonstandard speech. The de-centering of the self, a self-destructive irony, a radical fragmentation, a reliance on irreconcilable sociolects, and a violation of grammatical rules characterize the short texts of Endre Kukorelly (b. 1951), who consistently tries to avoid the characteristics usually associated with poetry. His activity implies a dissolution of the work-concept, in so far as his constant preoccupation is with the question what makes the difference between literary and nonliterary discourse when there is no perceptible morphological difference between them. Needless to say, this acceptance of everyday speech or ungrammatical discourse represents continuity with Apollinaire's "poèmes-conversation" and with texts by dadaist authors. Kukorelly's texts served as inspiration for the younger generation. As the interactive installation called *Cryptogram*, inspired by Leonardo's sketches for a sculpture never realized, shows, the distrust of newness in creativity goes together with the use of computers and a blurring or even collapse of the distinction between literature and the visual arts as well as between art and non-art. Other examples, texts published in the journals *Új Symposion* and *Kalligram* (published in Novi Sad and Bratislava, respectively), would also suggest that in Eastern Europe poetry may have given a decisive impetus to postmodern creation.

3. The Status of Postmodernism in Postcommunism

It follows from what has been said so far that it may be somewhat unwise to accept the idea that postmodern literature was born in the West and later received in the rest of the world. Those who insist on a radical break between the West and the other parts of the world may continue to represent the logic of modernism, in the sense defined by Jameson: "The moderns thus, with their religion of the new, believed that they were somehow distinct from all the other human beings who ever lived in the past – and also from those non-modern human beings still alive in the present, such as colonial peoples, backward cultures, non-Western societies, and 'undeveloped' enclaves."[15]

Since much of Eastern Europe, Asia, and Africa is involved in a love-hate relationship with Western culture, there are serious risks in speaking about the infusion of postmodernism in these regions. Hermeneutics has taught us that appropriation is a dialogue of great complexity. Some of the interpretations current in the U. S. and in Western Europe seem vulnerable from the perspective of the rest of the world. It is certainly unacceptable complacency to assert that "the history of world art since 1945 has been pretty much the history of American art centered in New York."[16] The explanation for such provincialism is related to the lack of historical consciousness which Henry James regarded as the basic weakness of American culture: "the flower of art blooms only where the soil is deep," he wrote, "it takes a great deal of history to produce a little literature."[17] The belief in the hegemony of the United States in contemporary art is inseparable from the misconception that between the end of the Middle Ages and the rise of the avant-garde there was no paradigm shift in artistic conventions, "perception itself undergoes relatively little change over the period in question – let's say from about 1300 to 1900 – otherwise there would be no possibility of progress: the progress has to be in representations that look more and more like visual reality." Such a conception is bound up with a simplistic and ahistorical attitude to mimesis. The assumption that "seeing is a lot more like digesting than it is like believing"[18] is in contradiction with the hermeneutic principle that history is part of the meaning of all works of art. The conclusion is inescapable that if reception is taken into consideration, it is by no means easy to perceive the dividing line between modernism and postmodernism.

The idea that there is a consensus on the definition of literary postmodernism will not hold up under scrutiny. The late Hans Robert Jauß described a "Horizontwandel" in terms of a strong reaction against the "nouveau roman,"[19] whereas Douwe Fokkema included such early works by Robbe-Grillet, Butor, and Ollier in his list of "French postmodern texts" as *La jalousie* (1957), *La modification* (1957), and *La mise en scène* (1959).[20] While Jauß insisted that the history of twentieth-century literature could be written in terms of a teleological sequence leading from modernism through the avant-garde and late modernism to postmodernism; others defined modernism either in a narrow sense, in almost provincial terms, or lumped it together with the avant-garde. Julio Ortega, for instance, started his essay on Spanish-American postmodernism with the following hypothesis: "I will use 'international modernism' (or modernism in its broadest context) to refer to that innovatory artistic movement that was carried by Pound, Joyce, and Eliot, but that also coincides with the systematic program of the avant-gardes."[21] A definition of modernism based on a very limited canon of works written in English by authors whose emphasis on tradition was at odds with the goals of most avant-garde movements may lead to a rather one-sided interpretation of postmodernism.

To what extent are Western theories of postmodernism helpful for an understanding of the culture of Eastern Europe? Of course, it is undeniable that in some of the countries of this region there was hardly any full-fledged modernism. This absence would make the flourishing of postmodernism rather dubious. Moreover, it is not possible to speak of consumer society and information industry in all parts of the former Second World. Still, if we limit ourselves to those countries that can claim to have an important avant-garde legacy as well as a market economy, the difference between Western and East-European literatures seems to be striking at least in one respect: in the former communist countries the rewriting of such popular genres as the Western, the detective story, science fiction, or pseudo-historical fiction is far less wide-spread. It is difficult to find works that bring out the emptiness of the generic conventions they invoke. *Enciklopedija Mrtvih* (1983) by Danilo Kiš or *Khazarski rečnik* (1984) by Milorad Pavić prove that in Central and Eastern Europe the dichotomy of canonized history versus the falsification of the past makes no sense. For some Croats Serbian history is pure fiction; the history of the Soviet Union, Czechoslovakia, and Yugoslavia has lost its credibility since the dissolution of those states; the Hungarian and Romanian versions of Transylvanian history are irreconcilable. The communist interpretation of the past can be called retrospectively a willful distortion but it is still quite difficult to see what may replace it. The contingency of history seems so self-evident that no postmodern rewriting of the historical novel could emerge.

As an "Epochenbewusstsein," postmodernity has certainly reached the former communist countries. In the words of Arthur C. Danto, "we have entered a period of post-historical art, where the need for constant self-revolutionization of art is now past." What I find questionable is the idea that "we are entering a more stable, more happy period of artistic endeavor where the basic needs to which art has always been responsive may again be met."[22] The age of pluralism may lead to a decline of taste. Danto's optimism hardly applies to the postcommunist world, in which the younger generations often have no sense of direction. Writers who are at the start of their careers seem to be convinced that everything has been written, the criteria of progress and overcoming have lost their relevance, value has been reduced to exchange-value, and a distinction between good and bad writing can no longer be made. Their "Lebensgefühl" corresponds to what Jauß described in the following way: "Das Paradoxe der wirklichen Welt, in der wir heute leben, liegt darin, daß sie zwar noch nicht geschrieben und doch alles schon gelesen ist, bevor sie für uns existiert."[23] The negation of the places that had traditionally been assigned to aesthetic experience is simultaneous with the decline of the middle class. The concert hall and the book have lost their popularity and it is still an open question whether the informational technology of the Internet can help us to develop new cultural institutions that can replace the old ones. The thought underlying the ideal of open society that a citizen should not commit himself to any particular value-system may lead to a sense of frustration.

While Danto may be right in maintaining that "possibly it is the work of Post-Modernism that anything can become an influence at any time, a disordered past corresponding to a disordered present and future,"[24] his definition needs to be modified in terms of reception aesthetics. If something is art when it is declared to be art, the question arises: declared by whom? If the Musée d'Orsay represents an attempt to restore the aesthetic value of nineteenth-century academic art, it is possible to ask: by whom is the tradition of modernism called into question? One of the reasons why some definitions of postmodernism are vulnerable is that they are based on a sociologically indiscriminate concept of the public.

"Postmodernism is both academic and popular, élitist and accessible," writes a prominent critic,[25] but it seems relevant to add that accessibility is a relative concept. Postmodern novels may be readable for more people than modernist texts, but it might be somewhat misleading to take it for granted that they can also achieve the goals of modernism. The complexity of *Il nome della rosa* is negligible in comparison with that of such works as *Der Mann ohne Eigenschaften* or *Finnegans Wake*. Let me admit in parenthesis that I cannot share the view held by some that Joyce's late work or Musil's unfinished masterpiece can be associated with postmodernism. If postmodernism is inseparable from the enfranchisement of the commonplace or at least from a desire to supersede the dichotomy between experimentation and a reliance on popular culture, if it is closely tied to a postindustrial situation dominated by a powerful cultural industry, information technologies, and mass media, the two long novels just mentioned still belong to modernism. In any case, they are very different from clever, opportunistic consumerism. Warhol's appetite for money and huge earnings are in violent contrast to Webern's lack of interest in financial considerations and commercial success. It would be a mistake not to admit that such highly talented artists as Eco, Warhol, or Philip Glass make evident concessions to be more immediately grasped by a wide public. This demands a partial renunciation of the legacy of such masters as Joyce, Schwitters, and Webern. With some reservation it is true that while in modernism the artist is a producer against, in postmodernism she or he is a producer for society.

As for the dialogue between high and popular culture, it has to be remembered that there were periods in the past in which the borderline between elevated art and vulgar taste was muted if not erased. The relevance of "noch nicht" and "nicht mehr" was at least suspended in Biedermeier and Art Nouveau culture. It is hardly accidental that it is relatively easy to find examples of kitsch in these three periods. The attempt of Western postmodernism to bridge the gap between high and popular culture has inspired a kind of conformity in Eastern Europe. The acceptance of international mass products goes together with a condemnation of élitism that is used by some as a pretext for reviving the artistic eclecticism of the communist decades. Recently a critic of Chinese birth spoke about a "combination of 'socialist Realism' and American pop,"[26] thus reminding us that socialist Realism may appear acceptable in a situation in which the legitimacy of high culture is seriously questioned.

4. The end of Postmodernism?

It is not possible to generalize about the relations between postmodernity and postcommunism. To understand the role of postmodernism in China one has to be familiar with Chinese history. The same applies to Eastern Europe. I am not qualified to make any statements about Asia, but I can risk hypotheses about the former Warsaw Pact countries. While in the 1980s Postmodernism seemed to be the dominant literary trend in Yugoslavia, Czechoslovakia, or Hungary, by the 1990s this trend has lost much of its power. The deaths of such prominent writers as Kiš, Hrabal, or Heiner Müller were a serious loss. Others disappointingly seemed to repeat themselves, and several works appeared that are unrelated to postindustrialism and the cult of pastiche. There is a general feeling that East-European culture was more exciting in the 1980s than it is since the political changes that occurred around 1990. Esterházy is fond of saying that he has no words for the present situation, and his latest books are collections of articles – with the exception of *Harmonia caelestis* (2000), a long narrative that may be read retrospectively, as a novel dominated by a genealogical imperative. Although only the followers of György Lukács, commuting between the New School for Social Research and Budapest, would accept Jameson's idea that postmodernism is a First World invention, the cultural dominant of late capitalism, it could be argued that the shift from communism to postcommunism may have led to a decline of postmodernism.

One of the most memorable works of fiction published in recent years is *Sinistra körzet* ("Sinistra District" 1992) by Ádám Bodor (b. 1936), a frightening account of the political nightmare of Ceausescu's Romania, written in a style that has none of the structural tricks, metafictional or self-referential devices usually associated with postmodernism. Although some would point to multiculturalism and autobiographical character in Bodor's fiction, such analogies are misleadingly superficial. The Transylvanian-born writer's prose is extremely economical and free of any allusions. The fate of the hero of *Sinistra District* is no less or more an extension of the author's life than the destiny of any first-person narrator. In fact, the narrative perspective is somewhat ambiguous: in some chapters the main character is the narrator, in others a third person refers to him and he is portrayed with as much "impassibilité" as any other human being. He is a survivor whose story is about a form of existence in which there is no individual freedom and human fate is regulated by invisible forces. The world of totalitarianism is presented in terms of heightened fictionality that suggests no traffic between high and low culture. There is no trace of rewriting, recontextualization, or overcoded playfulness. In comparison with this world, the absurdity of *Malone meurt* may appear to be a somewhat tongue-in-cheek seriousness. While some readers may find humour in Kafka or Beckett, there is hardly any trace of the witty in the work of Bodor. His characters live in forests surrounding the river called Sinistra. Except for some bureaucrats the only inhabitants of this district are people who have been sent there by way of punishment. The hero is visiting this region with the purpose of finding his adopted son. The young man follows the example of many others by committing suicide in an astonishingly cruel manner and the hero escapes from the territory.

In the West the complaint is often made that the collapse of communism has given rise to nationalism in Eastern Europe. Bodor's work suggests that the reaction against international capitalism and postmodernism is not necessarily tied to ethnocentrism.

Several other works could be cited as confirming the thesis that more and more artists seem to reject postmodern eclecticism. A recent example is *Az élősködő* ("The Parasite," 1997) by Ferenc Barnás (b. 1959). It is the first novel by a writer who has a university doctorate in literature but earns his living as a flautist in Western Europe. Characteristically, in 1996 the manuscript was rejected by a publisher for the reason that it seemed unrelated to any current literary trend. Although a careful reader could possibly detect the influence of Hesse and other German writers in this book, intertextuality is almost entirely absent from it. Like *Sinistra District*, *The Parasite* is the confession of a man whose only meaningful experience seems suffering. The difference between the two works is that while in the earlier book the narrator is able to leave the world controlled by torturers, in the later novel the narrator-hero faces self-destruction. From this refusal of resolution comes the aptness of the style for the representation of anguish and the macabre. This kind of writing has nothing in common with the recycling of the elements of popular fiction. The confessional tone is combined with a passionate interest in selfhood and "Dasein;" that is why *The Parasite* has been compared to an eschatological meditation.[27] Being is understood as corporeality and language, and the words seem uttered prior to and beyond all distinguishing between bodiliness and spirituality. The struggle to find words concerns the relation of language and body. It is presented as the most profound struggle in which one can engage. The

278

emphasis on the linguistic nature of experience is in harmony with the tradition of Nietzsche, Heidegger, and Gadamer. The idea underlying the narrator's confession is that we do not use language. Rather, we require it, because "Sein, das verstanden werden kann, ist Sprache."[28]

The most interesting literature coming from Eastern Europe is closely related to the sufferings of the people who spent their formative years in communism. Bodor has left Romania for Hungary but is haunted by the memories of the activities of the Securitate, and the nightmares related by some other writers are also linked to the political system that cannot be forgotten by those who had lived in it. *The Parasite*, on the other hand, represents an ontological discourse with no apparent political implications. Both types of writing are a far cry from postmodern literature. What they seem to suggest is that it is a simplification to believe that global changes in society call for a certain kind of writing. Ironically, arguments about postmodernism as the cultural dominant of late capitalism may remind those with a lived experience of communism of the ideology of a totalitarianism that can hardly be forgotten.

Notes

[1] *Polyphony*. Budapest: Soros Center of Contemporary Arts, 1993, 294.

[2] For a brief description of the project, both in English and in Hungarian, see Zoltán Szegedy-Maszák "http://.c3.hu/cryptogram," *Magyar Műhely* 102 (Spring 1997), 58–60.

[3] Fredric Jameson, *Postmodernism, or, The Cultural Logic of Late Capitalism*. London and New York: Verso, 1991, 96.

[4] Joseph Kosuth, *Art after Philosophy and After: Collected Writings, 1966–1990*. Cambridge, MA: MIT, 1991, 118, 154, 70.

[5] *Biennale di Venezia, XLV. Espozitione Internazionale d'Arte Padiglinone d'Ungheria 1993*, 105.

[6] *Polyphony*, 292.

[7] Fredric Jameson, 1991, 271, 273.

[8] I am more than willing to admit that on the basis of the historical experience of the Third World one might draw an entirely different conclusion.

[9] Fredric Jameson, 1991, 10, 312.

[10] Georg Lukács, *Die Eigenart des Aesthetischen*. Aufbau, Berlin und Weimar, vol. I, 1981, 779.

[11] Susan Rubin Suleiman, "The Politics of Postmodernism after the Wall," in Hans Bertens – Douwe Fokkema, eds., *International Postmodernism: Theory and Literary Practice*. Amsterdam–Philadelphia: John Benjamins, 1997, 54.

[12] Suleiman, 51.

[13] Terry Eagleton, "The Contradictions of Postmodernism." *New Literary History* 28 (Winter 1997), 6.

[14] Hans Bertens, "The Debate on Postmodernism," in Hans Bertens – Douwe Fokkema, *International Postmodernism: Theory and Literary Practice*, 11.

[15] Fredric Jameson, 1991, 389.

[16] Arthur C. Danto, *The State of Art*. New York: Prentice Hall Press, 1987, 192.

[17] Henry James, *Hawthorne*. London: Macmillan,1967, 23.

[18] Arthur C. Danto, *After the End of Art: Contemporary and the Pale of History*. Princeton, NJ: Princeton University Press, 1997, 49.

[19] Hans Robert Jauß, *Wege des Verstehens*. München: Wilhelm Fink, 1994, 329.

[20] Douwe Fokkema, "The Semantics of Literary Postmodernism," In Hans Bertens – Douwe Fokkema, eds., *International Postmodernism: Theory and Literary Practice*, 28.

[21] Julio Ortega, "Postmodernism in Spanish-American Writing," in Hans Bertens – Douwe Fokkema, eds., *International Postmodernism: Theory and Literary Practice*, 315.

[22] Arthur C. Danto, *The Philosophical Disenfranchisement of Art*. New York: Columbia University Press, 1986, xv.

[23] Hans Robert Jauß, *Studien zum Epochenwandel der ästhetischen Moderne*. Frankfurt am Main: Suhrkamp, Frankfurt am Main, 1989, 276.

[24] Arthur C. Danto, *Beyond the Brillo Box in Post-Historical Perspective*. New York: Farrar, Straus, Giroux, 1992, 123.

[25] Linda Hutcheon, *A Poetics of Postmodernism: History, Theory, Fiction*. New York and London: Routledge, 1988, 44.

[26] Sheldon Hsiao-peng Lu, "Art, Culture, and Cultural Criticism in Post-New China," *New Literary History*, 28 (Winter 1997), 119.

[27] József Szili, "Barnás Ferenc: Az élősködő (A testiség eszkhatológiája)." *Kalligram*, September 1997, 59–7.

[28] Hans-Georg Gadamer, *Wahrheit und Methode*. Tübingen: J. C. B. Mohr, 1986, 478.

Printed in Hungary
Budapest